# WHEN THE GODDESS CALLS

A TINA PAVLOU COLLABORATION

# CONTENTS

**DISCLAIMER:** This book is not intended as a substitute for the medical advice of physicians. The reader should regularly consult a physician in matters relating to his/her health and particularly with respect to any symptoms that may require diagnosis or medical attention.

# TINA PAVLOU

*E*ver since I was young, I have known that the universe is on my side.

My name is Tina Pavlou, and I am the founder of the Goddess Rooms in Ramsgate, Kent. I am a Clairvoyant, Clairsentient, Clairaudient, and Claircognizant; I see, I feel, I hear, and I know. I am an Angelic Reiki Master and Theta instructor, and I teach these forms of healing at the Goddess Rooms along with many other healing modalities. I also instruct on the Sacred Femininity to the Tantric Arts for Women, work as an intuitive spiritual coach, and practice EFT and sound therapy. I will soon begin training in Kundalini Tantra Yoga as well. My gifts are blessing which have been bestowed upon me so that I can teach people who they truly are. I work on the Angelic Realms, and help people connect to their Angels, to their higher self, and to the Creator of All That Is.

I HAVE SEEN SO many things in my life; I see Angels on a daily basis and have been in the presence of miracles. My intuition affords me some incredible abilities, such as being able to scan a person's body and know its internal workings: from being able to sense hormonal and nutritional imbalances, to knowing when there is a presence of unhealthy tissue such as tumours. I just know, like I know. I have also helped many women conceive children with my healing hands.

A LOT of my teachings and healings work with the Goddesses, the Divine Feminine. I see and work with these Goddesses and Ascended Masters on a regular basis, including Anna, Grandmother of Jesus, Mother Mary, Isis, Mary Magdalene (the most beautiful woman who is extremely misunderstood) and her daughter Sarah. I love teaching about these ladies; it is my purpose. Waking up the Divine Feminine is my passion. Connecting women back to their souls, hearts and wombs is the driving force in my life.

CURRENTLY, I teach in the UK, Australia and America, and my intention is to bring a global sisterhood together, something which is already beginning to manifest. With the founding of the Goddess Rooms, I am able to nurture and provide a safe environment where people can grow and be vulnerable without feeling weak. Everything I have done has come from the heart. I have been driven by my experiences of 'lack' throughout my life, to create the safest and most loving environment possible; a sanctuary of safety and security. Authenticity is who I am.

I HAVE CREATED the most amazing community and beautiful sisterhood of women from all over the globe. It is a community of healers, psychics, and goddesses, all founded in loyalty, sisterhood, genuine friendship and love. My dream is to light up the world. I decided to put this book together with a group of my soul sisters to show others that they are not alone, and that the consciousness of this planet is changing: we are waking up. A new way of being (and a new way of thinking, feeling, seeing and doing) is arising. We as women are reconnecting, finally stepping away from the patriarchal world which has been created by man to keep us in fear of each other and the power we possess.

THE GODDESSES RETURN.

OF COURSE, I did not manifest all that I have in my life overnight. Life has not always been sweet for me, and I have been on a long and difficult journey to discover all that I am now. My story begins when I was a little girl, around four years of age, when I saw my first vision of an Angel. It was Mother Mary. I have no idea why she came to me, but I will never forget how she leant over me and looked deep into my eyes. Then, when I was eight years old, I saw a vision of a future event that I was to encounter in my thirties. I was presented with images showing myself in hospital, undergoing some kind of operation, and it was accompanied by a strong acrid smell. However, being so young I didn't understand the meaning behind these visions, and I blanked this out for years.

BETWEEN EIGHT AND THIRTY, I had a relatively normal life, though I was a very sensitive child. I was affected a lot by the symptoms of ADHD (my mum would call me hyperactive) and I always felt so much, I always felt other people's emotions. I was an empath, something which I didn't come to understand until much later in my life. Still, on the whole I was the typical teenager that had some issues with bullies, made it through school, and later moved on to get married and have two beautiful daughters.

· · ·

FAST FORWARD TO when I reached my thirties, and I entered into a period of my life which would turn out to be the beginning of my development and initiation into spirituality. I had so looked forward to entering my thirties. I was told it was the best time of your life: you looked really good, you felt really good, your children were older, and you had a little bit more money in your pockets... but my vision of being in my thirties was not anything like I had imagined.

I FOUND myself faced with one devastating obstacle after the next. My marriage broke down as a result of betrayal. I was continually let down by 'friends', and I reached a place in my life where I thought I was all alone; I wanted to die, and my whole world collapsed around me. I was smoking Cannabis and drinking red wine to relax my manic brain at night, and I soon became submerged in a dark murky pond of depression where I drowned and could not breathe. It was then that I suffered a mental, spiritual and emotional collapse: complete psychotic breakdown. The psychosis lead to me suffer delusions and hallucinations, to the point where I was convinced that people were trying to get me through the TV.

I WOULD LAY on my bed, day in, day out, praying to the Angels to be put to sleep; not to die, but to sleep, until all the pain had disappeared. This was the dark night of the soul, but it was also my initiation into something greater.

SOMEHOW, through inner strength and pure determination, I managed to raise my head out of the mud and darkness and breathe again. It was a slow process, but over the next nine months, with the help of a psychiatric nurse who came to my home, I started to recover. I began to rebuild, looked for jobs, and resumed life again; how I did this is beyond me, but I do know now that the Angels were with me the whole time.

A COUPLE OF YEARS LATER, I was still very weak, very vulnerable. But I was functional, and able to hide the remaining fear that everyone was against me.

SOMETIMES WHEN I think about this, think about that time, I just want to go back to myself and hug her. That thirty-something year old woman was so alone, so frightened, so scared... I don't believe any human being should have to go through that kind of pain. I remember sitting on my bed, and swearing at the universe, Creator and the Angels and saying, 'how dare you let a human hurt so much'. I was so angry with them, I had so much anger inside me. So, I would drink a lot. I would go out and party, because it was the only way I knew how to deal with my pain, the only way I found myself able to cope with life.

AND THEN MY father fell ill. At the time, I was working as an airhostess, finding joy in the role of the glamourous hostess travelling around the world. I loved being able to tell people what I did for a living because it was the only thing I had which made me feel good. However, while on a material level it looked like everything was going well for me, on the inside I was still really hurting.

THEN ONE DAY, I came home late after attending a flight to the Czech Republic. I sat on the sofa and was suddenly overwhelmed by the massive urge to go to my mum and dad's house. In my tired state, I fought it off the feeling, and I decided I would go in the morning. I was so exhausted that I fell asleep on the sofa for a few hours before heading to bed, and I forgot to lock my front door. As I finally got into bed, I had a vision. My dad was lying in a glass coffin, and sand began to pour inside with him in it. I couldn't fully comprehend the vision at the time, so I just resolved to go to see him in the morning, telling myself everything would be okay.

THE NEXT THING I heard was someone calling my name from inside the house. I jumped out of bed and ran to my banisters and looked down to find that my mum, daughter and sister had let themselves in where I had forgotten to lock the front door. I looked at them and said "It's dad isn't it? He's gone." and they confirmed what I already knew to be true. I knew he'd gone; I'd seen it happen before he died. That was my biggest wakeup call on the spiritual path.

THE NEXT MORNING, after having gone to see my dad in the hospital, I knew I would have to go home to sleep for a few hours because it was going to be a busy few weeks; my father is from Cyprus, so we had family coming in from all over the world to pay their respects and say goodbye. When I woke up, I went down to the front door and there, lying on the ground, was the biggest white feather I had ever seen. And I knew that it was a message from the Angels.

YOU SEE, I had been reading more and more about the Angels. I had even bought myself some Angel cards and would sit at home and try to heal myself by talking to the Angels through the cards. That's all I did; I wanted to heal. Three days after my father's death, I was asleep in bed and in my dream I was sat on a white cloud, watching my father walk towards me. He had a full head of hair and he was well. He put his arms around me, and he said "Darling, everything's going to be okay now". I was overwhelmed by this love which I had never felt before in any human existence, and the magnitude of the feeling woke me up. It was warm and it was beautiful; it was true love. I felt it in every cell of my body.

I KNEW THEN, that all of the stuff that I had been seeing, all the stuff that I had been feeling, was real. But I didn't know where to go or what to do with that knowledge.

I WAS STILL VERY vulnerable from the breakdown. I was a shell really. I was just a shell operating like a robot. I needed guidance and healing. Unsure of what else I could do, I decided to turn to prayer, asking the universe to help me through my father's death. I had read somewhere that if you read a prayer every day for twenty-one days, you would be healed (though I understand now that prayer doesn't work like that - you might not receive everything you ask for through prayer, but you will receive help and Divine guidance). I scrolled the internet trying to find a prayer which felt right to me, but when I couldn't find one which resonated, I decide to write my own.

ON THE SEVENTEENTH day of consecutive prayer, I was sat on my bed, at five-past-five in the evening and the sun shone on my face. I was bathed in warm light when, all of a sudden, two beautiful Angel wings wrapped themselves around me. My whole body froze as if it was paralyzed, unable to move anything other than my eyes. It was a startling feeling, but I wasn't afraid as I knew it was an Angel, and that it was a sign that they were with me.

FROM THEN ON, the Angel cards continued to be my biggest channel of communication to the Angels and Creator. The more that I used them, the stronger my connection to the cards became, and as I would sit and shuffle them, the cards would fling out of the deck and give me messages. Occasionally, I could even see the hand of an Angel flicking the card from the deck. So, I started to do the Angel cards for some of my friends, finding that I was really accurate in my readings. I was quite shocked by the knowledge that was coming to my mind and the visions that I could see. Then one day I was asked to go to a psychic fair to do some readings. The next thing I knew, I had around sixteen people stood in front of me speaking of the 'Angel lady', and that is how I came to be known as the Angel Lady by many of my clients.

IT WAS this experience which started me down a path of working in the daytime at psychic fairs giving Angel readings. As I began to gain more and more interest from prospective clients, one day a friend of mine turned to me and said, "you need to do this for a living". So that's what I did.

I STARTED to save the money I was earning from the psychic fairs to go on my first self-development course, which was a Reiki course. I threw myself into self-development, buying books and going on lots of courses. All I knew was that I never wanted to return to the dark pit which I had so recently surfaced from.

EVERY EVENING I would go onto YouTube or read my books. My favourite book was 'Many Lives, Many Masters' by Brian Weiss, all about reincarnation. I knew I had been here before, and my inquisitive mind led me to want to learn more. I also read the Louise Hay book 'You Can Heal Your Life'; I was doing anything I could to improve myself and my life. The more self-development courses I did, the more I evolved, and the more that I grew. Every time I was getting better, and better, and better and then something else would come along to test me, and I would grow even more, and more, and more. I just kept reading. Just kept throwing myself into me, throwing myself into knowledge. I was getting there – I finally felt really, really good.

AFTER TWO YEARS OF THIS, I felt really really good, and I was in the mind-set that the only way was up. Unfortunately, I then became quite poorly, and had to go into hospital for an operation. I was put under anaesthetic, and when I woke up, I was given the news that the surgeon had accidently punctured my bladder. I was in so, so much pain. Somebody else had hurt my body and there was nothing that I could do about it. Again, I was put into a dark place, but it was then that I recalled the vision that I had when I was eight years old. I remembered I had seen myself unwell and in hospital, surrounded by the pungent smell of urine: an echo of exactly what I was going through now.

THIS PROVED to me that I had been blessed with my gift for a very long time, prompting me to remember many visions which I had been having from the age of four years old, right through my teens and through my twenties; memories which I had completely blanked out.

THE COMPLICATIONS from the operation served as one of the biggest lessons that I was to be taught: to love my body, and to love myself. I was in so much shock, so much pain, and the doctors couldn't tell me if I would ever be able to use my bladder again. I was horrified, mortified and broken hearted that after everything that I had been through, I was faced with yet another life altering problem. My thirties were certainly not shaping up to everything that I had hoped.

THE HEALING PROCESS from the operation was a slow one. The doctors gave me morphine, and guess what? After three weeks of morphine my poor little body became so dependent on the drug that, when I tried to come off the morphine, I was literally having fits. 'Not another thing to do', was all I kept thinking. 'Not a nothing thing to deal with, please not another thing'. I was plagued with the thought that my mum would have a drug addict for a daughter, and I couldn't do that to my mum. I couldn't do that to me! So, I decided to just cut out all drugs completely. For three days and three nights, my body went into strong palpitations and fits. Eventually, after four or five days, I came out the other side and I was able to begin to heal, and around five months later, my body was completely healed, but I was left very fragile and very vulnerable once again.

I STARTED to live in fear. Fear of the next thing to come along, fear of what was going to happen, fear of future failure. When I look back on my thirties now, I understand that everything happened because it was to bring me to who I am today. It gave me the ability to help people before they ever fall that far. But still, when I look back I want to cry for the girl I once was; it hurts me to see her in so much pain. I want to go back to that girl and hold her tight and give her what she needed the most: love.

WHEN I CAME into my forties, I continued to go on to do more and more self-development; it was my main focus. In this chapter I can only tell you a few pieces, but my intention was to heal as many people as I could, so that I could stop them facing the pain that I felt. No human should go through such deep pain. I know we all come here to learn lessons, but even now I think to myself, 'when I get up there, I might have to have a few words with Creator about how tough it can be down here!'

OVER TIME, more and more people were coming to me for help. I could resonate with so many people, and that was my biggest strength in helping them. I went on course after course after course, and I was growing. But something still wasn't right. I couldn't work out what it was, but something still wasn't quite there. I was still falling back into old brain patterns, old ways of self-sabotaging, and still feeling as though I wasn't good enough.

IT WAS THEN that I discovered Theta. Theta was my life saver.

BECAUSE IT DOESN'T MATTER how many courses I did, I still had that low self-worth inside me, carried through the DNA lines which make us who we are. We all have stuff which comes from many different levels within us, such as our soul level, the core level, an ancestry level, and a history level, and these reside within our DNA makeup. So how is someone to heal, if we don't know how to clear ourselves on all of these levels first? This was my question to the Creator. How many people are out there working on themselves, but they can't quite get it right?

THEY KEEP FALLING BACK into their old addictive ways, back to self-sabotaging. I'm so glad that the universe brought me to Theta, because it changed my subconscious. It changed my religious beliefs. It helped me understand the seven planes of existence. It taught me about grudges and forgiveness, hatred and prejudice, about genetic blood-lines, family histories and releasing ancestral grudges. Through Theta, I learnt to journey to the root of each issue and the origin of every thought, questioning everything. One of the greatest things I have learnt is to set boundaries, to know myself. Learning to say no is one of the greatest things I have achieved. Most importantly, I learnt to take responsibility for myself.

. . .

You see, working through Theta is designed to help you release beliefs which are holding you back. The processes of the Theta Healing technique are not specific to any age, sex, race, colour, creed or religion. Anyone with a pure belief in love, and the Creator, can work with Theta. I tell you, Theta is a miracle healing modality which allows us to not only work with the law of attraction (everyone assumes this is the only primary law), but all the other laws which exist within the universe too.

Theta also enables us to work through other planes of existence. You see, there are seven planes in total. There is the first plane, where you have your crystals, your ores and minerals. The second plane is where your flowers, your trees, and your elemental fairies exist.

Then the third plane is where the humans live. I call this the matrix. This is a matrix. You are all in the matrix. Here you are all being downloaded with how to live, what to eat, how to dress, what to say, what to think. It's a mass consciousness, something which can only been seen once you separate yourself from this way of thinking and raise your vibration.

Beyond our plane, we have the fourth plane of existence, this is where the ancestors are. This is the plane where our families transition to, and where our shamans reside. Then we have the fifth plane, which is where the ascended masters are. This is also the plane of the Angels and the ArchAngels; a place of pure beauty.

Next, we have the sixth plane. This is where we have sound and vibration, all the laws, and all the languages and symbols for any kind of Reiki that you've heard of. There are so many symbols, and so many languages which you don't know about yet; and I say yet, because we are all waking up. Everybody on this planet is raising their vibration and waking up.

FINALLY, we have the seventh plane. The seventh plane is the Creator of All That Is. This is the energy where you can create anything in your life, and now that I am a Theta Healing instructor and Angelic Reiki Master Teacher, this is what I teach people; this is how I help people grow. How I assist them in growing in their relationships with themselves, how I help them to release their old limited belief systems, their self-sabotaging; removing all of the things which are holding them back. This is how I can help you, by lifting your vibration through the Angelic Realms, and teaching you Theta Healing so that you can work on the highest vibrations which we are gifted with on this planet.

I HAVE my own healing workshops and modality called the Awakening of the Angelic Goddess. I am so blessed to be invited around the world to teach this, from the UK to Australia and America, with some amazing results.

SADLY, it is important to be aware that not everyone who works within the healing community has such high vibrational intentions. As I went onto my spiritual path, I naively believed that everybody who worked with the same modalities as I do, worked in the name of the light. I didn't realise that there were so many charlatans out there, and I was absolutely horrified when I encountered so many of them. So many people who I still see out there working now, and I am still so gobsmacked by the ways in which they work.

. . .

A PRIME EXAMPLE of this was an occasion where I was asked, by a so-called healer, if I would like to engage in a treatment swap with her; I would give her a reading, and she would give me a massage in return. At the time, I was delighted by the idea, and naturally agreed.

ON THE DAY of our treatment swap, I headed to her house by car, leaving myself plenty of time for the hour drive. However, to my horror, I hit every single traffic light, every road diversion and every type of traffic problem that you can imagine. There were so many hurdles during my journey, that by the time I got there, I only had twenty minutes left of our appointment time. I was so embarrassed, and just kept apologising. I just couldn't understand how it could have happened.

THE WOMAN who I was going to meet accepted my apology on arrival and told me not to worry, saying that she would just give me a back massage, and that we would rearrange to finish the treatment swap another time. As I lay down for the massage, innocently assuming that everyone worked for the light, I turned my head to the left, and I saw the mighty Archangel Michael stood before me. I felt this over-whelming love was over me; it was so beautiful, and I knew it was being sent to me by him. Then, all of a sudden, I saw him lift this mighty sword and exclaim 'Oh no you don't', before swinging his sword across the form of the woman who was about to massage my back. This completely dazed me, as I didn't understand what was happening. Then, during the massage, I started to see things. Visions of what seemed like dark covens and spells, but I didn't quite under-stand what that meant either.

AFTER THE MASSAGE, I left the woman's house and got back in my car. It was then that I heard a voice. All it said was 'Body scrub. Twenty-

One. Three pm.' So, I picked my phone up and called the local beauty salon near my home. I didn't even know that there was such a thing as a body scrub, but I decided I might as well as ask anyway. The woman at the salon said yes, they did do body scrubs, and that there was an available appointment at three pm that day, stating that it would be twenty-one pounds. I explained to the woman that there had been a number of diversions on my way out of town, and that it might not be able to make it back in time for three pm, but that I'd try and make the appointment. To my amazement, it took me exactly one hour to get home, and I did not hit a single diversion, red light, or section of traffic the entire way. I arrived at exactly three o'clock and had my body scrub. When I got out my purse and looked at what money I had to pay, I had exactly twenty-one pounds in cash inside my purse.

IT WAS THEN that I grasped what happened. During the massage, the woman had tried to place some kind of psychic attack on me, but I had been protected against her evil intentions by Archangel Michael. Then, when I got in the car, because of the residue which had been left on my auric field, I had been told to get a body scrub to remove the residual negative energy from my body.

IT STILL HORRIFIES me to think that some people are out there masquerading as beautiful light workers who secretly harbour such evil intentions. Though I am thankful that the experience taught me how truly loved and protected I am by the Angels.

I HAVE BEEN BLESSED with many other experiences with Archangels throughout my life.

ONE AMAZING EXAMPLE was with a client of mine who came to me a few years back for healing. As she lay on the couch I noticed that she didn't look particularly well, but I didn't say anything to her at the time. As I placed my hands on her head, I saw two hands going into my hands, and I felt that it was Archangel Raphael. Then out of nowhere, I saw white lightening begin to spark from my fingers, passing from my hands into my client's head. I was totally in awe of this, hand no idea what was going on, but I knew something special was happening.

WHEN THE LADY sat up after the healing, she told me that she had just been diagnosed with high blood pressure and narrowing of the brain arteries. I was totally blown away. I explained to her what had happened, that archangel had come to me and placed his hands into mine. I had witnessed another miracle.

SHE WENT BACK to her doctor, and her doctor asked who I was, because guess what? Her high blood pressure was back to normal, and there no longer appeared to be any narrowing of her brain arteries. I am so lucky to have witnessed this miracle, and the fact that the Angels used me as a channel to perform this miracle is something I will cherish forever. I saw this. I know this to be true.

BY NOW, I have witnessed so many miracles that I will have to leave those stories to another book, because this has now become a day to day occurrence for me.

I WITNESS AND AID MIRACLES, and I have no doubt in my mind, or in my heart, that in everything that I do I have the Angels walking beside me, helping me to assist humanity. The Creator loves me and has my back; the Angels love me and have my back. They've always had my back, having carried me from when I was a young girl, right through my thirties when I needed them the most. They were carrying me the whole time; I was never alone. Never, ever alone. The universe truly is on my side. The universe has my back.

So, I am now in my fabulous forties, about to turn fifty. I am so excited to go into my fiftieth year; I am so excited to be alive. I am to become a grandmother this year, on June the Twenty-first - the Summer Solstice, my favourite time of the year. I am going to Bali to learn to become a Divine Feminine sexual energy teacher. I will also be training to become a Kundalini Tantric Yoga teacher, and I have two books being launched. Not bad, considering where I started as that young girl who had found herself buried in the mud, and could not yet see her way out.

LIFE IS AMAZING.

FROM MY FIRST self-development course fourteen years ago to now, I have built up over ten thousand clients worldwide. I have healed many, many people along the way, from those diagnosed with mental illnesses such as depression, to those facing physical and chronic illnesses, emotional pain and trauma, and spiritual crises. I have helped people find their true calling; I have helped them wake up. The Angels whisper and I hear them, using the knowledge which they bestow upon me to help others. My aim is to help people to wake up, to realise they deserve happiness, fulfilment and love, because if you believe you deserve it, the universe will serve it. The universe is on your side, the Angels are on your side, but they cannot work with you unless you ask them to, because they work on the law of free will. You have friends in high places. They will guide you, they will protect you, and they will nurture you.

. . .

I UNDERSTAND NOW, that all I went through in my thirties was my initiation, my wake up call. If I hadn't gone through all that, then I wouldn't be here now. I wouldn't have this opportunity to write a book with all of my beautiful soul sisters who I have met along my path. I am blessed to have had the privilege to mentor and instruct these women in the most amazing healing modalities which we have been gifted by the Angels and God (or Creator, or The Universe, whatever term you would rather use - at the end of the day, we are all referring to the same energy on the seventh plane of existence; the Creator of All That Is.)

THERE AREN'T many people who teach in the ways which I teach, and I own that. I own that I am special, and I can say that whole heartedly without any egotism. I am here to help wake up the world. Your vibe does attract your tribe, and I have the most amazing people around me. That is where the idea came to me to create this book, to collaborate with all of my beautiful sisters who I have assisted onto their current path, so that we can help you on to your path. So many of you think that you have to hustle to align, to fully invest yourselves into the matrix so that you can become successful... come and work with me, and I will show you the real truth.

THIS 'SPIRITUAL MALARKEY' as everyone calls it, this supposed 'new age,' is real. You cannot go on living in the matrix, being fed foods from supermarkets which are cultivated in labs and sprayed with man-made pesticides. You cannot continue to exist being pumped full of poisons in the guise of medications whenever you become unwell, only for a vicious cycle to be brought into existence once those medications cause further issues within your bodies and minds. It is time to wake up. You have the power to heal anything, you just need the right tribe around you to help you. And that's who we are; we are here to help you.

ARE WE 'AIRY FAIRY'? Are we 'new age hippies'? Call us what you will, but we are just normal women, who have led normal lives. We have all suffered deep trauma and come out the other side. This is the first book of its kind, and it is an honour and a privilege that you have this book in your hand now, reading our stories and being allowed to share in our journey's. While I am able to talk to and teach you, I also found it hard to sit down and write about myself, to tell everybody my journey. You see, I am still learning, I will always be learning. But I need no longer learn though pain; I am learning through love, a path which I would like to help you to find too. All I ask, is that you trust me, and we can share this journey called life together.

YOU ARE in the presence of a Goddess.

# ABOUT THE AUTHOR

## TINA PAVLOU

Tina Pavlou is a Clairvoyant and an intuitive Coach and Mentor.. a seer into the Spiritual realms, who works with the Seven Planes of Existence and the Spiritual Laws; a Theta Healer Instuctor, an Angelic Reiki Master and teacher, a Suara Sound Therapist and a Divine FEMININE Taoism Sexual Energy Teacher from Kent in England.

Tina specialises in empowering people to live their best lives by giving them the spiritual tools to do so.

After experiencing the Dark Night of the Soul, she made it her passion to help as many people as she could, so they would never have to experience as much suffering and pain as she had.

It is impossible to be around Tina without feeling anything other than positivity and love as she vibrates on such a Divine, Goddess high frequency. Her passion is just love.

**CONTACT**
    EMAIL: Pavloutina@yahoo.co.uk
    WEBSITE: tinapavlou.com

# ANNA TOKAROVA

*W*ow! What a beautiful journey it has been so far. I am writing with excitement and joy sincerely hoping to share these vibes with you my dear reader. I have been told on numerous occasions to share the wonders and miracles of my `story`. When Tina Pavlou offered for me to participated in her collaboration book I was grinning from ear to ear thinking the universe works in wonderful ways indeed. My experience of life led me to believe our life is as we allow it to be. We have the choice, power and strength to do anything we put our brilliant minds to, if we truly believe it will benefit us or to others in meaningful ways.

## Me Me Me

Without further ado let's jump right in. We all have fascinating and story worthy lives (even if some of you might think you do not - You Do!!). You are alive and reading this and I am telling you "WELL DONE! You have made it this far through all the ups and downs. What a brave soul you are! I admire you". Pointing a finger back at me oh boy - if anyone knows how to mess their life up on solid ground it is me. I dropped out of university a year before my graduation, fell in love with a major lesson in my life, had the blessing of my son being born and a step daughter joining my "team".

I MADE a lot of money by running a little beauty salon and lost it by miss investing it. I had to take myself out of an abusive relationship and became a single parent. I was 23 with 2 kids and a realisation something had to change profoundly.

## Change

In our heart of hearts, we all know or have that tingly feeling in the gut that you have got to stop, look and assess where you are at, what led you here... do you really want to keep moving in the same way and direction? I did not. Due to the relationship I had with my children's' father I was in isolation so had few friends...If I'm being honest - I had no one I could turn to for meaningful help.

THIS WAS the moment I learnt that in a world this huge you can feel completely alone. At first the feeling is of a hollowness inside, but once you embrace it and see it for an opportunity of ultimate freedom it's easy to become very curious and childishly excited. I thought so, and in theory I can decide a new story, a new start where I choose, and how and what will happen. This was a liberating thought. I can choose to reinvent myself, who I am, what I stand for and how I make my daily choices.

## GETTING STARTED

And so, I decided what to keep from the old ways, habits and responsibilities and what to let go. The children stayed! The house stayed as I had no financial means to move. But I gave my notice in at work and decided to work from home as a beautician. My treatment room looked like something from a horror movie (I used it as a storage room) and so much of the place required redecoration. Hey, but like I said money issues. Oh, and a one big O ...I am not from the UK.

## Early Days

I came to this country by myself when I was 10 years old for a month to study English in a London school. To the host families shock I was not 18. Poor them. They were kind and patient, and for me it was all a bit overwhelming. I did fall in love with London, charmed by its unique energy.

I came back to Cambridge to continue my college education and after went to Bath University to study Sociology and Human Resource Management. As a foreign student back in the day student finance was not an option. I came from a modest family so studied and worked since I was 15, at my busiest point having had 4 jobs and was studying full time. Providing for myself has always been very important for me.

As a non-EU citizen, I did not have access to the standard social safety net. I was never good at asking for help. Always wanting to do everything myself, I am stubborn that way. So as a result this had a great positive side effect. I had a strong motivation to excel in my business, success being the only way forward. I decided I will make do with the shabby looking interior and facilities I had at my disposal and build on it best I could.

So, whatever I lacked in opulence I compensated for with attention to detail in treatments, offering a unique individual approach to every person, I also had buckets of enthusiasm. The result was outstanding. People were coming back from day one because I cared. I was happy that people who came to see me were happy as that was my main focus. Money came in as a natural result of my work, my effort was paying off.

OVER THE YEARS my business grew to its peak, I was managing a team of 12. In the last 2 years I have chosen to focus on maintaining steady healthy business. I found a strong drive to grow the consultancy branch of my work as it enables me to help people in more profound ways.

## FROM BEAUTY SECTOR to Personal Coaching

My natural motivation has always been to make myself and people around me happier. This took me on a path of discovering for myself what happiness means for me. It took me some time to recover from a manipulative marital relationship. Next, I felt it was important to find out who I really was. What did Anna really want, crave, feel, enjoy, without the influence of others. This bit took a while and honestly, it's still a work in progress. I love learning, discovering and finding out more about myself each day. It's my belief that in this way we can be more skilled, effective, useful and helpful... and further thoughts came of why service to other people has been so fundamental to me.

A FRIEND of mine introduced me to Theta Healing meditation technique and after seeing success in and after sessions I trained to get my Instructors qualifications. Why stop at improving peoples lives on a physical level? I wanted to take my expertise further and allow my clients work on their emotional and energetic issues as well as physical ones. My goal was to make the experience whole.

. . .

## BRAVE SOULS

I went on to practice and discover extensively with clients and at further classes different healing modalities and

methods as I do not believe a "one fits all" solutions exist. Each of my clients is a unique individual with their own inner and outer cosmos. Looking into people's most private aspects of life, having that level of trust is a privilege. I have experienced abuse of various types first hand. It can be very straightforward, super embarrassing and often leaves physical and emotional.

OTHER ABUSE IS VERY SUBTLE HARDLY noticeable and quite often hardest to deal with because as soon as you put your finger on what it is ... it slips away from you ... you question yourself did it really happen the way I perceived it? And with time our perceptions change.. just as well as memories. I always admire clients who find the courage to seek out and ask for help when they realise it's needed. I met Tina at one of the courses and was fascinated by her vibrant and radiant personality. In my eyes she has been an inspiration, someone to follow your heart and dreams and believe in miracles as well as trusting the universe.

## MIRACLES

For miracles to happen in your life I find you need to believe in them. The more faith you have and the stronger it is that miracles can happen, and that you are willing to allow for them to happen, that you are worthy, the more they will. Their magnitude will increase as your faith grows. At least that's what I noticed myself over the years. If a person is very down (I am talking from personal experience here, so I avoid embarrassing someone else) and you feel like nothing good is going to happen you are then withdrawing your consent from anything good actually happening to you. Giving the universe, god, you name it, permission to help bring in the great stuff, I feel is crucial..

## Trust

Me and trust we like to tango. Who do we trust, when, and in which circumstances? I have struggled with the concept and had what feels like a lifetimes share of let downs, betrayals and disappointments. However, after doing some inner work I came to the conclusion free will is a founding block of creation. I have allowed others to victimise me, so I have learnt how to stand up for myself in all sorts of environments professional, domestic and social. I now wake up and choose instead of living in victim energy, to follow the concept of - I am the creator of my own universe and day, I choose as much as I can, what will happen to me today.

OF COURSE, there are sides to every concept but this one I find empowering. Situations arise and things happen daily. What we choose is how we react and deal with them. So fragile and yet so important for healthy relationships with others.

## Intuition

I have started working on developing my intuitive abilities as I needed to find a better way of discerning what was happening around me. I work closely with various people daily. Everyone is different and has a varying baseline of what is an acceptable code of behaviour. I wanted to learn how to have healthy boundaries with people asking me for help, so I avoid wearing myself out. Regular Theta meditations and classes truly helped me to start seeing further and deeper into truths of situations.

· · ·

BY STEPPING AWAY and looking at the situations from a higher perspective it saved me from making rushed decisions in the heat of the moment. It helped me not to pick sides in arguments and look beyond singular individual versions of truth. I came to an understanding that everyone has their own truth and that's ok. I also learnt that it's ok for your truth to be different from others'.

MY TRUTH IS what feels truly right and light to me in a given moment. This allows for more flow and flexibility. It gives me a chance to admit to myself or others if I was wrong or made a mistake. Learn from the experience and go forward in life as a slightly better me to myself than I was.

## MY PASSION

What I offer my clients is an opportunity to have a listening ear, a supportive and patient mind of someone who has been through quite a bit and came out the other side sane, well, and successful. I am a survivor. I relate to both women and men that have been through hardships of various kinds and might need some guidance of how to start looking at the world around them with joy, happiness and trust again. Business wise I offer guidance on how to create a business depending on your strengths and passions. I also work with people who seem to have it all, but feelings of happiness and fulfilment elude them for various reasons. Many of us have been taught happiness is unattainable or as soon as you feel it, it fades away. Many of people I work with (including myself at the start of my healing journey), feel they are undeserving of lasting happiness. A lot of us choose to punish ourselves for mistakes we made on a subconscious level and this brings barriers to achieving goals set for success and fulfilment on any level or happiness of any kind. Limiting beliefs in our subconscious mind can sabotage not just our happiness as a whole but all sorts of life aspects.

28

. . .

I WOULD LIKE to offer my personal example of a limiting belief that messed me about for a while. I have taken it on from my ex-husband who until the present moment has been a strong believer that you cannot have both love (or more specifically true love) and financial abundance at the same time. In his universe you are either in a loving happy relationship and struggling for survival, or you are wealthy but miserable since in such a scenario love cannot flourish. This is a generalisation of a complex underlying issue he has been working through during his life. One strand of it has been his belief that big money can only made in illegal ways. This belief he took on from his parents who used to say all wealthy people are frauds of one kind or another.

ANOTHER ONE WAS the fact that this way any responsibility for failure could be avoided. It's not me not trying hard enough, it's the laws of the universe working against me. So I followed suit without even realising it and went down the same rabbit hole. After a while one of the beliefs that came up is that money is evil. Evil destroys love and following this logic money destroys lives.

I WOULD LIKE you to think about it. What stops you from being happy? What blocks your abundance and success? What rules you? Is your own personal cosmos blocking your awesomeness from coming through to full on radiant blinding brightness. For a long time I could not wrap my head around why I would achieve considerable success only to lose everything by trusting someone I shouldn't have. I have tempted fate many times for no solid reason whatsoever apart from needing an adrenaline rush, chasing some sort of divine proof of universal love, support or intervention. First lesson I learnt is do not tempt fate in vain and don't gamble with it unless you are 200% ready to deal with a loss. Most of us are not that good at loosing.

SECOND LESSON, to my surprise was, your relationship with money requires just as much inner work as with people. If you want to have a healthy lasting happy relationship with anything -person, money, plants, animals, work etc then work on it. Taking the good times for granted and becoming complacent has rarely taken anyone far.

THEN AGAIN IT is useful to work on a belief around allowing good and easy luck be part of your daily life and accepting it just like anything else with joy and gratitude.

THIRD LESSON WAS the more joy and gratitude you practice and experience the more of what you need and crave appears in your life. On occasion this even comes in the shape of miracles.

ONE SUCH BLISSFUL occasion of a miracle was when I was having a super tough, full of challenges day and half way through it, Tina Pavlou contacted me about joining her Angelic Reiki class. The timing of it, the gesture and the love coming from Tina was beautiful. I was on the verge of a collapse from fatigue that day. What Tina did changed the day, week and month for me just in the moment when I needed it most.

THIS IN TURN inspired me to be the person Tina was for me for other people. I always say to friends and family when they observe someone unnecessarily rude or nasty and start passing judging comments: " we do not know what kind of hardship that person is going through, who messed up their day so badly that they cannot handle it and are taking it out on others just to ease all that pain, worry or anger somehow ".

IN MY COUNTRY we have a saying that roughly translates as - –'another person's soul is full of darkness' -not in a sense of darkness being bad, but meaning that there will always be part of, or aspects of that person unseen and hidden away from prying eyes. That is our defence mechanism. Few of us are comfortable while being vulnerable. What would it be like for you? What does vulnerable mean for you personally? Is being an open book vulnerable? Is it safe? Or you would rather cover yourself with various shields and masks? Just food for thought.

I KNOW how to feel safe. Do I really? Yes, in the world of probability where everything is possible, I find it is quite easy to overthink. Healthy boundaries and due diligence in every life matter are vital as long as they are in balance. Find what balance you are most comfortable with today. What is good, safe and happy for you today is not the same what will be tomorrow. And that's ok. You are not going crazy. You are just growing, changing and adjusting to the shifting and ever evolving world around us. And if you do get kicked off balance all of us in this book are here for YOU!

THANK YOU BEAUTIFUL SOUL. My gratitude flows to you. May you find your own cosmic self within this amazing cosmos we are sharing.

P.S.: As for me I have joined university at the age of 32, to study Business and Law. Three years will surely fly by and it will be a wonderful journey filled with new friends, experiences and joy. My spiritual journey flies effortlessly filled with magic and unconditional love and support. I wonder daily how lucky I am to have my life, body, health, family and friends, people that I meet daily, strangers that pass me by and inspire me through tiny acts of being human. Thank you all! All of you have made my journey unforgettable and filled with love. To all the people or situations that I deemed hurtful thank you for being my best teachers. Last but not least to all my teachers: Thank you! I would not be where I am without your patience, wisdom and guidance.

# ABOUT THE AUTHOR

## ANNA TOKAROVA

Anna a persistent London based entrepreneur and holistic wellness consultant. She has Sociology and Business Administration educational background as well as a successful business venture running over 8 years.

Anna is passionate about promoting wellbeing in all aspects of life and is a certified Theta Healing® Practitioner and Instructor. A part of her unique approach is a fusion treatment method involving meditation, essential oils healing properties and massage therapy.

Anna has built her beauty and consultancy businesses from scratch and has first-hand experience of what it's like to go through all the ups and downs of such an endeavour. She is an immigrant and a single mom to a son and a step-daughter who according to her have been her guiding stars and pools of inspiration.

Anna chose to be based in Kensington, London as the creative energy in the surrounding area provides continues flow for ideas and new concepts that arise in the fast paced time we find ourselves in.

Her moto professionally is "Go above and beyond for my clients" and personally at present "There's always opportunity for growth and development if one is willing".

**CONTACT:**
**EMAIL:** atokarova8@gmail.com
**LINKEDIN:** www.linkedin.com/in/anna-tokarova
**WEBSITE:** www.letsgetinspired.co.uk

facebook.com/anna.tokarova1

instagram.com/777anicka777

# ASHLEIGH EDWARDS

*I*t has been quite a rollercoaster, growing up always knowing I was a bit different, a total empath which is ok when you know how to deal with others energies, but as a teenager not so easy because I felt everything from everyone most of the time and I was constantly around energy vampires who totally drained me. I have suffered the loss of loved ones and severely damaging relationships which pushed me to where I am today. So I thank the universe for that, but dark times I have been through but always risen from. I have always been very psychic, a clairsentient and claircognizant which has got stronger as I have progressed spiritually.

IN MY YOUNGER DAYS I suffered with depression, and after having my two children the doctor put me on antidepressants and diazepam, I now know better, but I was un-awakened and uneducated then and thought tablets were the answer. They really aren't! They just mask the problem then you get side effects and have to take more tablets for the side effects and so on. You are not dealing with the cause of the problem.

· · ·

MY MIND SET was always "it's just my luck" and everyone would say "Ash, you have the worst luck" and I was totally stuck in this energy and thought process and funnily enough nothing ever went right for me. Then in august 2016 I was visiting my mother in Craon, France, whilst at dinner chatting to a lovely couple they literally flicked the switch for me. The husband and wife told me all about the law of attraction and 'The Secret' and suddenly it all made sense. All I wanted to do was learn more, I was so thirsty for this new information and I knew this was my life from now. I'd been told by several psychics that I would become a healer, and this was the beginning of my journey.

I READ 'THE SECRET' straight away and it all made perfect sense to me, your thoughts become things! Of course, my mindset was still programmed in my old thought pattern, so I started to retrain my brain by consciously being very aware of what I was thinking and putting it out there to the universe, and then my life started to change for the better. It started with finding £20 in my jeans pocket, then a random refund for something I wasn't expecting, it went on from there. I totally transformed my thoughts on money because the more I worried about it the worse it got. Now, no matter what financial state I am in there is no fear or worry because I trust that it is going to be ok, and it always, always is! Switching my frequency to being grateful for the abundance of money that I have has given me such relief.

MY PATH then crossed with my now dear friend and soul sister Katie who introduced me to EFT(Emotional Freedom Technique) which helped me so much to clear emotional pain. Every day we would do some tapping and I could feel the release of emotions leaving my body. Katie said she had a special friend she wanted to introduce me to. Little did I know that this lady would change my life! That's when I met Tina Pavlou (Angel Lady) we met at a girl's lunch but didn't get to chat much, but I could feel her powerful energy, she was like a bright shining light. I knew I wanted to connect with this beautiful Angel lady.

A COUPLE OF MONTHS PASSED, and I was in France again for New Year when I met a truly amazing lady, Chantelle, we instantly connected like we had met in a past life. As soon as she mentioned Reiki that's it, we were off! We chatted deeply about our passion and that we both wanted to heal the world. Chantelle was already Level 2 Reiki and was kind enough to give me a session. I was so excited, I had never had Reiki before, but I had always been drawn to it. My first session was amazing! I was unsure what to expect but Chantelle reassured me and told me to relax and just go with it, taking in the energy. It was a surreal experience I saw lots of different colours and shapes and felt the energy tingling up and down my body. Chantelle's energy was intense. I was so grateful for the session and felt totally away with the fairies afterwards. I knew this was my path and what I would be doing, I could see this in my future. Shortly after I received an invitation to one of Tina's classes on Facebook which was Reiki 1st degree. I knew this was my calling, so I booked on to the course for January 2017.

I WAS QUITE nervous about doing this course but also extremely excited. Tina welcomed me with open arms and gave me a short reading. She said I would become a master teacher and also saw me in India with her in a few years. The energy in the room was so loving and safe. I felt very much at home at the Alders Healing Sanctuary. I have made some amazing new friends some of which have moved on and some are flying high in their spiritual development.

· · ·

NOT LONG AFTER being attuned I had a healing crisis, which is the old energy that you've cleared leaving your body. It's not nice, I cried, was emotional, up and down but Tina kept reminding me, it isn't real. Accept it and go with it,and once it's gone it's gone. Of course, I felt better after and saw the world so differently. It was like I had shed a layer of old energy away.

A MONTH later I did my Reiki 2nd degree which blew me away even more, I did doubt myself a lot putting so much pressure on myself, unsure whether I was feeling what Tina said we should be feeling. Was I doing it right? Can they feel my energy? Then something happened whilst I was giving healing, a small quirky Japanese man came to me and said, "you are doing fine, keep going". He is one of my guides and that was the first time I had met him. He gives me a lot of confidence when I need it. Another one of my guides is a wolf, he always shows me the way. Something I keep having to remind myself I always ask the angels and guides for assistance. Just ask.

AFTER THIS COURSE I had a very strange experience, this really got to me because at the time I had no idea what was happening. I was meditating one evening when I left my body and watched myself die, I was crying over my dead body screaming "you can't die, what about your children" I was so deep in meditation I couldn't come out of it. What was happening to me? It all seemed so real. Afterwards I felt traumatized, was this a warning that something bad was going to happen? I messaged the group to see what their thoughts were, and they were all so reassuring, I had been reborn the girls told me! Makes perfect sense now, I felt a massive shift after and everything was so shiny and bright! I had shed old energy and been reborn into a higher state of consciousness. How amazing is that!

. . .

LAW OF ATTRACTION manifestation class - this was a big thing for me. Tina ran a class on manifesting your desires. She took us up in to Theta during meditation and asked us to send out to the universe what we would like to manifest, being very specific I asked for the most compatible soul mate and then wrote down everything I desired in a soul mate being very careful of my thoughts, because your thoughts become things and what you put out there you get back! Fast forward two months and along he came!

DEAN CAME in to my life and was everything I had asked for, he helped me feel at peace with myself and made my soul content. Also, being fully aware that you should love yourself so much that a partner should complement that, not rely on someone to complete you. I have never had this kind of true love in my life and it scared me as I had only ever known the wrong type of attachments and over the past two years we have grown and developed together wanting nothing but the best for one another. Our souls are so connected and in tune and forever will be, for that I am eternally grateful. Everything I was teaching him he totally related to and understood, and he fully supported me with every single aspect of my life! He taught me how to love and how to be loved. This really did validate how powerful my manifestation skills were and gave me so much more drive to create the life I wanted.

IN JULY 2017 I did my Usui Reiki masters. This was a very special time because Chantelle came down from Essex to do it with me! This was a corker of a course learning to attune people to Reiki. The energy was intense, everyone was buzzing after, we couldn't believe how far we had come. To be able to now attune people to Reiki was an absolute privilege. Again, my vibration got even higher.

.   .   .

I GAVE it a few months before working on people because I wanted to work on myself more, plus I was a little scared. Dean encouraged me to set my Facebook page up for my business. I called it R&R Holistic Therapy for Reiki and Reflexology (I am not a reflexologist yet, it's on my to do list!)

THE CLIENTS STARTED COMING in fast which was brilliant, and I received amazing feedback. It was so rewarding, and I was doing what I loved! I was naturally becoming more psychic and reading peoples energy. Some people were more intense than others, especially if I forgot to protect myself which was a habit I needed to get into. I was very drawn to using crystals with Reiki too and just went with the ones I was drawn to for that person. My vibration was rising higher and higher and I was attracting great things. Your vibe attracts your tribe, and it really does!

MY LIFE WAS amazing everything I was asking for was coming to me and I was very conscious of showing gratitude for everything I had.

IN MAY 2018 I had some major surgery which set me back. I was confined to my house for 6 weeks and didn't see my children for nearly 4 weeks, and I hit an all-time low. I got stuck in a massive hole and my vibration was lowering. Then some personal issues a few months later tipped me over the edge and I crumbled, anxiety hit me along with post traumatic shock. I wanted to touch on this briefly because I think this was a major part of my healing journey. I shut myself off from the world and fed my fears, forgetting how powerful I was. I did not want to admit I was not ok. I had never really suffered from anxiety ever. So, where had this come from?

· · ·

A LOT of people who come to me for healing suffer with anxiety and I understood it, but not having been through it I couldn't imagine what it felt like apart from me feeling their emotion and energy. I believe the universe made me go through this in order to help people on a deeper level, I have learnt new ways of coping and to live in your soul not your mind and also for me to rise to a higher level on consciousness.

So, with some absolutely amazing support from Chantelle speaking with me every day, helping me step back into my power, until I was actually ready to take control and do the work by myself again. Theta healing helped so much and cleared some beliefs and also confirmed that everything I was going through was for me to become not only a better person but a better healer. This lasted around 6 weeks, and I am very proud to be out of the other side using all of the knowledge and tools that I have.

THE UNIVERSE ALWAYS has your back you just have to believe, and also remember that you get what you ask for so change the frequency if it's negative. This was a huge lesson for me, dealing with the personal issues and letting go of the resentment and guilt I was holding on to and addressing my own problematic thoughts. I learnt how powerful our minds are also how destructive they can be. I feel like I am a Phoenix that's risen through the fire! The strength I have now is more than ever before.

SEPTEMBER 2018 WAS a massive game changer, I was finally doing the Theta Practitioner DNA course which is something I have felt so passionately about since I first learnt about it, having watched Tina grow tremendously over the past two years progressing up to a teacher. Witnessing her life transform and opening The Goddess

Rooms which is our beautiful space to learn, give and receive healings and meet for shares. This healing modality is truly amazing because you are clearing subconscious beliefs of all different levels and working in the 7th plane of existence where there is only truth.

AFTER THIS COURSE I was mind blown and felt truly blessed to be a part of this, it really wasn't easy, I have had to face a lot of demons and working on myself, all the time pulling old beliefs out. A month later I did the advanced DNA Theta course which was going deeper into it and understanding more, performing healings, doing belief work, receiving hundreds of downloads, future readings and so much more. I let go of a lot of stuff I had a belief that I wasn't worthy and that I didn't deserve to be loved and love was abuse, it was great to get rid of that! This was really was not serving me one little bit.

THETA HEALING HAD OPENED up my eyes and was like a whole new world to explore and learn. I have only just scratched the surface. When we heal ourselves, we heal the next generation that follows. Pain is passed through the family line until someone is ready to feel it, heal it and let it go which is exactly what I am doing.

SOME VERY IMPORTANT things I have learnt over the last two years;

FIND YOUR SOUL FAMILY, mine are the CChicklets which is Tina's group that she set up. I cannot describe the love that we all give and receive. There is no ego here just love, you feel extremely safe. We have all laughed hard, cried hard with absolutely no judgement of anyone's past. Everyone is on the same mission: to light up the world. We fully support one another in development and courses and most importantly heal one another! Someone is only a phone call or a message away and will give whatever type of support you need.

WE ARE all on our own individual journey but at the same time learning together and sharing our experiences. Everyone has their own unique gift and their own amazing energy. I have met some truly amazing healers who will be lifelong friends. Myself and some of the CChicklets attended Tina's spiritual retreat in Glastonbury in 2017 which was absolutely amazing and something I would highly recommend. I love watching my soul sisters/brothers grow.

IT'S ok not to be ok! We put way too much pressure on ourselves. I have been through some drastic changes emotionally and physically and I have learnt that you have to accept what you are feeling in order to move forward. Acceptance is key.

I HAVE big things planned for the future, I trust that the universe will deliver as long as I do the work on myself, and my vibration is not ever lowered to meet other people. This is actually a very big lesson I have learnt; let people rise to meet me, because I am the one who will suffer.

YOU HAVE to do the work : work on yourself! Mediation, grounding, Reiki, Theta Healing, Reading (you can never know enough, and knowledge is power!) Connect with nature, surround yourself with likeminded people.

GRATITUDE IS THE ATTITUDE! Be grateful for every little thing you have. Show gratitude daily even if it's something as small as being thankful for the tea bag for your cup of tea. Write lists of everything you are grateful for.


Do not feel bad for charging people. It is a business and I am providing a service. This was a subconscious belief I had to work on because sometimes I undercharged and then kicked myself after.

These are the all-important boundaries to set:

- It is not my job to fix others
- It is ok to say no
- It is not my job to take responsibility for others
- Nobody has to agree with me
- I am responsible for my own happiness
- I have a right to my own feelings
- I have a right to express my needs honestly
- I am enough

The only energy is love. Unconditional love, not ego.

Practice what you preach! I have come across people who talk the talk but do not walk the walk. Be your true authentic self!


As your vibration rises new people and opportunities will come into your life and old friends/family may back off. That's ok because they do not match your frequency and are stuck in one place. Let them be, they are on their own journey. When you can't control what is happening, control the way you respond to what's happening. That's where you find your power.


Pay attention to your intuition. If something doesn't feel right in your gut, then it usually isn't. I am very good at reading people's energy and know when someone is lying however, I am now at the place where I accept it is them with the problem and not let their energy affect me or my vibe.

WHAT I FIND TRULY AMAZING IS that my children are learning and are awakened at such a young age! They go to children's Meditation classes and love learning about crystals, and also enjoy Reiki from their mummy!

SO MUCH ENERGY has been released and old beliefs gone, new beliefs have come. Everything starts with you. Healing can be painful, healing can bring emotions up, healing can make you cry, a lot! But it's not real and once it's gone it's gone. We all have subconscious beliefs that control our thoughts and the way we behave, making us self-sabotage, or not able to move forward. If someone says or does something that triggers you, it's you that needs to work on yourself.

I AM FINDING things that trigger me and am working on myself to clear these beliefs with Theta Healing, along with the amazing support from Tina and our soul family. You have to take control of your life and create the future that you want and truly deserve. Trust me, it is totally worth it! Tina, I would like to thank you for giving me this opportunity and for the past few years of teaching me to be my true authentic self and believing in me.

THANK-YOU FOR READING and feel free to contact me link in bio.

LOVE AND LIGHT,
**Ashleigh xoxo**

# ABOUT THE AUTHOR

## ASHLEIGH EDWARDS

Ashleigh Edwards is a mother of two boys who lives by the sea in Ramsgate, Kent. The eldest of four & coming from a large family, caring became natural for Ash. Mr & Mrs Edwards owned a residential care business which was also their family home so instinctively she followed in her parents footsteps going in to the same profession.

At 16 Ashleigh attended college studying Early years and child psychology obtaining her level 3 and then later on her level 4 management in Early years. Ash worked in a nursery school for 7 years, showing her leadership skills with an early promotion becoming assistant manager. Motherhood soon approached & after having two lovely boys of her own she decided that nursery work wasn't for her anymore taking some time to spend being a Mum.

The still quite young Miss Edwards moved to Adults with learning disabilities, supporting the elderly, and worked very hard to obtain her level 5 management of care homes but again, this was not what she really wanted to do. The stress of being a manager and a single mother was not worth it. Although she thoroughly enjoyed helping people and thrived on this deep down knew there was something else she should be doing.

After having her spiritual awakening in 2016 Ashleigh's life totally changed. Still working part time in the care sector, she started her exciting journey completing the Usui Reiki 1$^{st}$ degree learning to heal herself, 2$^{nd}$ degree learning to heal others and finally Master Teacher, which is being able to attune others to Reiki.

Ashleigh has a fast growing number of regular and new clients with amazing feedback and testimonials. She then went on to start her Theta healing journey which has given Ashleigh a totally new perspective on life and healing others through clearing subconscious beliefs. So far, she has completed her Theta Basic DNA and Advanced DNA course and is steadily working her way through the series of courses.

Ashleigh is also a Crystal healer which she finds very effective along-side Reiki healing.

Ashleigh spent some time doing voluntary work with adults who have learning disabilities running group healing sessions and discussions on Reiki and plans to do this again in the near future.

Becoming the master of her own future, she learnt how to manifest great things into her life. Ash feels that her mission is to help people to help themselves and to give them the tools and knowledge to create the life they want and work with her sisterhood spreading love and light across the world.

**Contact:**
    **EMAIL** ashleigh_757@hotmail.com

       facebook.com/ashleighedwards11

# CLAIRE MILLER

*I* have a very happy and positive outlook on life and always put a positive spin on thoughts and situations. I am an ambitious character always wanting to experience new things. I have been told since a child that I am an old head on young shoulders and give wise advice. I always see the best in people unless they prove me otherwise. I think you should be the first to smile, you could lift someone's spirits. Life is about love. Love for yourself and others you encounter.

Gratitude and love are the key to inner peace and a harmonious life. Each morning I set my alarm and it says 'thank you for today' then I step out of bed and say thank you in my head. I am brushing my teeth I repeat thank you, I can instantly feel my mood lift. If you practice gratitude daily for the little things you will notice your life change for the better. 21 days changes a habit. Your mind is a powerful thing; when you fill it with positive thoughts your life will start to change.

. . .

I ENJOY READING and listening to audiobooks mostly around self-development and people. My happy place is with nature whether that be woodland walks or beach walks being around animals and the unconditional love that they offer. I am a good listener and can empathise with people and their situations I have always been sensitive to others energies and a good judge of character. I know when someone is lying which can be useful and I feel others emotions and pains.

PEOPLE HAVE ALWAYS SAID to me over the years what a calming influence I am to be around and what a calming voice I have. When I was younger I would think 'really?' if only you knew how much I had going on in my head at one time you wouldn't think so. I was always thinking of my future ambitions, family, love, relationships, generally what I wanted to do with my life and how I could better myself.

I LIVE in a small town by the sea called Whitstable famous for its oysters. Walking down the high street people say good morning to each other. I find it sad when you go on the tube in London and give someone eye contact they automatically look away and think there is something not quite right about you. What is life for, if not for the relationships we build daily sometimes with strangers. My Dads family are from South London and I love his roots growing up to such phrases like 'I'm just going up the apples and pears to go for a jimmy and take my whistle off' means 'I'm going upstairs to go for a wee and take my suit off!'

I'VE BEEN TOLD before that I need to toughen up. Always thinking of how my reactions affect other people due to how other people's reactions have affected me in the past. Rightly or wrongly I tend to protect myself from the mainstream news. Historically, I would get quite upset by seeing horrible things that happen to helpless people. I realised I have no control over this although I can always send the situation love. I can only control what is in front of me and the people that I encounter on a day to day basis. I can help these people realise that kindness exists and they may then go away and do the same to the people they encounter; like a domino effect! There is so much good in the world – when will the media start covering these stories?

I AM grateful and thankful for my Mum, Dad, Brother and Auntie Linda. They are the reason I am who I am. The love and support they have always shown me is priceless and I am so lucky. I feel abundant with love from my family. We were fortunate enough to have had some wonderful family holidays over the years in America, The Caribbean and Europe. We are part of a large extended family due to both of my Nans being one of ten! I have lots of cousins who I have had loads of fun with over the years. I would definitely choose this lovely lot as friends if I had the choice and I am lucky enough to call them my family! How blessed am I! Family parties with the older aunts and uncles were such fun as kids and these days showed me how important family is to me.

MY EARLIEST MEMORY is me when I was 18 months old having a cyst removed from my neck. All I remember is a nurse playing peekaboo with me and feeling very safe, she was obviously trying to take my mind off of things and just doing her job, but this act of kindness and the laughter stuck with me for a reason. Kindness and thoughtfulness cost nothing but can make a difference to someone's life that you may not even realise.

WHEN I WAS a child my Nan and my brother and I would go to the beach and collect shells and take them back to my Nan and grandpas house and paint them. I would always feel so content and so loved. My Nan always said, 'it's the simple things that mean the most'.

I ENJOYED LEARNING AT SCHOOL, I had good grades and met some really good friends who I am still fortunate enough to be close to now. Who needs a councillor when you have close friends that you can talk to about anything? There are 10 of us now always there for each other through thick and thin. We are a real mixed bunch of characters but all good, genuine hard working people that may not see each other from one month to the next but still have so much love for each other. We span from Canada, Liverpool, Ascot, Margate, Whitstable and Canterbury. All with different lives some with children some without but we have helped each other through some tough times and been part of some of the best. They say your vibe attracts your tribe and these girls are my tribe!

I'VE BEEN WORKING in sales for the last 17 years and I am always learning. I have been on lots of sales and management courses always wanting to better myself. I started working with my Dad at 19 selling new and used cars. I ended up working there for 11 years, working my way up to sales manager. Working with my Dad was fun but also a challenge. I learnt a lot from working with him and one thing that has stuck with me is that you have two ears and one mouth for a reason listening is so important. People buy from people they like, and we would look after our customers like they were our family.

DAD RETIRED and the plan was always for me to one day take his position if I kept working hard enough to impress the owner. To follow in his legacy was the goal but this was not to be after losing out on a promotion. I stayed for a little while afterwards, but the place was just not the same; I felt like I needed a new challenge where I could move myself forward and had exceeded my time limit there. Sometimes what you think is for you is not necessary the path that the universe has for you. The universe always has our back and the next step is always the right one. I felt this was my time to grow and change and rise up to the challenge of something new.

I STARTED WORKING with a prestigious car brand selling and working my way up to business management. They are my work family, we work so hard and have a good laugh in the process. We work with each other ten hours a day sometimes six days a week so share most of our lives together. I really enjoy working with them and meeting new people. The motor trade is a great place to work.

WHEN I WAS 24 a good school friend decided she was going travelling around the world and asked me to go with her. I said no, I was doing well at work and heading towards a management position and saving hard for my own home. I had stayed doing this job working 60 hours a week when I changed my mind and decided to set off on what was one of the best times of my life.

I WENT to Los Angeles for a short break with my Mum before setting off Business Class around the world to Australia, New Zealand, Fiji, Thailand and Japan. All the money I had saved for a house I spent whilst exploring. I have never regretted this. You can always make more money but you can't always make memories. I had so many great experiences and met some wonderful people from all sorts of cultures and it really opened my eyes to the fact that there are a lot of good people in this world.

I BECAME SO CHILLED and go with the flow after spending most of my life rushing about here and there, trying to fit everything in with the hours I was putting in at work. I had an irrational fear of moths which was cured by showering with a load of dead ones around the shower cubicle in a hostel in Broome!

I HELD a gigantic python at the Steve Irwin Zoo, skydived, and bungee jumped twice. We skied in New Zealand, chilled and took in the beauty of Fiji, Island hopped around Thailand and stayed with a Buddhist community in Japan. I felt so grateful of the beauty and history, experiencing the different cultures, food, people and adventures.

TRAVELLING the world with nothing but a back pack living with such limited resources really simplified my life. In New Zealand my friend and I were driving our campervan through the North Island and decided to camp for the evening. We were cooking our dinner and a man approached us; he was older than us and looked like a hippie. He was a happy friendly man and just wanted to be our friend. The following day he asked us if we would like to meet a couple of his friends we agreed and followed him in our bright orange campervan through beautiful hills and windy roads. We eventually reached this tiny house; very remote and were greeted by an equally friendly couple who invited us in for a cup of tea.

MY FRIEND and I often speak of this experience and look back on it fondly. We walked through the tiny house into the garden and wow there we were - surrounded by acres of beautiful luscious green hills with a tree swing for the children to play on and a tree house that the children slept in. The mum had lit some wood underneath a free standing bath so they could all have a hot bath later. The children were so happy and excited to meet us and show us their tree house so we climbed the ladder the father had built into the children's bedroom. Three of them slept up there and it looked like so much fun as a child.

THIS WAS such a beautiful experience to see the family's happiness from the simplicity of life. This was a great lesson to what is really important. For someone that always wanted the latest phone, nice cars, clothes and makeup this really opened my eyes to a simpler way of living. This goes back to what my Nan always said, 'that it's the simple things in life that mean the most'.

I REMEMBER COMING home to my bedroom and feeling like it was Aladdin's cave but also remembering that I didn't need it all. I have been very fortunate in life to visit some wonderful countries and meet some amazing people. Travel is good for the soul it gives you balance in life.

PEOPLE ARE such an essential part of my life! Love and relationships with my partner and family and friends are very important to me. If everyone could work from a place of love and kindness the world would be such a better place to be. You don't know what burdens of life people are carrying around with them. By showing a little compassion or kindness you can give people hope, that there is good in this world.

I AM AN EMPATH. Naturally, you hear empaths can be drawn to a narcissist behaviour in a romantic partner. I have had a brief encounter previously and I can identify why. I felt vulnerable from a previous long term relationship ending and an old flame came along and made me feel like it was meant to be. It wasn't. I wasn't myself and felt totally out of character. I realised I had given away my power trying to help this person feel better, trying to help him fix his problems which he had opened up to me about from his childhood. This person needed professional help and as soon as he realised I couldn't help fix him he left me the following day.

I USED to be a YES kind of girl but learning to say no can be a very powerful thing. Find what makes you happy and not everyone else. I have learnt you can't fix someone you can only fix yourself, so you are no longer attracting these types of people. You must work on yourself and learn to love who you are before expecting someone else to love you.

I DECIDED I would write a list of manifestations of what I wanted in my next partner. Mainly life values, personality traits. In September 2015 I met him – kind, generous, funny, sensitive, makes me laugh and also doesn't mind putting me straight on things. I feel very fortunate to have this connection. At Christmas 2017 he proposed, and we are getting married next year, very exciting.

THE POWER OF MANIFESTATION! You truly can get what you want from life. You just have to believe you already have it. I have always had a good relationship with money I believe that if you think you will always have money you will. I think of myself as wealthy therefore I am always looked after financially. Once I was driving home from a meeting hours away from home and I thought to myself that I would love not to have to cook, but really fancied a hot chicken dinner. I couldn't believe it when minutes later my friend rang me and said she had plated an extra dinner up for me and she would drop it round. I was delighted. Such an act of kindness on her part and manifestation at it again! Whether it be a chicken dinner or a promotion or a future relationship I urge you to give it a go.

I KNOW that I will always be looked after in this life I have good intentions towards everyone I encounter. I have met people whose intentions are not as pure as mine and I have learnt that you're always your number one priority! You are the person that lives your life no one else. Of course you have life partners, friends and family but if you are not happy with yourself then how can you expect the people round you to be happy? Working on yourself through a path of self-development is so fulfilling.

I HAVE learnt to choose my audience over the years when speaking about spirit, crystals, energies etc as some people will ridicule what you have to say and think that you're crazy. Maybe a little crazy is good... wouldn't it be boring if we were all the same! It is important for you to not be affected by these people.

MY RESPONSIBILITY to myself is to maintain healthy boundaries, especially with those who are unhealthy. One day they will be awakened too and will look back and maybe remember the things you have said.

EVERYONE'S spiritual development is at different stages and paces; we are all on our own journey. Thinking that you are better than someone else is not only incorrect, but you are also working from your ego. We are all equal and have the same tools available for self-growth. What are you going to do with yours?

I EMPATHISE with people in such a way that before I learned how to protect myself, I would take on the energy of peoples' problems and would walk away feeling down or confused, that person however would walk away feeling great! I have learnt to be thankful of this gift of sensitivity and say in my head if I feel like I am empathising too much 'Thank you this is not mine' and I noticed that this feeling I had taken on from that person would disappear and once again I would feel myself; although enlightened and grateful of this gift.

A LOT of physical pain can be bought on by emotional pain that has not yet been healed from the past. By helping this emotional pain and getting to the root cause you can switch your mind set into good things for you. Why wouldn't you try it? I decided that I wanted to help people; if not to heal them completely but make their life easier somehow and give them hope that they too can heal themselves.

AFTER HEALING myself over the years I have set up a business Whitstable Holistic Therapy which I run in the evenings from a healing room in my home. I wanted to help others be able to have a safe space to come and be treated without any judgement, my ethos is everyone should always leave me feeling happier.

I would always encourage self- reflection and self-development, being self-aware is so important.

THE AMOUNT of people that I have come across in life that are quite happy to talk about themselves and some very rarely ask how you are as a person. Over the last few years I have taken this is a compliment. I must come across as someone that really has my 'shit together' so no need to ask me; however trust me sometimes it's just nice to be asked.

I FEEL energies from people and animals. I can feel if they are upset or happy I do need to protect myself from these energies as I have been known to take these emotions on myself and then wonder why I feel rubbish. Now I can work from a space of sending them healing and not taking it on. I like to be able to send love to these people. My energy tends to drops in crowds and I feel the need to protect myself. I despise arguing or fighting partly due to the fact I hate loud noises and have very sensitive ears.

As WELL AS being a Usui Reiki Master I trained in reflexology, Indian head massage, Hopi ear candles, Swedish massage and Angelic Reiki. My purpose in this world is to help others, which I feel is everyone's purpose in life. After you have helped someone doesn't it feel great? When you know you have helped someone realise there true potential within themselves it doesn't get better than that.

I FIND self-care such as meditation, reflexology, Reiki, massages all help to balance your body, mind and soul. If you do not deal with emotions from past or present this can turn into illnesses and diseases in the body. By talking and releasing these emotions you feel so much lighter.

THE BEST PIECE of advice I have received is not everybody is the same as you. I would have high expectations of people as I am kind, considerate, and thoughtful and in turn I expected everyone else to be this way. Growing up you realise not everyone is the same and that's ok. Everyone has their day to day challenges that they are facing and some people have invisible illnesses. Just be kind it's that simple. When you learn to interact with everyone from a place of love it does affect your environment. You will come across difficult people – god knows I have! The test of your character is how you behave and react to these people.

. . .

DON'T SHOUT AT PEOPLE! Raising your voice is unnecessary and a loss of control. If you feel someone did do something on purpose to hurt you, then that is their issue and their drama. Send them and the situation love. This is hard. Forgiveness isn't easy but when you are in a place of forgiveness that person cannot hurt you anymore. Ultimately we are all one of the same.

HOW YOU DEAL with your emotions and react to those people around you affects your soul. Don't give anyone your power! That's your power, your body and your mind. You can share yourself with people but don't give it all away. If you react with love and kindness and remain calm in difficult situations you feel so much better.

I REMEMBER a powerful post from a friend of mine years ago on social media declaring that she was sorry to the man she cut up in the car this morning she was sorry that he was angry with her she has just left the doctors and found out she had breast cancer and wasn't thinking. Thank god my friend is now happy and healthy but Wow! You never know what's going on in someone's life so give them a break!

EVERY MORNING and every night I lay my hands on my solar plexus and feel the love and healing energy from the universe. This knowledge that you are unconditionally loved by the universe and your angels is such a wonderful feeling.

I HAVE MET people over the years who have been so affected by their childhood they carry their emotions into adulthood and therefore affect the people they encounter. I have seen how childhood interactions are so important to who you can become as an adult. Children are special and gentle souls whose soul is conditioned by its environment. A baby is not born a sexist or racist person its life's conditioning that can make you that way. Every child is born a fresh new start the parents are the ones that teach values and show children how to react and children copy you. We could learn a lot from children; keep your childlike wonder, it is so important to be silly and light hearted sometimes.

I AM VERY POSITIVE HOWEVER, I am a realist and sometimes life will throw you people or situations to deal with and you are the only one who can work through it. You are the one who has to look at yourself in the mirror each day and be happy with who is staring back at you. Ultimately your life is about you. You are the director of your own life. You can do anything you set your mind to and if you really want to do something you will do it.

ONE OF THE worst times of my life was when my Nan passed away and during this period I felt helpless wanting to be able to heal her or at least ease her pain somehow. Tina came to me around the time of her passing and gave me Reiki which helped me with the grief. Could this help in healing pain too? Emotional and physical.

I HAVE KNOWN Tina now for nearly seven years. We met at a local pub when she was part of a psychic evening giving out readings. I went with a friend and as we walked in Tina waved at me from across the room. I tried to sign up to see Tina but she had a long waiting list so I had a reading with another lady instead. A month or so later I saw advertised that Tina was going to be at another local pub, so I went along early with my cousin in the hope to see Tina this time around. When I had my reading with her she told me 'if you're the only person

I meet tonight this whole evening will be worthwhile' her energy was so uplifting and I instantly felt drawn to her. She is such a positive and genuine presence. She invited me to have Reiki with her. She blew me away with her energy. She suggested I learn Reiki to be able to practice on myself so I attended a class.

I'D HAD Reiki a couple of times before when I went to a health spa with my mum over the years and I found the experience uplifting and very relaxing. I felt like I was on a hamster wheel working long hours and not truly connecting with myself. I knew there was more to me.

I WENT BACK to Tina and learnt Reiki 1 for practicing on yourself, Reiki 2 is for healing others and became a Reiki Master in 2016 enabling me to teach Reiki to others. It has helped me clear my mind even if I close my eyes for a minute, I can centre myself back to a natural state of euphoria.

SINCE LEARNING Reiki and practicing with clients I have found an inner peace and quiet and can create a natural place of calm within, which is priceless considering how fast pace my head used to be. It really is great for deep relaxation and stress relief. When having Reiki I often see green, purple and white glittery colours like you would see in a lava lamp I see this in my mind's eye. Everyone has different sensations when having Reiki like feeling heat from the hands and just feeling relaxed.

IT HAS BEEN a pleasure getting to know Tina and I have always felt like she was looking after me as I was one of the youngest in the Chicklets group. I have always felt fiercely loyal towards her and I know that she has my back and I have hers. She has been through some rough times and has come out the other side and is a true inspiration to us all. that we can all do it if we want to. After spending just five minutes in Tina's company you feel uplifted.

SHE HAS GIVEN me some fantastic opportunities one of which is being a part of this book. She invited me to one of her friend's yoga retreats a few years ago. I was not so great at the yoga side of things, but I gave it a good go, I enjoyed the classes, workshops and sound baths and just being around like-minded people. Our signature song for this weekend was the 'power of love' and I remember at the end of the retreat listening to this song and just all of a sudden sobbing – healing – what a powerful release of emotions, that I didn't even know were there to release, until it came up!

RELEASING IS EXHAUSTING but oh so worth it, it strips the layers away from yourself that have been stored in your body – yukky emotions that you have experienced through your life released away and you feel so good afterwards. It is a happy buzzy feeling and you feel lighter in body and mind. Healing, self-development and having the right people around you are important for your growth as a person.

TINA INTRODUCED me to her Reiki master Samantha Trew the author of 'The Wakeup Call'. Sam is a lovely lady; in 2015 I had seven sessions with Sam with two weeks apart. Having this two week break enables your body to realign the chakras to the way they should be – sometimes they can be out of sync due to experiences or people you may encounter. Reiki realigns your chakras and moves you forward into a new and improved you.

SAM WOULD SIT and listen to me for well over an hour and we would talk about each other's lives and experiences. She is a fantastic life coach and I would recommend her to anyone. She has shown me how to let go of things that no longer serve you. She worked on my chakras noticing any blockages or stored emotions and removed them. I could have cried for days on end, and at times I felt so drained and down in the dumps, but then I would feel so much better. Like a new updated version of myself. This is called a healing crisis and it can last a couple of days. The key is to listen to your body if you need to be alone then do it, if you need to have an early night then do it.

YOU DO NOT REALISE the emotions that affect your day to day living and how they can be stored in your body. When receiving Reiki you literally feel the emotions attached to these problems and worries being removed and being replaced with love, light and happiness.

MY FIRST CRYSTAL I bought was an amethyst, I was drawn to the sparkly purple colours it has and did not really know much about crystals apart from I liked this one. On my Reiki one training Tina gave me a large rose quartz which had a beautiful light and fluffy energy around it. Its purpose is unconditional love. It's always a good idea to pick up a crystal and see how you feel when you touch it to see if its energy suits yours.

EACH OF THE seven major chakras have a set of crystals that help balance and heal areas of your life. My current favourite is celestine and clear quartz they make me feel at peace and closer to my angels. Now I have crystals everywhere in my bra, my purse, my car, my home and at work. All crystals have different healing properties. I have a good crystal collection and would encourage anyone to look into buying a crystal to help; you can get crystals to help with anything.

. . .

I AM ALSO interested in Numerology and Synchronicities. I first started encountering number sequences for example looking at the clock and seeing 11:11 or 22:22 or 3:33 or 4:44. All of these numbers hold meaning and I guarantee if you look out for this you will see what I mean. This is a way of your angels sending you messages to connect; other signs of this is feathers, robins and pennies. I started seeing 11:11 the awakening code and googled it and blimey how many other people see the same. I always say thank you when I see this and know that I am on the right path.

AFTER NOTICING 11:11 I realised that the number 37 pops up for me regularly in my life before I even knew that numerology is messages from your angels. The synchronicity is incredible. I had a private number plate, phone numbers, bank accounts, house numbers, and I often see it on the TV or table numbers in restaurants its everywhere! Is this just a coincidence....I don't think so.

SYNCHRONICITY IS your angel's way of communicating with you and giving messages of reassurance to show that you are on the right path and everything is ok. The number 37 means independence and getting things done yourself. I can relate to this I have always been a very independent person knowing that I can do anything I put my mind to. Look out for these little reminders that the universe has your back!

EVERYONE HAS guardian angels you just have to remember to ask them for help! There is such a thing as free will, which is where angels can't intervene in your life unless you ask for their help. I can imagine angels looking at us sometimes thinking please would you just ask me to help! How amazing….a dedicated team always there for you waiting to help at a moment's notice, you just have to remember to ask them!

I WOULD LOVE for you to get in touch with me if you want to work on yourself and realise your true potential. We are all evolving daily I am not the same person that I was 6 months ago. Each day is a time to expand and update to the best version of yourself. You create your story, you live in that story, and if you don't like the story, only you can change it.

I ALWAYS KNEW this was the path for me all the love I have received in my life it's time to share it with others to let others know that there is so much good in this world.

THERE IS ALWAYS something to be grateful for….Thank you Universe xxx

# ABOUT THE AUTHOR

## CLAIRE MILLER

Claire Miller is a 36 year old woman born in Canterbury, Kent and lives in the seaside town of Whitstable. She is a holistic therapist and sales business manager for a prestigious car manufacturer.

Claire has always been ambitious and wants to help people. Claire has spent 17 years in the corporate world climbing the ladder and working within a male dominated environment.

Claire has also experienced and recovered from burn out during her time in the corporate world giving her an understanding of how today's world and its challenges can affect women, their minds, their bodies and their soul.

Claire is a healer, a Usui Reiki Master and Angelic Reiki Practitioner. She also practices Reflexology, Indian head massage, Swedish massage and Hopi ear candles, from a healing haven in her home.

Claire loves to help others realise their true potential and believes in positivity, affirmations and taking time for you to refresh yourself. She is someone who radiates positivity and no matter what sees the light in the dark and helps others to see joy and happiness.

Claire believes positive attitudes breed's positive outcomes and wants everyone to leave her feeling happier.

Claire is engaged to Stuart and away from work she can be found enjoying her hometown, reading books, spending time with friends and family and travelling as often as possible.

Contact:
   **Email:** whitstableholistictherapy@gmail.com
   **Website:** www.whitstableholistictherapy.net

f facebook.com/whitstableholistictherapy

# DIMPLE THAKRAR

*little Indian girl conceived in Uganda, evicted by President Amin overnight. She survived, her family survived, but the riches didn't. Born in Bolton 1973, to a beautiful, now known to be spiritual mother, and a father who knew no better. Born on 30th April 1973 and she felt her love, her protector, her soul mate, her plane traveler, her hero with her and here the love story begins.............*

MY FIRST CHILDHOOD memories were of my mother's blood on the wall, my first feelings were of pain as she was beaten while I was in the womb. Fast forward, a few years, going to school with my beautiful mother. She was a stunning woman, a delicate, joyous flower. She blossomed and shone but people around her didn't understand her and wanted to dull her shine. It was impossible, looking back at what I felt and know now to be true, is that nobody else can dull your shine, only you. She wasn't giving them the power. So, to protect her light she became, according to the 'doctors' a paranoid schizophrenic. I call it living in a parallel universe where her shine was acceptable, and her glow was appreciated.

.  .  .

She was joyous, loving and acknowledged for her beauty in this world. She was happy and her girls were happy with her. She wasn't a threat to me or my two sisters, just to herself and so they drugged her with Lithium, and it killed her soul. She hated being on it and would often stop taking them to go back into her happy plane. The family used to get frustrated with her, but for her it was worth her not taking her tablets enabling her to shine and feel alive.

Childhood memories of joy and love filled our home because of my mum's "craziness" she showed us how to live with feeling and be fun. To laugh out loud and not care what people thought, to garden bare foot and feel the earth in her toes, to sing until your heart song sings. My father worked and provided. He did protect us but was brainwashed by mass consciousness and his mother. He was a good little Indian boy, the eldest of 8. He didn't know any better, my mum found her happy place and despite all of this she raised 3 beautiful girls with so much love, beauty, joy, laughter and a little bit of crazy!

When we moved to England, we were refugees. My mum left overnight with her in-laws and my then 5-year-old sister. Her husband (my dad) was left behind to sort the millionaire business that the family had built over the years or be killed by President Amin's "soldiers". Mum did not know if she would see her man again. The love of her life. She adored him and was being sent to a faraway country, 7 months pregnant with a woman that was the source of her beatings. What the f**k! What a woman.

Her legacy of strength and trust lives on through each and every one of her daughters and granddaughters. We are warriors. We are angels of the light. We are gods' creation. We are Lakshmi.

SHE ARRIVED in a refugee camp having traveled for days. Unfamiliar with the language, scared and vulnerable. She was alone. No, she wasn't – god always protects the light. My now father-in-law rescued her, he was sent to protect her and protect her he did. He lived at 77 and we lived at 22. He provided her with her family sanctuary, a place to escape and be, a place to be loved and to heal. The house of pure love and light.

THEY HAD two boys and the youngest took care of her, and as he grew to a strong 6 ft. young man – he physically stopped the pain and said no more. My beautiful family knew no different. They had been seduced by the demons within. I know that now. It was the cultural norm. Still wrong but they were weak. He had the internal battle of having the love of his life being gifted to him shining so bright and yet the demons inside him were blinded by the light and tried to dull it. He found a way. He never left her despite the demons telling him to send her to an institution and get a fresh wife. He knew that this love was pure, and he would never have a love like this again and he never did.

FAST FORWARD A FEW years and always knowing that I could see and feel things, but they frightened me. So, I became scared of the dark and being alone because I could feel and dream things I didn't want to know or understand. I couldn't control it. I was going mad like my mum. I was going to be the embarrassing crazy lady that gardened bare foot in the front garden in view of the posh neighbours. I was going to be the crazy lady that laughed so loud and freely that everyone stared with envy! Hell, no I wasn't. I was 13 and I needed to take control! And boy did the universe provide it for me.

Be careful about what you wish for. The trigger arrived! "You are fat, aren't you fat?", my sister and now husband said to me in the kitchen. I remember it so vividly. They didn't mean it in the way I took it, but I was going to control this one and boy did I control it. What strength of character! I remember thinking that "I will show them who is fat". I started to exercise 3 times a day and became a walking Encyclopedia for the calorie content of foods. I knew exactly how many calories I was expending and how many I was using. I balanced the numbers perfectly every day but did not allow any calories for breathing, my heart beating or living! It sucked the life out of me, and I lost a third of my tiny childlike body. It was brutal. My periods stopped for two years. I lost myself, I forgot to smile and laugh.

I was in control of my self-destruct button. Game over! No way. I am my mother's daughter. I am my mother's light. I am light. I have her strength to survive and even at that tender age I knew I had work to do on this earth. I had a path laid out for me. The universe wasn't done with me. I survived the anorexia. I learnt from it and it drove me to search for the truth. The truth about nutrition and love. Self-love.

I became a dietitian.

In 1995 I married the love of my life, my soul mate, my protector and my lover. The beautiful young man that lived at 77 that I met the day I was born. He loved me unconditionally. He was there the day that I was born. I knew we were connected in past lifetimes. I just knew. We had been raised as brother and sister but our hearts grew to be lovers.

His kindness and generosity to others was so seductive and our love was explosive, our love was strong. We married a year earlier than we wanted to – at my father's request. He had had my charts read by an astrologist at birth who determined the year I should marry would be 1995 and not 1996. It was immediately after I graduated from university. This was my first encounter with numbers and spirituality, although when I look back, I was truly guided. This was the biggest gift and I am so grateful to my father for insisting, as you will discover what happened to mum in 1996. In fact, when I look at how I was raised, with chanting and bhajans (Hindu hymns), and my Hindu heritage the path had already begun. I simply wasn't aware of it.

WE BOTH WANTED a small intimate wedding, but this was not our path. My mother insisted on a huge Indian wedding and so it was to be. You see despite my parent's rough beginnings; my father was a true romantic with huge gestures! Like the way he took mum to the solicitors on their 25th wedding anniversary to sign their wills, or so she thought, and he had arranged with the solicitor to give her the keys to her new dream house. Not only that, but he had completely re-decorated the house and it was ready to move into! He was so in love with her and he was finally free to express it. So, when she asked him for our big wedding, her wish was my father's command. So Atul and I became husband and wife on 20th August 1995 in front of 1200 people. Yes, you read it correctly 1200! We didn't care, we had the most amazingly funny and joyful day.

I HAD AGREED to move in with his parents and naively agreed to live with them forever as I loved his parents dearly. However, going from the freedom of university life to living in a moderately sized love filled home with my new husband and his parents, proved to be more challenging than I had anticipated. The arguments began. I had started a new job and my mother had become ill. So, the hospital appointments began and the responsibility of it all fell on my shoulders as both of my sisters lived too far away. The stress took its toll on our new marriage. We were kids trying to make the most of the situation in a small space. The clash of the two cultures was difficult for me.

THE BELIEFS and constraints I had put on myself to be the perfect traditional Indian daughter-in-law were suffocating and it resulted in me building up resentment and anger towards Atul and his beautiful parents. I needed space, I needed to breathe. I spent too much time at work and Atul did the same. We had no idea on how to communicate with each other, never mind live together. When my mum's health turned in November 1995 it was so difficult for both of us, because Atul was the son she never had, and he was struggling with his wife's emotions as well as his own. He was building our future with his businesses and I didn't understand it – why couldn't he get a job?

MY MUM WAS DIAGNOSED with stage four ovarian cancer on Valentine's Day and died on 16th March 1996. I knew she was passing before anyone else. I knew she was going. I was frozen in time, helping and supporting my family. I was angry at her for going so early. I was angry because she had been taken in her prime. She had only just, in her last weeks of life being given the love and respect she deserved from her family. It's like the anger turned a switch in me that I would never trust god again. I mean what kind of god takes a beautiful innocent woman at the age of 47! She was scared when she left. But she was with her beloved and he held her as she passed. She was granted her wish. Thank you. I was angry with god, the world, the doctors for missing it, myself for not picking it up and I took it out on my husband for 20 years.

·　·　·

WE HAD HAD ENOUGH, love wasn't enough, and we made each other miserable. The bad times started to outweigh the good times. It was too much for the children and for us. It was time to call it a day. The outwardly perfect power team were throwing the towel in after 20 years of a roller coaster of a marriage. We decided to plan our exit strategy, just like in a business. On our 25th wedding anniversary we would split and go our separate ways, when our youngest daughter was 18 years old. The journey of splitting the assets had begun. I was so hurt and so frustrated that this beautiful man could be so amazing for everyone else except me, or so I thought. I became resentful and bitter and hurt by the years I had put my life on hold to have the children, while he pursued his dream.

DON'T GET me wrong I was a very successful dietitian, having completed research, presented it at national conferences, and represented dietitians in Europe and on the BBC1. As well as 15 years supporting people with Motor-Neuro Disease, Parkinson's, Multiple Sclerosis and Strokes to die a dignified pain-free death, free from starvation and dehydration. It was here that I really did my apprenticeship in the intuitive healing space. I was able to know when someone was passing and what they and their family needed. I was an empath and didn't even know it.

DURING JULY 2016 I left the NHS after 20 years of service, it was time for me to start my business and write my book. I was scared, I didn't believe I could, who would want me? What if I got it wrong!

I KNEW IT WAS RIGHT, it was now or never. I took the plunge and was so successful. It was the right thing to do and before I knew it, I was making 3 times what I had been making in the NHS and teaching other dietitians how to shift their mindset from the NHS to business, as my husband had always said, he had had faith that I would be amazing! My business coach at the time introduced me to Tony Robbins. A very big guy who talked a lot of sense. I watched a few videos on you tube and I felt my heart opening. I felt my vulnerability opening to feel love and release the anger. The pain I had carried for 20 years. The shutting down of my soul was starting to awaken. I booked to see him in London in 2017 and was so excited. The universe drew me to his Platinum Partners desk, and I had signed up as this was my last chance with my marriage. I was so desperate to keep the love of my life and I needed to understand how.

TONY WAS HOLDING a relationship event and I had to get Atul there. Firstly, I had to tell him what I had done. I was scared. I called him at midnight and said, "please don't shout but I have done something crazy!" He replied, "Whatever it is we can sort it, just tell me." He had been travelling for 48 hours was exhausted and I think he thought I had had an affair or something. "I said I have joined Platinum Partners and the cost is $xxxxx ". I was scared because my business was going well but not that well! How would I afford it financially and spending the time away? Wait for it, ladies, his reply is going to make you cry! He replied – "20 years ago you took a job so I could follow my dream and my passion, you invested in me and now it is my turn to invest in you. So, the way I see this is, it's an investment in you, your business and all those souls you will impact. We will make this happen." Remember we were getting divorced. We were getting ready to split. The beautiful man literally loves me unconditionally! I cried.

THE NEXT HURDLE was getting him to the relationship event in Maui.

THE EVENT just happened to be the same week as his brand-new company, a company that he had just acquired, was at the biggest trade show in France. He had an internal struggle, work or love? Which, for a serial entrepreneur was tough. He chose love.

WE ARRIVED in Maui after 2 days of traveling. He had never even heard of Tony Robbins let alone been to an event. Meanwhile I had already been to 4 by this time and established my friends. I was still angry at the world and yet felt this conflict with my inner true self. The battle of the awakening had begun.

DAY 1 and Tony asked the room (400 people) "who in the room doesn't want to be here?"

I NEARLY DIED as 3 people stood up and my man was one of them! How could he embarrass me in front of Tony! A part of me was also proud because he was man enough to stand up for his truths. Tony looked him straight in the eye, man to man, it was so powerful that in that moment it felt like it was a slow-motion movie, life slowed right down, as Tony said directly to Atul – "I just ask you keep an open mind please?" Atul looked him straight in the eye and nodded. It was done the male seal of approval, Atul trusted him as a man because he had honored his integrity as a man. It was done.

DAY 2 and of course we have a fight and I don't want him anywhere near me and I get him to sit by himself while I sit on the front row with my friends. The whole day he tries to make up for something that is not his fault and I push him away. Then at 10.30 pm it starts by me saying something that Tony disagrees with and 2 hours later he has broken me and awoken me to the magnificent love of my life. My beautiful man that would defend me to the death, would stand up against Tony 6ft 7 Robbins to save me from the big bad wolf! I was awakened, rebirthed and found my soul again. Let the spiritual journey begin. The door was opened, and I had stepped right in. Thank you, universe. Thank you.

18 MONTHS later I had attended 18 events all around the world in the space of 12 months and I was a transformed woman. I was coming back. I had the greatest awakening and teachers. Learning and growing spiritually and serving as I grew.

I HAD SHIFTED and my vibration started to attract people and situations into my field. I found my best work was when I was guided and words would come from nowhere, almost as if they weren't my words. I felt people's souls as opposed to *thinking* what the right thing is. I worked from love. But it was inconsistent, and I was unable to command it and serve on demand. I didn't know how to tune in. And so, my business, home life with my girls and relationship were very volatile, like the ocean, and my income became very volatile. Some days I made more money than I could ever imagine and then I would have dry spells and blamed it on business with the belief that that is how business operates.

I KNOW NOW that is not the truth. The truth is that my vibration was volatile and explosive, just like a child learning to understand its power. Learning how to use language, understand relationships and the dynamics of their impact on the world. So, if they cried or laughed, they learnt the reaction of others around them! Of course, the universe had plans for me and I needed a guide and naturally when the student rises the teacher appears. But I needed evidence of the teachings and the modality that this would take. Serendipity was about to prevail.

. . .

ON MY FINAL Tony Robbins trip – an adventure trip in Cannes, France, one of our many expeditions was driving vintage cars. Now I am not really a car person, I don't like driving and I am very uncomfortable with driving on the wrong side of the road. So, the thought of driving an old car for 2 hours on the wrong side of the road didn't fill me with joy! We had to partner up and it was almost as if the universe sent me my knight in shining armor. William appeared from the heavens and offered to drive me both ways. He loved to drive, and I am guessing he sensed my fear and reluctance. The two hours we spent together I will never forget. We laughed, we talked, and I learnt so much and most of all, we connected. I trusted him with my children's life! He made me feel safe. He is the epitome of elegant masculine energy.

I RETURNED home and weeks went by and we stayed connected through Facebook and then one day I saw his advert for something called theta healing. I had never heard of it, but as I was guided with Tony Robbins, once again I had found myself booking a session. I must have known this was the path to my next spiritual awakening. The answer to me understanding who I really was, am, and learning my identity of trusting all is Divine timing.

I HAD 3 sessions with William over the months and was blown away by what he could tell me over the phone especially as he was in Australia and I was in the U.K. During this time serendipity occurred again because William's wife Joanne, was very active on Facebook with live posts and organizing events with a lady called Tina. I was curious! Who is this Tina? What does she do? And as if by "magic" I tuned into a Facebook live at a time when I wouldn't usually be on Facebook and it was Joanne's live interview with Tina. Tina was doing a reading, there were 30 plus people on and she picked my question first and answered it! I was blown away! You see the universe always provides exactly what you ask for.

I AM A SCIENTIST, so I needed to experiment and experience firsthand to trust the teacher. I was hooked. William had sent me a theta healing meditation to do and I had been doing it daily because I was hooked on the high. Weeks pasted and several messages later, I asked Tina if she ever came to the UK assuming she too was in Australia. Nope she was based in UK! What the f**k. I asked when her next course was and how could I find out more. I was in Spain at the time, and she was in Australia and would come back to me. That was 2019 January. The dates arrived and it was at the end of February. I was dishearten as my husband and I had booked to start our spiritual journey in India at O and O University. The dates had been booked, paid for and scheduled. As Tina sent me her dates for May I knew it wouldn't be May. I just knew that it would be February but didn't concern myself with the "how".

THE UNIVERSE ALWAYS PROVIDES, and it did. The course in India got cancelled (unheard of) and the universe sent me to Tina. I had not asked any questions about the course or the length of the course or content. Tina sent me the dates for a 2-week course (or so I thought) and organized it all. It would be our first valentine's day apart in 23 years. I realized that it was okay because every day with my beautiful man had become a valentine. We had grown so much and continued to grow. It was beautiful, he once again supported and trusted me on my path and took care of all the logistics back home with Kiera, our 14-year-old gift – and there's a whole other book about the gift of our two angels Maya and Kiera. How they came into the world is truly a miracle.

· · ·

So, I arrived on the 13th February 2019 not knowing where to go or what I was doing. I didn't even have an address. I remember my husband saying, "It might be worth me having an address?" – lol. I later found out that he wanted to send me a dozen roses for valentines. Bless him. He did and all the ladies in class enjoyed them.

THE SECOND AWAKENING of my spiritual journey began. The student presented and the teacher appeared. I did 5 theta healing courses back to back over 13 days. Unbeknown to me this was unheard of. Once again, the creator had guided Tina and I had trusted. She taught me that people look at me not because I am the only Indian but because my inner beauty shines bright. To love me.

MY STAMINA and commitment for my mission, to transform relationships with yourself, your significant other and the food you eat, possess me like an angel from god. Like Lakshmi. I find inner strength effortlessly for this work. It comes with ease and grace. I travel this path hand in hand with all my sisters and brothers. This mission is greater than me. My king has been with me in this lifetime and many more before as my protector.

MY SOUL HAS BEEN AWAKENED through the teachers that have been presented. I am light. I am love. I am justice for the beautiful dance of masculine and feminine energy within me and the others. I am light. I am joy. I learnt self-love, not only to give it but to receive, acknowledge and accept it. In fact, cherish it because we are all worthy. We are all whole. We are all love. We are all light. I now know how to use my power and guide it and people, to a place of peace and joy. My path is so clear. My soul is pure. I have no fear except to warn me, but I am light. I am safe. I am protected. I am loved. Love is pure. We are a gift on this life time. Use it to serve and you will be taken care of. I thank all my spiritual leaders along the way - past, present and future. I honor and respect you.

ON THE 26TH February 2019 I performed my first healing on my beautiful king. I asked the creator "how do I explain to him what I have learnt". He is so curious and yet I can't find the words. Then in a flash while meditating it came to me. "He needs a healing." He trusted me. I healed him on a matter that was unresolved for 10 years and he changed in that moment. Our lives will change forever because of the law of attraction. Because his vibration will now attract exactly what he deserves and desires. It is time ladies and gentlemen rise, rise, rise! Let us change mass consciousness for the good of all. Let our children learn and accept spirituality as the norm. It is time.

MY PATH IS SET. I am a global speaker, an author as a contributor, and in my own right with my book Your Food Freedom, I am a healer and I am a mother and wife. Most of all I am me, whole and complete. I am beautifully me. I attract people, not because I am Indian but because I am beautiful and light. I am me and proud to be my beautiful self finally.

GOD BLESS each and every one of your beautiful souls on your journey of finding your truth. X

# ABOUT THE AUTHOR

## DIMPLE THAKRAR

Dimple Thakrar the founder of Dimple Global, is an international speaker, author and TV expert for the BBC and appears in The Times, The Guardian, Huffington Post and Good Housekeeping Magazine.

She has devoted over 20 years as a Dietitian, NLP (Neuro Linguistic Programming) Practitioner and Theta Healer to transforming entrepreneurs' relationships with themselves, their intimate others and the food they eat.

Her purpose is to save marriages and prevent eating disorders. Stopping the pain of divorce and emotional eating!

Her mission to serve has been driven by her own childhood challenges with Anorexia and transforming her own 23 year marriage, to a serial entrepreneur, from near divorce to teenaged lovers. Now transforming 1000's with her one to one, group, online and speaking healing/coaching globally.

She is well respected in her field and has been mentored personally by the best like Tony Robbins.

She invests heavily in her own personal development and walks the walk and talks the talk. She is supported by her soul mate Atul

Thakrar and her two daughters Maya and Keira. She adores people, serving and fast tracking people with her relationship hacks to the relationships of their dreams!

Catch her at Dimpleglobal.com or ask to join her on Facebook- The Love Tribe; where she offers daily support and pearls of wisdom on transforming your relationship.

**Contact**
Email: dimple@dimpleglobal.com
Website: www.dimpleglobal.com
Facebook Group: The Love Tribe
LinkedIn: https://www.linkedin.com/in/dimple-thakrar/

facebook.com/dimple.thakrar
instagram.com/dimplethakrar

# JAN COULSON

## MY STORY - MY LIFE SO FAR

*J* was born in a hurry into the commode, so my mother told me. I was eager to start my life!

IT WAS in the early hours of the morning on the 6th December 1956 with the brightest, carrot-coloured ginger hair and the fairest of skin. Of course, my parents were surprised and puzzled at my fiery colouring, as both of them had dark brown hair; so did my older brother and younger sister.

I DON'T REMEMBER VERY MUCH about my early years. Apparently, I was knocked over by a car when I was three - I just ran into the road, no fear at all. I got dragged along behind the car as my clothes got caught on the bumper of the car. Thankfully it was moving at a low speed, but I was still taken to hospital to be checked. I was so lucky not to have suffered any physical injuries. A year later, I had whooping cough which was life threatening. I survived that too.

· · ·

As I was growing up, my parents argued all the time. I think I just blocked it out, living in my own happy little world, drawing and colouring was one of my favourite things to do. My brother said he used to comfort me and my sister when my parents were in the throes of another argument. Still, it wasn't all bad. We had some lovely family holidays together although there was always some friction with mum and Dad. Mum used to keep us looking good, in hand-crocheted knitted tops and lovely hairbands with matching dresses.

Mum came from a large family of nine, so when visiting our grandma and grandad, there was always a large pot of tea on the table in a big brown tea pot with a crochet tea cosy. Dad had four siblings and his mum was known as our 'Little Grandma'. She always got out her best china on a Sunday, only using the front room on this day. Where she would bring out all of her homemade cakes, served on posh bone china and tea served from a beautiful teapot.

In the posh front room, my nan had a pyramid poem on the wall, which I loved to read on every visit. When Little Grandma transitioned, Dad asked me if there was anything I wanted of hers. I chose the poem and a picture of animals in nature. As I got older the poem meant more and more. It was called the Desiderata: it's a poem about life and the universe.

I have this on my play list and listen to it often. Now I truly understand it.

When I was four and my sister was still unborn, Mum had to go into hospital for an extended amount of time, so my brother and I were looked after by each set the grandparents and an aunty and uncle.

Something happened with my Little Grandad that I had blocked out, but, over the years as I've been on my healing journey, I've had a vision of my Grandad and have been shown something I didn't want to acknowledge. I went to see a healer who confirmed my visions.

As I was growing up, I loved to play outside on my bike and roller skates. I loved being out in nature; visits to the parks and open spaces was always a highlight. Going to the seaside was my all-time favourite. The salty sea smell, noisy seagulls and crashing waves used to make my soul sing. I was happy when we moved to the countryside when I was around ten. Dad use to take us on walks along the country lanes where we would march along behind him, thanks to his younger days in the Army. I wasn't much of a communicator; my family knew me as the quiet one. Dad even told me off for not speaking much. This was confusing to me; when I did try to talk, I was told "Don't speak until your spoken to!" or something along those lines, so I went into my own world of drawing and reading.

There was a modern church near our house where I used to go to Sunday school, something I really enjoyed, especially as we were given postcards with pictures of Jesus on them when we left. I loved looking at the images on the cards. School was a coach ride away and was something I didn't like to do - to me, being told what to do was awful. As I became a teenager, I rebelled. I've never liked to follow rules.

For example, I'd never come home at the time I was told to, so I'd be grounded for days, then only go and do it again. One thing was for certain; I didn't like the restrictions of being in the family environment. Saying that, I did enjoy rural studies, learning about plants, nature, growing vegetables and flowers from seeds. I adored art as I could lose myself in creating pictures. Music was another thing I enjoyed. I learnt to play the recorder and loved playing in school concerts.

WERE BOYS INVOLVED? Of course they were! My friends and I would all hang around the park in groups, so I always wanted to stay out, and then I'd get grounded, but I'd always do it again. I never learnt! I'd had a few boyfriends on and off as a teenager but when I was 19, I met a loving and kind man. He worked as a groundsman, looking after trees, plants and flowers. It wasn't long before I left home to go and live with him. My parents were devastated as he was somewhat older than me. Sadly, Dad did not see nor talk to me for a number of years, although I still used to see mum. Things became harder for her as the pressure from Dad about me was tough for her to deal with . In time this rift was healed between myself and my Dad then both my boyfriend and Dad got on well.

WHILE WE WERE LIVING TOGETHER, I met a person who I became friends with, and she was interested in the same things as me. It would light me up when we talked to each other.

I WAS INVITED along by her to a group of people called 'Emin' (meaning 'mine' when you moved the words around). It was all about the spiritual world; astrology, tarot cards, numerology, clairvoyance and everything to do with the spiritual realms. I looked forward to the weekly meetings; it felt like there was a purpose to life. Every week, as I learnt more and more, I started to feel and believe there was something else to life. When growing up I was always asking my parents, "what are we here for?" and I'd always get the reply "'cos you are."

. . .

DURING THIS TIME, Little Grandma was admitted to hospital. On my way to visit her she had sadly passed away. On arriving at the hospital my Dad told me something she said that has never left my mind. It was; "I'm going now as they've sent the silver cord for me". I now know the silver cord she mentioned is the chord that keeps us connected to the spiritual world, like an umbilical cord.

LIFE CARRIED on and I eventually married. We and had two beautiful children and over the years, I carried out motherly duties with so much love for my children. I still went to the Emin meetings; being with people who talked about the meaning of life plus attending classes on all aspects of spirituality was interesting to me. The more I was growing spiritually, the more my husband was convinced there something wrong with me for wanting to go to this spiritual group. He thought I was being brainwashed. Sadly, we divorced after being together for ten years and married for seven. The year before we split up, we hardly communicated which caused a strain on the children too. One evening when putting my daughter to bed, I heard a very loud message in my ear. It said, "Don't worry it won't be long now." I even answered with a simple "ok!"

IT WASN'T until the following year when I left. I moved in with Mum. She had just gone through her own divorce and lived in a house on her own, so the children and I lived there. At this time, my daughter was nine and my son was six. It was an emotional time for us all, although the children adjusted very well. We were free form the heavy energy we were living in. Everything was fine for a few months. Mum got a new puppy - it was her constant companion. That was until she met a new man. The poor dog started to be left for hours on end. I was working, and the children were with their Dad at weekends. I observed that until this new man came into her life, the dog was her world but now he was around, she threw everything into the new relationship - and I told her so! Sadly, she let the dog go as more of her time was spent staying away with him.

I EVENTUALLY MET HIM; he seemed ok enough. He made Mum feel loved, but I couldn't shake the feeling that he didn't want me and the children around. On one occasion, Mum was annoyed that I'd done a machine load of my sister-in-laws washing whilst her machine was being repaired. We had an argument and I couldn't help but say; "Just evict me if that's what you want!". Sure enough, that's what she did. I didn't think she would actually go through with it!! I had a bailiff come to the front door to serve me eviction papers and there was an altercation with Mum's new man which was upsetting. The day came for us to move out. I ended up in a halfway house for a few months and then a three bedroom flat further away, where I didn't know anyone.

I HELD down a full-time job to support us. The children were still visiting their Dad, although a new woman came into his life. She didn't like the attention he was giving to them and the children didn't get on with her. They stopped wanting stay with him at weekends, so he would see them after school. One morning, I had a call from my ex-husband's sister to say he'd had a massive heart attack whilst playing badminton. I couldn't believe what I was hearing; he was a fit man and this news didn't seem real. I sent the children off to school and I got my head around what had happened.

WHEN THE CHILDREN GOT HOME, I broke this sad news to them. We were all devastated. Sometime before the death of my ex-husband, I'd met a fun-loving kind-hearted man, he got on with the children and had two children of his own who were similar ages and went to same school. My new companion was very supportive to us during this time. I used to pray for my life to turn around as I felt the negative events in my life were relentless.

MANY YEARS later in September 2005, I'd had what felt like a pronounced and memorable dream. A female voice spoke to me and took my hand, saying, "Come with me, I want to take you somewhere. It will be very bright and wobbly. You won't be able to stand up, you'll have to kneel down." As the voice was saying this, I felt like I was going up a kind of spiral staircase. The voice then said, "Don't take your hands away from your eyes, the light will be so bright, it will be ok." As I removed my hands the light was brighter than the sun, however, it was not golden yellow, it was the brightest light I'd ever seen.

IN THE DISTANCE was a figure sitting with his arms outstretched. It looked like my children's father. He had long hair and was glowing in a luminous light. I could recognise just his face very briefly. I held out my hands to his and they started slipping away as he was disappearing from my sight. His message was, "Tell them I visit every day." And then he was gone. The time was 4am. I got up to write this important message down for my children. At first, I thought it was a dream, now quite a few years into my spiritual journey, I know it was real.

I REMARRIED and moved in with my new husband and all the children got on so well. Our life was spent running them around and doing everything for them all. We eventually moved and brought a house together. The children grew up and moved out and then I started searching again for why I was in this world. How could you have so many things happen without there being a purpose to it all? There had to be more to life. I started to have more spiritual happenings.

·  ·  ·

EARLY ONE MORNING I was awoken, still sleepy, I felt this uncondi-tional love of something so very large behind me whilst I was laying down. It felt like I was being cocooned in softness. I gently opened one eye to see if I was imaging this, or if it was truly real. I had never felt so nurtured and loved, it was like I was being held by this enor-mous being behind me. I closed my eyes as I never wanted this feeling to end. Eventually I woke and remembered what had happened. I knew I'd had a vision in my head where I had seen this image. I went to my drawer and I found a leaflet from a company who made Angels out of crystal, I already had the Mother Earth statue. There it was, a person being held by an Angel. I couldn't wait to go to the exhibition that was coming up to purchase this Angel.

THE DAY of the exhibition came and the first stall I had to find was the crystal sculptures. I was looking to buy a chakra Angel, although I couldn't get to this part of the stand as there were so many people looking and admiring them. I then picked up this bronze Angel .... wow! It felt like its heart was beating in my hand. The owner of the stall turned to me as she was serving others and said, "That's Archangel Sandalphon, a high vibrational Angel, he is connected to the Dolphin energy." I had no idea what this energy was. I had a reading with her husband at the stand who makes the Angel figures. The reading made me emotional as he said, "The Angels are so proud of you for all the healing you have been doing for others that have come to you." I had been channelling Reiki for them. I had to purchase this Angel sculpture as I felt so close to the energies.

I SHOWED the bronze Archangel Sandalphon to a very loving friend of mine who channels energies, and she also felt the heartbeat. Like me, she felt maybe there was a message for me. I let her take the sculpture home to cleanse any energies on the Angel where it had been picked up at the exhibition. She said she would place the Angel on her altar. A few days later I went back to her house and as soon as she opened the door the energies hit me. They were so strong. My beautiful friend made us grounding healthy food to eat before we entered into a mediation as the energies were so high.

To bring in Archangel Sandalphon's energy, we chanted and prayed together and then she tuned into channel to see if there was a message for me. The energy got stronger until I felt it come down through my crown chakra, it felt like a tingling fuzzy feeling. I felt I had no control over my face. The tears of emotion were uncontrollable. Never have I felt so loved. I felt my body was on fire. I was just sobbing with happiness, I can't describe in words how this felt. I had a message of ... FLAME ....RELEASE....TRUST.....SMILE.

Then the energy started to fade. My friend said that Archangel Sandalphon wanted to leave me a gift and I was channelled .... SUNSHINE, GLOW, RELEASE, TRUST. After this we sat quietly, letting this experience subside. My friend was there to hold the space for this experience to occur. I then started to search for the meaning of why I was given these words.

The next day on waking, I was given another message to say my endocrine system was being cleared. For a few weeks I was having black and white image flashbacks in my third eye to when I was younger. It was like a fast movie being played backwards. There were words too, but it all moved too fast for me to understand. Maybe it was from what happened with the channelling with Archangel Sandalphon.

At the same time there were other things happening to me at night.

On one occasion, I woke up and felt like I was being lifted up. I could see there was a bright golden glow approaching my bedroom door, the glow became brighter and then I could see a group of illuminous beings grouped together coming into my bedroom.

THERE APPEARED to be a fire in the corner of the room too. (my husband was fast asleep). It disappeared to be replaced with a golden ray of sunlight on the wall and a tree that looked like it was falling down. There was the head, shoulders and face of a man with white hair. I remember saying, "Help! The tree is falling down we have to save it!" Once again, on waking, I remembered every detail of what happened, and I knew I had seen this man before on a Facebook page that I follow. I searched her pictures and there he was, a Bulgarian spiritual teacher. Why had this man come into my life? My friend explained there was a lot of symbology in this occurrence/dream, so I started researching as maybe I could get some kind of explanation.

IN 2010 MY Dad passed away suddenly. He had no illnesses, in fact, he appeared to be a healthy and active man, so it was a surprise when he was taken into hospital so abruptly and ended up with a burst Aneurysm over his Stomach area. He underwent a twelve-hour operation but he had another bleed and only survived a few more hours. I'm so thankful we were all with him when he took his last breath. I remember looking to see if anyone had come for him (I remembered the silver chord and Little Grandma). I asked Dad to keep the telepathy with me as we'd always had a strong telepathic connection. My Dad comes to visit me often. I always smell the familiar scent of him; Golden Virginia tobacco and it's right under my nose! That's how I know he's around. Over the years, he's given me messages for my brother and sister too. My brother accepts the message; however, my sister is not so sure.

·  ·  ·

THE SUN SHONE wherever my Dad went. He was always such a positive man. When planning his funeral, the vicar asked us what songs we wanted for the service. In that moment, Dad whispered to me, "What a Wonderful World", so of course, that's what we played. With whatever was going on in his life, he always maintained it was a 'Wonderful World'. On the day of his funeral, the sun even shone through the windows of the vehicle carrying him to the crematorium. He had ordered the sun to shine on that day.

TWO NIGHTS after my Dad's passing, I woke up abruptly. It felt like someone was sitting on the end of the bed. In the morning the two bedside lamps were on. I knew my Dad was giving me a signal. A few days after his transition, the reality of what had happened hit me hard. Once again, I questioned, "what was the real purpose of us being in this world? To be born and then die and that's it?" There just seemed no point to it all.

NO ONE COULD ANSWER the questions I'd asked for years. My pathway and search for meaning in life then became so strong. It was something I just had to know. His passing sent me spiralling down. I took time off from work to come to terms with my grief and I went into depression. The GP prescribed medication and asked to see me again in two weeks, so I did, and gave the prescription back. I asked for counselling as I felt it would help me more. I've never been one for medication and felt the natural route was for me.

THE COUNSELLING DIDN'T REALLY HELP. It didn't seem to take me away from all I was feeling. After leaving the session, I found an Angel healing shop. On stepping inside, straight away the lady said she could see my Dad around me, without me even telling her. This was when I started to think more about the Angels. To help bolster my mood, we took a trip to a seaside town in Sussex. I had a tarot reading with a man. He asked me how I felt, "I feel like I am just hanging around waiting for something to happen," I said. He guided me to meditation to get me to the 'next level…'whatever that was. He said I'd find out in time.

ONCE I RETURNED TO WORK, there was a colleague that always had Angel figures around her desk. We never really spoke until my return from being off work. This lady was loving towards me and we befriended each other. She told me she would send the Angels to be with me. We started to go to various workshops on Angels, crystals and meditation groups. We went to a Reiki workshop and eventually, both got attuned to these healing energies (Usui Reiki Level1 & 2) by a very beautiful and loving soul. My life began to change. I started to see glowing colours and swirls when closing my eyes. I started to read about 2012 and the paradigm shift. I was understanding more and more what was happening with the world.

I CONTINUED to meditate and ask,"why am I here?" I felt like I was taken towards the stars. A voice said, "you are from here. Every day we will guide you and show you your purpose". In every meditation I would ask for direction. I received direction,"you know where you are going, you have much to learn. You've earnt it. You're going to the next level, like a graduate, you are moving on and shifting," said one voice. I carried on living my life, knowing there was something else for me. One morning after cleaning my teeth I heard another message, loud and clear in my ear, "you are here for love." Is that it? I questioned myself. For Love? Was there not something else I should be doing?

IN MAY 2013 my husband and I visited San Francisco, where we'd done all the tourist things. But I wanted to take a journey out through California to a spiritual mountain I'd been reading lots about called Mount Shasta. We hired a car and took the long drive. As we got closer to the area (we were still quite a distance away), we could see the top of the mountain. It seemed so near yet we still had a while to travel. I started to feel the energy of this mountain; it was very intense. On arrival, I found the town was very hippy and loving, with so many crystal shops. In fact, at one point the assistant in the shop sat me on the stool made of crystal as I felt so dizzy. The crystal stool helped to balance me. We shipped so many crystals back to the UK!

I ALSO PURCHASED some Lemurian seed crystals that I carried with me. As I held them, they put me in a trance-like state and in my third eye, I could see a stunning firework display. We drove up to the mountain as far as we could go by car. We then just sat in the energy of Shasta. We also visited Sedona in Arizona. There were so many crystals shops there too. The energy felt electric. We took a trip to feel the energy vortexes of masculine and feminine. It was amazing to sit amongst the red rocks at The Enchantment Hotel. I felt so much happen on that trip

IN AUGUST 2013, I was sitting in the garden on a very sunny day and I drifted off to sleep. An illuminous light surrounded me, the same light that surrounded me when I was taken to see my children's Dad in spirit. There was such peaceful feeling with this light. I remember coming back from the drifting just crying and saying, "I just want to go home!" Of course, I was at home in my garden. I now know it was my spiritual home I wanted to return to.

MY FRIEND USED to talk about feathers appearing from nowhere. I'd never had this happen until one morning in my kitchen, a small white feather drifted down from above my head onto the kitchen worktop, right in front of my eyes. It appeared from nowhere. It seemed so many things were happening. I had a crystal candlestick holder that sat on the window ledge. As the sun used to shine through it, it would create amazing rainbow colours in the house. One particular morning, my attention was turned towards the window where the candlestick was. There, in front of the candle, was this massive pink heart. Wow! I got my phone camera and took so many pictures before it faded. Looking back at the pictures blew me away. There were so many different coloured orbs of all different sizes. I sent them to a lady who told me they were Angels of love bringing love to whoever was in the room at the time.

I TOOK some more courses in massage and Anatomy and Physiology. I decided to concentrate on Lastone massage as I felt this amazing modality was for me. The stones use to show me by flashes of light where I need to place and use them. The love just flowed through these basalt stones as I gave a treatment. They guided me to areas of the body the client was having problems with.

MY DAUGHTER WAS VERY much interested in the spiritual side of life too. She told me about a lady she'd met called Tina who was running Angel workshops in Ramsgate, Kent. Together we went to one of the workshops. Tina's energy was so loving, giving and electric. The Angels were truly with her, speaking through her constantly. Tina's energy just uplifted you by being in her company.

WE LISTENED to visualisations to take our energy up to the higher realms. She told me she could see mountains all around me. I showed her my Angel orb pictures that came in through my crystal candlestick too. She said Archangel Chamuel and Archangel Raphael were present in those images.

MY HUSBAND and I put our house up for sale, knowing we wanted to move and not be in that particular house anymore. We were going out on a whim as we had no idea at all where we wanted to live. But at this time, we didn't have many viewings. At the same time one of our loving Cavalier Spaniels, Oli, who was five, was diagnosed with Lymph cancer. We had no idea he was so ill until we found a lump around his neck. A visit to the vet confirmed he was in stage four and had only a few months left in this world. Sadly, it was just three months later when Oli transitioned to the light, his beautiful sister Bo was heartbroken as they had such a large bond. Bo started having small seizures herself, on and off, which we later found out were mini strokes.

WE DID GET a bit despondent with the sale of the house, or lack thereof, but out of the blue it eventually sold to first time buyers who wanted to be living there within the next three months.

FINALLY, we decided that we would move to Sitges in Spain where our son was living with his Spanish wife. My husband ran his own business so could work from anywhere in the world, and I gave up my job. We found a place to rent that was surrounded by mountains, as Tina had said to me months before. I moved to Spain two weeks before my husband as he had more to sort out with his work before joining me. Only a few days after arriving I had an inner knowing that a deeper inward journey was only just beginning. I started to be triggered by so many things. I wanted to blame others for everything I was feeling, when in fact, I used to tell my clients when they came for Reiki that all healing is back to the self.

. . .

IT WASN'T easy to admit to myself the reflections from others was triggering my own stuff. It took a few weeks to finally own it as my own, coming up to be healed. Once it started, I was on a roll. It was like someone had shone a light in a cupboard for me to see all these emotions I'd hid away, finally wanting me to look at them. This time I had no choice. I couldn't go back to how I was. I had to face it all, years' worth of stuff.

I WAS TAKING time to visit my sister in Majorca as it was a very easy journey from Barcelona. My sister had breast cancer so spending time with her was good for the both of us. My husband began sending pictures of properties in France as he felt it was where we should be especially as some years before, we had a holiday home by the sea. So, on our quest for a new home, we spent weekends driving up from Spain and staying in France.

WE FOUND a stunning house in a village between Carcassonne and Narbonne, right by the famous Canal Du Midi; the area is steeped in the Cathar trails, an hour away from Rennes Le Chateau, Monsegur and Bugarach a region that has stories centred around Mary Magdalene and Jesus. Our new house was only an hour's drive to Lourdes, where Mother Mary made a visualisation to a young lady many years before. It was also one and half hours to the Spanish border, so we could still visit our son.

THE HOUSE HAD beautiful shutters and a stunning roof terrace; the views were spectacular over towards the Pyrenees Mountains and the lush vineyards of the Languedoc area. The house was enormous, and it had a beautiful energy. In fact, one bedroom had a very strong energy presence, my dog Bo could sense energies very well. I took her in to this room with the energy that I felt, and she seemed fine by it. In a house we previously viewed she did a poo on their carpet! So, we knew that was not the house to buy. The idea of us moving was to downsize, however this place was twice as big as our UK house. My husband had amazing ideas to make it into a B&B with a room for my therapies. The house was owned previously by a French couple, the lady taught Yoga and worked with Feng Shui. We had some changes to do in the house before we could open.

I COULDN'T HELP but question why we were buying this large house when we were meant to be downsizing. However, everything about it was drawing me in. As I entered the house, there was a big picture of a Buddha which the owner was leaving. At the front of the house the owner said there had been a figure of Mother Mary that had been stolen. She'd replaced it with a beautiful bronze Angel that couldn't be removed. The house was also number three. In numerology it means that the Ascended Masters are near and want to help.

WE MADE an offer which was accepted a few days later. We moved in on the 21st July 2014. We were still surrounded by mountains, as Tina had previously said. Work began on the house. I realised quite quickly I was doing things I just didn't enjoy; building and painting became my new existence. On the contrary, my husband was relishing in this work. He loves to make and create things. In the same way the house was progressing, my inner journey was full steam ahead. I started to feel the immense control my husband had, or rather, the control I was buying into. I was metaphorically being pulled apart; I no longer knew myself. It was like my identity had been removed.

I FOUND DOING the simplest things ebbing away my confidence like driving for instance which I'd been doing for years with no problems. It felt like I was at the start of being reborn, and it wasn't the easiest thing to experience, I'd started to open up deeper layers of healing and it was uncomfortable. I wanted to blame and judge my husband for so many things, that again, I knew were all my own deep inner resentments. I would use all the healing modalities I knew; EFT was amazing. It helped put my meridians back from a negative state to a positive one.

THE VILLAGE we lived in was a melting pot of many nationalities, plus some were holiday homes. There was not a shop in the village, so the bread lady came in a van from a neighbouring village. It really felt like I'd gone back in time. The village in the winter was so quiet; most people closed their houses down for winter and returned to their other homes. There was no one I could befriend, no like-minded women were to be seen. It dawned on me that this part was a deeper healing journey with my husband. There were days when I just wanted to run away. All that was coming up was so emotionally painful.

MY HUSBAND HAD MET an English lady who was one of our immediate neighbours, living just around the corner. She was into crystals, so thinking we'd get along, he introduced me to her. At first, it was good to have female conversation. She would tell me about her fire bucket and the spells she'd done, a spiritual side I didn't know much about. She'd tell me about the traumas she'd faced in her life too. We would invite her round for dinner and she would ask my husband to do small electrical tasks that she'd repay by cooking dinner for us. Her energy started to feel overpowering and over a short amount of time, I could see how she would pull me in, something that became a pattern.

. . .

ONE EVENING she'd invited us over, I didn't have a good feeling about going but my husband convinced me it would be fine. The first hour was bearable; but as the wine began to flow and they drank more and more (I couldn't drink more than two glasses; I didn't like the way it made me feel the next day) things became hostile. He got cross and verbal, telling her he didn't have to put up with her rudeness, walking out of her house, leaving me sitting there not knowing what to do. She turned on me, saying, "and you with your Holy ways!" I stood up and said, "that's me done too, I don't have to put up with your talk" and I left too. I felt so proud that I'd stood up to her. It was a night I never wanted to repeat so we avoided her from that day on.

MY HUSBAND MET another man at the builders' yard, helping him carry wood to his car. They spoke for a substantial amount of time before the subject of Angels came into the conversation. He gave my husband his number and we met him and his wife on a few occasions. He'd written a book and he gifted me a copy. We talked about Angels more in depth and it became a pleasure to meet with them as we all had something interesting we could talk about. They were from New Zealand and lived between there and France; winters spent in France and the summers in New Zealand.

THAT YEAR, we spent the summer running the B&B and I was doing occasional therapies. I met a beautiful French lady who used the chan-nelling method to write. She didn't speak English, nor I French but we got by just fine. She would always leave me a gift of fruit from her trees and things she'd baked. We had several Reiki sessions, she loved it so much that she'd found someone in France so that she could be attuned herself.

THE ENERGY in France started to become quite heavy in a way I can't explain. I found I was becoming increasingly unhappy and I didn't want to be in France anymore. I felt the neighbour who we'd fallen out with that time may have been casting spells. I'd never met the dark in this form before as I always see the best in everyone. I felt village life was not for me. It felt like my life had ended.

LUCKILY, we kept a flat back in the UK that we were renting out. Never did I think we would be living in it. We had to wait three months before we could take it back as we had rented it out to the local authority. When we eventually took it back over Christmas time, it had been left in a mess. We had to live in a holiday cottage in the countryside whilst it was being done up. We also found out that a previous tenant, sometime before we brought it, had taken his life by hanging himself over the balcony. Did I really want to live there? My husband's brother had passed away in our last months in France and I could see his mood dropping. To be back near family was good for him, especially as the business he had with his business partner had collapsed at the same time, something which only impacted his ever-decreasing mood.

IN THE FEBRUARY of that year, I took a phone call from mum's husband to say that she'd been taken ill. I couldn't make sense of what he was saying, being 90 and in a panic, so I drove over from Kent to Essex, on the dreaded M25 through the tunnel that seemed to always be traffic-clogged. I prayed I wouldn't get stuck in any traffic as I needed to get to Mum fast. The Angels were with me as I virtually flew there in no time.

WHEN I ARRIVED, my stepfather was delirious, crying and speaking to the doctor on the phone. I grabbed the phone off him and flew upstairs but as I went towards the bedroom, I could see Mum's hand with a glass of water just ready to fall out of her hand; she was unable to move, looking like she was swallowing her tongue, purple in the face. I threw the phone down and tried to put her in the recovery position, but I was unable to move her. I slowly lifted her head up, aware of her tongue, and as I got her up, she took a big gulp of air. I managed to wet her lips from the water in the glass and called the emergency services. The doctor also attended after I didn't respond on the phone.

MUM WAS in intensive care for eight weeks and ill for months after . The professionals didn't think she'd survive, but like a true fighter, she recovered although she was in respite care for another three months as she was unable to walk. I called her the 'Warrior Goddess.' During this time, I started to suffer from anxiety and depression. I was in my head all the time. I didn't know what was happening to me. I didn't want to go to GP as I didn't want to be numbed on medication. I was about to turn sixty and the thought of it just worried me and I questioned, "how did I get to this age and become like this?" I couldn't see my life ahead. What were we thinking coming back to live here? I just couldn't envisage my future.

I'D BEEN WORKING a few hours a day at a listed building near to our flat as a housekeeper. One day I tripped badly over a hoover cable and damaged my foot. I eventually had to have an operation to straighten my toes. During my recovery I started reading about the metaphysical causes of illness in the body. I learnt this fall was telling me I was unable to step forward on my life journey; something that resonated so true for me. I'd lost my purpose and direction in life.

MY HUSBAND HAD PLANNED a lovely family meal for my sixtieth birth-day, but being out and about made me worse, I just couldn't cope. I started a job in a supermarket, thankfully, I was put on the flower department, making up bouquets and looking after flowers, occasionally working the tills. I didn't know how I got to work each day, I just knew I had to. I'd started to think the worst about everything; fear overtook me completely.

SOME NIGHTS I felt the energy of the lady in France right beside my bed. I had to crystal grid the bed as she appeared so real to me. I felt sad as I walked up to our flat, like I couldn't breathe. I even got my husband to knock down the kitchen wall as it felt suffocating. Whilst we painted the outside together, I would have such a torrent of emotional tears I couldn't control. I realised I was feeling the energy of the man who took his life on the balcony. I burned so many big white sage bundles, the smoke that came from them was immense. I would be crying all the time while doing this. What was happening to me? I began to fall deeper into this dark place. At one point I felt I was going mad. I started taking flower essences to help. I took so many different ones at each stage of emotions coming up.

AFTER MUM RECOVERED there were so many things going on with my brother and my Stepdad (that's another story!) something I was being pulled into which had nothing to do with me. There had been some altercations between myself and my brother when I'd returned from France. I have forgiven him and myself for allowing this to happen. However, to this day it continues with them.

LIVING in the flat I started to feel that I was trapped in my emotions. To go outside the door was a real struggle, I didn't even want my husband to go to work. I felt such a need to be looked after and nurtured, and I even felt it was a struggle to look after my precious little dog who now had a heart condition. I'd done all of these healing modalities and wasn't using any of them! I didn't want to be here anymore, I couldn't cope with life and I wanted it all to go away. With all that was happening in my family, I couldn't even call on my siblings for support.

I COULD NO LONGER SEE colours in my third eye or feel the lilac orb that was always around me. I felt I'd been deserted by the Divine spirit. With nothing to lose, I contacted Tina, who I'd not seen for a number of years. I felt so desperate for something to change. On seeing her I just broke down and cried, unable to get my words out. She gave me some much-needed healing and she told me she was going into Theta to help me. She worked on my shock and trauma. I just wanted to cuddle her as she had so much love to give. The anxiety I'd been feeling subsided and the darkness started to lift. I also have another friend who lived near so went for Reiki with her. She cleared a mass of black slime from my solar plexus that felt like it was eating me.

OUR FRENCH HOUSE was not selling despite having lots of viewings. The couple from New Zealand came back to France and rented our house whilst they completed the building work on their French home, which was a bit of a relief. He put a protective shield of Archangel Michael around the house as he felt there was an energy there. He never had a good feeling when our neighbour who we'd fallen out with walked past. He would never give her eye contact.

I CONTACTED another friend at the time who lived in America. She'd undertaken the cleansing of people's properties who were having a problem selling. Sometime later, I'd found out whilst learning Theta healing how you can work remotely with Theta to protect your home. My friend put a protection all around the flat in the UK and also around our French house, and it was Theta she was using to do this. My friend came back and said someone nearby had put a spell on the house, so it wouldn't sell. And of course, it was the neighbour!

I KEPT GETTING a message in my head that someone from Paris was going to buy our French house. Three months later, a French neighbour had friends visit from Paris. They saw the sale board and they brought it in towards the end of 2017.

IT WAS around this time that I began to learn Theta healing. My daughter and I went along and was amazed about his healing modality. In February 2018, my Theta journey began. I started to heal old beliefs and began to feel unstuck - it felt like a new plan was coming in. Theta was so amazing; I'd been waiting for this for a very long time.

I'VE NOW COMPLETED several Theta courses; Theta Basic and Advanced, Digging Deeper, and Manifesting and Abundance. My life has changed beyond belief. I had to go through the dark shadow side to come out and return back into the light. There are many more courses I'm wanting to do on my Theta journey. I feel so much clearer! I started to manifest my dreams and visions. I now live by the sea, not far from The Goddess Rooms that Tina herself manifested.

I'VE ALSO BEEN ATTUNED to Angelic Reiki 1&2 and the Masters 3&4 with Tina. On a meditation, we were taken into the Angelic realms. Tina mentioned the Angels by name. As soon as Archangel Sandalphon's name came in, I could feel the immense energy surrounding me in unconditional love, the very same energy I'd felt previously, all those years back, way before I started my inward journey. I couldn't stop crying as I'd felt that Archangel Sandalphon had deserted me, but there he was, loving me as unconditionally as before. Tina understood this and said, "I can see you," and I really knew she could as she'd been on a journey herself.

WHILST I WAS on the Angelic Reiki courses, our new home in Herne Bay completed, and three weeks later I left my job. I've now been accepted on a Diploma course for Flower Essences which completes in February 2019, so I'm busy studying. I have been given a new name for my healing business by spirit and even shown the colours I should use. This message came to me in the early hours one morning, when I woke up just saying the name.

THERE ARE SO many more Theta courses to learn as once you start, you can really feel how deep they go. I'm ready for the next lot in 2019. I can't begin to explain how much they've helped me; I just want to share with others how amazing Theta is. I've felt for a few months that I'm in a kind of 'service work' everyday with everyone I meet; spreading the love to show others there is another way to heal yourself. Just recently, I landed a job with the new supermarket near to my house and out of 2500 people, I'm one of the 150 to get a position. It's only for a few hours a week, but what's important is it ties in with my purpose in life, which is to spread the love and to keep learning, with the view to passing it on.

I AM NOW ready to step outside of my self-worth issues and rise as a healer; the person I came here to be. I've learnt so much in my human life to take me through so many things that needed to be cleared before finally….stepping onto my true path.

# ABOUT THE AUTHOR

## JAN COULSON

Jan is a Theta Healing practitioner, an Angelic Reiki Practitioner, First and Second Degree and Jikiden Reiki Practitioner in Shoden and Okuden Levels. Jan is a qualified Indian Head Massager and La Stone therapist, working with hot, cold and Basalt stones as well as healing with crystals.

She is at the beginning of embarking upon her new ambition, learning to be a Flower Essence Practitioner with a Diploma being the end goal. And of course, treating others.

Today, Jan is the best version of herself EVER. I am that I am. I'm my own special creation.

A whole new world has opened up to Jan since learning and finding Theta Healing and Angelic Reiki with Tina Pavlou. Jan has dug deep and worked hard to clear old beliefs handed down from her ancestors, spending time getting to the core of her beliefs and not masking uncomfortable feelings with comfort eating, shopping & alcohol and many other unconscious things. Now, so many wonderful things are opening up to Jan, and this fabulous opportunity of putting her story into words is just unbelievable.

Jan is 62 and is nowhere near ready to give into doing less. In fact, Jan is now stepping into her power, to reclaim her life purpose as a healer. Jan loves living by the sea, with its soothing nature always around, bringing a calmness to her spirit. This was a dream Jan had for years, one she manifested on the Manifesting and Abundance Theta course with Tina.

Jan feels ready and can now bring a happy and vibrant energy into her later years. Plus, Jan now truly understands why she is here on this planet; to create a life that she can flourish in. One of Jan's passions is to be the voice of wisdom and lived experience, to help the people on the planet change; Jan has such a desire to help people love themselves more and to give them the tools they need to properly heal. Jan was given a message by spirit that told her, "You are here for love." This is the change that is so needed in the world.

When Jan looks back on her journey, especially not knowing where or how she wanted to live, it was clear she was being guided by spirit. Over the last few years especially, Jan describes she has been on a her 'shadow journey' to heal the deepest darkest parts of herself that she can no longer deny. Once Jan started to travel inwards to those deep dark parts inside her, there was no turning back.

One of the reasons why Jan is learning the vibrational medicine of Flower Essences is because she used these during her 'Dark Night of the Soul' and the power they yielded over her spirit and soul was immense. Plus, Jan has loved flowers from a young age, working in a florist upon leaving school.

It's incredible that she now has the first-hand knowledge in seeing just how much they help the emotional body. Jan can see sacred geometry in every living flower, plant and tree. Jan befriended an Oak tree in her previous home and every day she would chant underneath her.

Jan is ready to do more of what she loves. Jan says she has lived a rich and complex life filled with learning experiences and accomplishments. Jan will always continue to ask, "What's next?"

Jan.coulson@live.co.uk

# HELEN PORTER

*I* was drawn to healing at a young age, in primary school I was knitting jumpers for children in Africa and undertook my first 24 hr fast for famine relief at the age of 10, I was an avid supporter for both human and animal rights, and when walking through town I'd find the first charity collection pot and put all of my pocket money straight in it.

I WAS ALWAYS a little bit different and unfortunately attracted narcissistic friends. In my early teens I began to show signs of underlying trauma, I opened up even more to very unhealthy relationships both male and female, my relationship with my family began to break down and going into my middle to late teens I became very angry.

I HAD a will of iron so despite the emotional roller coaster I was on, I managed to run a second life parallel to that, at seventeen I was studying at college with 3 jobs, by nineteen I had my first business, from that point on work became the one thing in my life I could control. I had left school and trained as a Beauty Therapist, after a few years I moved into the holistic side of beauty and trained in Reflexology, Reiki, and various forms of massage.

I HAD A GIFT, I could feel my clients pain, I knew where it was, I could feel it in my own body. I believed at that age I was so strong that I could take the pain from them thinking I could handle it better than they could. Like I said I had a will of iron and pain would not break me, so I took my clients pain, for many years. The same way I also seemed to draw in friends who were troubled in some way. I felt that if I could heal them, I'd feel validated/needed.

BUT AS THE years went on the pain began to take form in my own body, the energetic absorption began to manifest in very real problems. Did I mention that I was a very physical person? I loved sport but most of all martial arts. I felt it gave me the balance of masculine energy that I needed after healing.

WELL DESPITE BEING EXCEPTIONALLY STRONG, my body began to deteriorate. I began to suffer with slipped discs in my neck and lower back. By this point, pain had become something I was familiar with, it was actually a driving force for me as it built my will power and I mastered the state of mind over matter. When I transitioned into the permanent make-up side of the business, I slowly moved away from the spiritual side got my head down and focused on being the best....

FAST FORWARD TO 2015...MY whole world changed, life as I knew it had ceased in no uncertain terms.

· · ·

I HAD IGNORED the messages from my body for so long that it took one huge side swiping message for me to wake up and see what I was doing to my poor body. I found myself having emergency surgery to save my spinal cord after the slipped disc I'd been living and working with for 3 months, had slowly crushed it. The nurses and physios that saw my scans said that I should have been paralysed, the damage was so severe I should have been in a wheel chair. But as I lay in the hospital bed at the scarily young age of 36 surrounded by old ladies, I realised I'd been given chance at a new life. It felt like all the pain and trauma had been removed from my body and I could start again. Now this could very well have been the morphine, but I was in high spirits all the same, I even got my PA to come to the hospital and from my bed I set up a new property sourcing agency to keep me occupied (it was a soulless business that I eventually said goodbye to, but it served its purpose)

PROBLEM WAS I still wasn't listening to the little messages my body gave me, so the healing journey was very rough, I was bed bound on average, 1 week out of every month for the first year. I continued to take the burden of others on my shoulders, the need to heal others by sacrificing my own emotional and physical wellbeing was over-whelming. I was being given lesson after brutal lesson and I just couldn't see it.

ONE DAY I was in the kitchen doing the washing up, just a normal day, no dramas or events just normal. I thought to myself with terrifying stillness that I had had enough, I was tired, my soul was tired. I'd lived a life most people only dream of. I'd travelled the world and had the most incredible adventures, but I'd also had more physical and emotional pain than anyone should have to experience, more than even I could bare.

. . .

So, I made an agreement with myself, I would let go of everything that caused me stress and pain, this included my business, old partners even challenging friendships. I would spend the savings I had in the bank, and then I would come back to this thought then.

This was the beginning of my new life, my rebirth. I booked myself onto a goddess retreat, it awoke something in me that had been sleeping... the feeling was liberating and addictive, I danced, sang, laughed and cried with total strangers and it felt wonderful. I went on to do several more, each time healing other wounds and discovering new layers.

I came home and began to share what I could remember with my friends and clients, the feedback was amazing, I couldn't believe how much we all needed these experiences in our lives, so I decided to do my teacher training and off I went to Thailand.

The 4 week intensive training was challenging on many levels and it gave me the tools I needed to create the foundations of my teachings... however it had just scratched the surface for me and left so many questions unanswered, the more I learnt the more I wanted to learn, so I have been on a pilgrimage/quest ever since, in search of the answers both within and outside of me.

I have invested a huge amount of time and money collecting life changing experiences and trainings to bring back and share with my sisters, this work is so powerful and so desperately needed. We have lost the beauty of the sisterhood in modern day society, we have lost the balance of the masculine and feminine within ourselves, our relationships, our community, our tribe.

. . .

MY PURPOSE IS NOW CLEAR... I have to share the beauty of awakening our true self by living an authentic life, we are sensory beings that shut down our senses to such a degree that we don't even know our own bodies or minds. My purpose is to show as many people as I can how to reconnect with their souls.

\* \* \*

MY BIOGRAPHY MENTIONED the wounded healer...I want to talk to you a little more about this, so you can recognise if this is you and at what point of recognition you are

THIS PATTERN IS when one has experienced great pain and trauma in their own life, they are aware of the need to heal but they have a subconscious block preventing them from healing themselves, they know how bad the pain and suffering can be and as they are generally strong empaths they cannot bare the idea of others suffering the way they do, so the pull to heal slips from being a choice to being a necessity.

YOU WILL FIND OFTEN that a wounded healer has a deep routed subconscious belief that they do not deserve to be healed, that the pain is a punishment for something they may not even know (this is more often than not a karmic debt or contract made before coming into this life and is not easy to pin down without the help of an experienced practitioner).

WHEN THE WOUNDED healer works from a place of such pain, they open themselves up to an extremely vulnerable position, they may end up taking on the energetic pain of their client and will sacrifice their own journey to heal another as it takes great discipline to offer and receive healing at the same time.

THEY WILL BE TEMPTED to heal or 'fix' their client, this is a dangerous place to be as we are not responsible for the journey of others, we are here to hold space and give them the tools they need to heal themselves with support and encouragement, but the responsibility is their own, and often a very important lesson for them to undertake.

ONCE YOU RECOGNISE yourself as a wounded healer, you can then go to work on breaking those old beliefs, for me Theta worked well, it was a quick process however each individuals 'awakening' is different, you will know when the beliefs have been broken as when you heal you are now coming from a place of pure love instead of a place of pain and you will begin to accept healing from others, you will truly feel and know that the healing is happening.

THE AMAZING THING about being a wounded healer is that once you have broken the old beliefs, it then allows you to treat your clients from a place of knowing, compassion and a 'safe' empathy, you can get straight to the route cause because it is something you recognise within yourselves, you have broken the patterns of, and know what is possible.

WHEN WE ARE HEALING from a space before understanding, we know deep down how to heal these wounds and we can heal them on others, but our own subconscious beliefs block our ability to selfheal, this is called self-sabotage.

. . .

THE SELF-SABOTAGE ELEMENT of our mind can show itself in many ways and can be very cunning and devious. I see it as 'the little devil that sits on our shoulder' it likes us to suffer and will do everything it can to stop us evolving. You won't even know it's happening until someone points it out to you but when you become aware of it and how it works it is an incredible revelation.

EVERY HEALER, psychic, spiritual worker I have ever met during my life tells me that I have great powers, greater than I could ever conceive and that I just needed to step into them, I always knew that I was different and that I had a bigger purpose than I could understand at the time. It was beyond frustrating, why could everyone else see it... I wanted to see it for myself not just hang off the words others were saying to me. This pattern has been going on for years and only came to light when I embarked on my Angelic Reiki training with Tina.

I WAS REALLY LOOKING FORWARD to the training, the first day was set to begin at 6pm however at 2pm I got a visual migraine, I couldn't see a thing, I sat in the dark until my vision came back nearly an hour later, but it left me with a raging headache. The stubborn will power that I've come to rely on got me in the car and over to the Goddess Rooms, I sat in the car and put my head in my lap and literally hid in the car.

TINA CAME out and sensing my pain gave me a huge cuddle and ordered me in to have immediate healing by one of her assistants. For reasons unknown to me I burst into tears as she worked her magic, I felt physically better but emotionally detached. That evening I gave some really powerful treatments, the girls I worked on had huge state shifting healing, but I felt nothing when the healing was reciprocated.

· · ·

THE FOLLOWING DAY the same happened, I felt myself disconnect even further and question what on earth I was doing there. Again, Tina felt the energy coming off of me and asked that I come in before class the following morning. After a session of healing she told me that I had made a contract when I was in my early teens, I was being bullied and the contract was for protection, which may sound ridiculous to some however it is highly possible as I was curious of the spiritual potential even at that age and had dabbled in pagan rituals unknowing as to what I was getting myself in to. Not only that but I was also carrying some huge Karmic debts with me from my past lives.

THAT MORNING I had one of Tina's assistants remove the contract that I had made all those years ago with Theata Healing. I cried for hours, I can't tell you the relief I felt afterwards but also the huge admiration I found for myself.

THE FACT that I have become as powerful as I am despite having these contracts and karmic nooses around my neck goes to show how that will of iron I've had since I was a child has served me so well... I've always felt the battle within me but never understood the degree of what was truly happening, it was an epic battle of light and dark, and so many times the dark has nearly broken me but each time the light has come out victorious and I thank my angels, guides, higher self for the guidance and support through this.

NOW THAT I see the self-sabotage at work, I look back at all the other times it has shown itself.

IN INDIA on a spiritual retreat I was bed bound for half of the course, in Thailand at my teacher training my back was excruciating for 3 weeks out of the 4 week course meaning I couldn't fully immerse myself in the physical aspects of it. There have been times when I felt grumpy and didn't want to socialise on the day of an event that may have opened me up to something new. It's amazing to look back now and see how powerful self-sabotage is. How the darkness of my mind so desperately tries to stop the light form coming in.

BE VERY AWARE OF YOURSELF... if a workshop, class, event or meeting calls out to your soul pay attention, especially if doubts start setting in, those doubts, challenges, lethargy, headaches whatever obstacle they are, is the 'little devil on your shoulder' , the self-sabotage, doing whatever it can to stop you from expanding, stopping your inner light from growing. Remember the saying...' feel the fear and do it anyway' because when you master that you open up the gates to a world that is full of opportunities and potential.

MOVING ON TO BUSINESS...My strongest piece of advice for anyone setting out in any business is to find a good mentor, when I look back at my life and compare my experiences, I can hand on heart say that the journeys I embarked on where I had a mentor were far more successful than any without. I'll give you an example.

IN 2002 I decided to train in permanent make up, so I booked myself on to a standard 5 day course, most people stop there, however, I felt I had un-answered questions so I went on to train with 2 other companies, the latter was the UK's leading cosmetic and medical training provider.

I WANTED to be the best I could possibly be which meant I wanted to know everything possible, I had so many questions that I felt had not been covered that I constantly bugged the training support staff, eventually they decided it would be easier to get me on board and join the team, so I began to work alongside trainers as a training assistant. I challenged certain theory's and techniques and went away and experimented with my own concepts, I went on to create new techniques that pushed the industry forward, I become recognised for my work and teachings and have been invited to lecture around the world to other technicians, surgeons and nurses in the cosmetic and medical field.

ON THE FLIP side I assumed as I had been so successful in my personal career the natural progression would be to open a large studio with 8 staff, so that's exactly what I did however this time I had no mentor.

I HAVE BEEN self-employed since I was 19 so have never had any experience in managing people but how hard could it be?? Famous last words, I learnt every hard lesson going and lost a huge amount of money in the process, I just couldn't understand why it was so difficult, but now I understand. I am a quick learner, when I'm shown how to do something I can then go off and do as I've learnt. However, no one has ever shown me how to manage people, this is a gift in itself, it is not like a piece of equipment you can fiddle around with until you get it working. Human beings are highly complex and individually unique, I chose the hardest thing on earth to try and fumble my way through, had I had a mentor, all of the problems I encountered would never have arisen, or they would have been handled in more efficient ways.

I DIDN'T KNOW BACK THEN that you could have a business coach, and to be honest even if I did, I probably wouldn't have wanted to pay for one. But with the experience I have now I know that the investment would have saved me thousands of pounds and an awful lot of heartache and stress.

I HAVE PREVIOUSLY BEEN WORKING with a wonderful mentor and friend that I met on one of her workshops in Spain, she has been my emotional coach working with me on my own personal development, we used to skype once a fortnight, it slowly went down to once a month and now I'll call her if I'm feeling a little lost, however, I haven't felt the need for some time now, as she has taught me how to find the answer within myself.

I THINK a lot of us fall in to the easy trap of looking to others for the answers. I have fallen into this before and it was a very good lesson in listening to my own intuition/gut instinct. I had booked myself and my partner on a retreat in India, this was his first one, he had seen the journey I had been on and decided he wanted to try it too, it was with a teacher I'd worked with before, the retreat advertised was in beautiful wooden cabins in the Himalayas, however there had been a problem with the booking and at the last minute the venue had been changed to a hotel in the city centre.

NOT AT ALL what I had expected as I hate noise and cities. The yoga studio was on the roof with building work happening all around, it was so hard to hear the meditations and inhaling pollution and fumes was enough to push me over the edge. So having a complete meltdown on day 2, I found myself sat sniffling in reception trying to get Wi-Fi so that I could book us on the first flight to Goa and escape, when the teacher came to me and said that this was my lesson, that life will never be perfect and that I had to drop this need to have control over everything, that if I wanted to learn how to be at peace in myself I had to let go of these expectations, against my gut instinct I stayed as I am not one to shy away from a lesson.

WELL THE UNIVERSE had given me a lesson and I had failed. But it wasn't the lesson the teacher had decided for me, the lesson had been to listen to myself, to have faith in my own instincts and knowing's, I decide when I'm ready to break my own limitations, when I'm ready to move onto the next level of learning and let go of old patterns. Me and only me. The repercussions to not listening were huge to my body, I spent the last few days bed bound with a slipped disc and a central nervous system that was in chaos... No one has the right to tell you when you are ready.

So, my lesson is also my advice to you, if something, someone, somewhere makes you feel uneasy take a minute, go sit in a quiet room with no distractions, close your eyes as this helps to tap into your subconscious mind and ask yourself... what is wrong with this situation?

IF YOU CAN'T IDENTIFY what's making you uneasy at this point, then just trust in the fact your body knows and distance yourself if possible until you can gain more clarity.

YOU CAN USE this method on a daily basis, all too often we get little adrenalin spikes that trigger our fight or flight response, but we have got so used to ignoring it that we have become desensitised. Start to pay attention to these triggers, it may be someone jumped in front of you and got served first at the counter, this is injustice, or someone cuts you up in the car and then shouts at you or gives you a fright, these events cause the FoF response which releases adrenalin.

· · ·

THE BUILD-UP of adrenalin if not released, starts to cause disease within the body when we overload ourselves then the last tiny little trigger becomes the spark that causes the explosion and release of it all. We work the same way as a pressure cooker, when we experience and ignore the stress, the adrenalin builds up like steam, we have a limit to how much the body can take, as it builds and builds it gets to the point where forced release happens and our body empties all of that stored up 'shit' that we have been carrying around.

THAT'S why more often than not people 'explode' over the smallest things at the worst possible moments.

IT IS crucial that we learn how to pay attention to these response signals and also learn how to release them.

A QUICK AND easy way to release adrenalin is to copy nature... have you ever seen a documentary on TV where a lion is chasing an antelope? Well if the antelope is lucky enough to escape you will see it stand and shake its body. That's how it releases the adrenaline that helped it escape.

SO, every night before bed and in the morning when you wake up, reset yourself for the day ahead. Have a good old stretch and then shake every part of your body, when you stop close your eyes and pay attention to what's happening, can you feel the cells in your body vibrating, energised and fresh?

FINISH off by having a good old sigh, breathing with sound is a fantastic way of releasing blocked emotions and energy. Take a deep breath in and urrrrggggggg sigh it out, listen to your body and its needs, sometimes it will want you to scream, other times you will feel more primal and will want to growl, pay attention and honour your body, the more you do this the more you will begin to notice. This practice is a great tool to use after you have had a stressful encounter, find a private space and get rid of any negative energy you have just picked up.

SIGN UP to my YouTube channel to see these exercises as well as many others
https://www.youtube.com/
channel/UCjuxY8ztRg1DuGVFVHuliUQ

DESPITE ALL THE challenges I have been through I been very successful in business over the last 20 years and I'm in a position now where I can let those businesses run by themselves allowing me to move deeper into more spiritual healing and teachings, although I now know how to run a successful business I have never run a spiritual business, this is new to me, I would be foolish to make the same mistakes again in thinking I can do this without the guidance or support of someone who has succeeded in this field.

TINA HAS COME into my life for what I believe is meant to be my spiritual business mentor.

I HAD BEEN aware of Tina for a few years, I had been attending the odd workshop of hers, just observing, somebody has to be very special for me to put my faith and vulnerability in their hands after the experiences I have been through.

.   .   .

125

THE WOUNDS of the feminine that had been ingrained into my subconscious were rearing their ugly head, so I waited, and I watched. And then Tina came to me and asked me to hold a workshop for her. She was trusting me with 22 of her very precious Chicklets, I saw then that she already had faith in me, it was after working with this group of women who had complete faith in her that I truly believed in her, her intentions, integrity, her passion and her vision.

I HAVEN'T PUT Tina on a pedestal (I don't put anyone on one these days) because no one deserves that expectation, she is very open and honest and makes no claims to be flawless, this openness and transparency allows others to show their vulnerabilities, that's what makes us human, we are after all just living a human experience. Each teacher will have strengths and weaknesses, I am highly evolved with my divine feminine, yet I have a weakness when it comes to self-protection. The women who attend my workshops come to learn the skills of empowering the divine feminine from me, but they also bring their own strengths into the group, raising the whole dynamic.

WHAT I SEE in Tina is someone who has the ability to see the gifts each person possesses, to nurture and assist individuals into finding their paths. She lives and breathes her belief every single day, her energy and positivity are relentless, she will give, love, and support to anyone who is willing to help themselves including myself, to which I am very grateful.

EACH TIME I have a new idea I have someone I can bounce off, I don't just have Tina, she has given me access to a sisterhood of powerful gifted human beings who are vibrating on such a high level that when you have bad days you have a tribe of warriors, mothers, sisters, even fathers that have your back, there is no room for egos or individual gain on this path.

TINA HAS INADVERTENTLY BECOME my spiritual business mentor and friend and I look forward to growing with her and sharing with her my passions and learnings as she has shared with me.

So, you may still be wondering how you can do this,

I CAME from a place where I was in a good financial position that allowed me to invest in training and travel, I own my own home and I have a partner who also has a house too, so people will look from the outside and say you're so lucky, you have the money to do whatever you want.. I don't have that. I can't afford to do it, well let me tell you, when I opened my first business at the age of nineteen, I didn't have a penny, what I had was a vision and nothing was going to come between me and that goal.

I HAD ARRANGED a meeting with the owner of a new gym, I wanted to set up a beauty room in his club, he asked me if I had equipment and stock, I said yes of course (I actually had nothing) he asked if I had a client base, to which I said absolutely (by this point I had built up a small following of trusty clients but nowhere near what was needed)

THIS GUY WAS NOT SILLY, he could see I was winging my way through the interview, but he saw something in me, he saw a passion and an iron will determination to succeed and he gave me the opportunity to prove myself. Back then post-dated cheques were accepted, so I took the plunge and ordered all the furniture, equipment and products I needed to set the room up.

THIS WAS NOT CHEAP, but I had 9 months to pay it back over 3 instalments. I had 3 part time jobs running alongside this new venture. I worked my little feisty butt off and when each cheque was due, I had managed to collect enough money in my account to clear it. Each cleared cheque was a moment of celebration, as the business grew, I gradually gave up the part time jobs until the day arrived when I had paid all 3 payments off and could finally give up all 3 crappy but necessary jobs.

AT NO POINT did I ever believe it wouldn't work, my vision was clear. I had embarked on a journey that filled me with passion and the universe provided me with everything I needed to succeed. It wasn't easy, I worked every hour under the sun and had nothing to show for it financially for the first few years as I ploughed every penny back into it, it was a labour of love, but it goes to show that anything is possible.

IF YOU WANT it badly enough there are no excuses that will stop you. If you have no access to any source of money then do you have something you can trade in exchange for training, do you have a skill, time, or a network of friends you can introduce to the person that you want to learn from, try thinking outside the box, people will respect your passion and dedication to learning and may well just work something out. It's always worth asking but make the proposal as attractive as you can.

I'VE LOVED SHARING these small snippets of my life with you and I hope they resonate with those that need to hear…but where does all of these experiences I've shared with you leave me know?

I'M NOW 40 years old and I'm sat writing this chapter in my partners beautiful 4-bedroom detached house enjoying the log fire for the last time. I have spent the last year letting go of all of my attachments, I have rented my beautiful home out, I have donated 50% of my belongings to charity and am slowly working through the last of my possessions, my clothes fit into 2 suitcases, my belongings will eventually fit into the other 2 cases. I have decluttered my entire world and I feel freer and lighter than ever.

WE COLLECT objects in the hope they will enhance our life in some way but travelling has shown me that the less we have the happier we are, my partner has decided to follow my footsteps into a life of quality not belongings. So we are saying goodbye to the security of this luxurious house to embark on a new journey, letting go of the financial chains and living a more modest life that will allow us to invest in ourselves.

I HAVE no idea what my future holds but I know that what we have been programmed to believe is needed for happiness, is a huge lie. I want a life that is full of experiences and connections and most importantly love.

IF YOU WISH to follow my journey: www.soulequilibrium.com

# ABOUT THE AUTHOR

## HELEN PORTER

Can you mix business and spirituality together... absolutely and Helen is a perfect example of how this can work so well.

Helen is the embodiment of the divine feminine, balanced beautifully with her masculine, she has a deep understanding of her shadow side and shows others how to accept and illuminate their own darkness. As a healer she is constantly evolving as she continually journeys into self-discovery, with each journey and lesson she brings new passion and teachings for her clients.

She has a deep calling to travel, each place she visits brings her a step closer to her life's purpose. She lives and breathes the lifestyle of her dreams, retiring from her main business at the age of 40 she demonstrates how you can break free from monotony and depression and truly live the dream.

Working in the cosmetic field for the last 20 years treating a mix of clients that include cancer survivors, trauma patients, alopecia clients as well as clients that just need a little boost with cosmetic and beauty procedures.

Helen has seen a huge increase in clients of all ages both male and female with depression, low self-esteem and lacking self-love, some sadly even suicidal. This has spurred her on to provide support, guidance and treatments for people ready to take their first step onto the path of their very own healing journey.

Most people are looking to be healed by someone else, this is something Helen is very firm about, she is not here to heal you but to give you the tools with which to heal yourself.

Over the years she has trained in a multitude of hands on treatments around the world from aromatherapy, Thai massage, reflexology, through to womb and fertility massages, she is an Angelic Reiki master and a teacher in the Shakti Spirit practices.

She is a highly intuitive and an extremely skilled healer... she heals on many levels, working both with individuals and groups and is no stranger to presenting on stage to large audiences

Helen's signature treatment is a beautiful divine feminine massage that helps reconnect the soul to the body, combining manual massage, trigger release points and wrapping with intuitive healing and Angelic Reiki, working on the emotional and spiritual attachments that need to be released from the cells of the body.

She runs a host of workshops that include the Divine Feminine Series, Empowering Women in Business and is currently working on the divine masculine programmes to name but a few.

She currently lectures worldwide on the emotional and physical effects of alopecia/hair loss for men and the emotional and physical effects for women who have undergone breast surgery/mastectomy, demonstrating the reconstruction of areola/nipple complex with tattooing. Bringing more and more of her spiritual practices into a very medical field.

In her chapter she will discuss the challenges she has had to overcome being such a sensitive empath and the fact that she carried the karma of a wounded healer for most of her life.

YouTube:
https://www.youtube.com/channel/UCjuxY8ztRg1Du-GVFVHuIiUQ

# KERRY SHUTTLEWORTH

*I*t was June 1970 when my first memory of spiritual consciousness happened. My birth. I was born aware of my rebirth into this life and as I grew I experienced vivid flashbacks of my past lives. I was being shown daily how life was, many life time's ago. This wasn't necessarily a good thing for a young child to experience who needed to fit in with her environment.

THANKFULLY I WAS CONSCIOUSLY aware that my mother knew. It felt lonely, confusing and at times in my young life frightening, especially at night, when my bedroom would fill with spirits.

I EVENTUALLY FOUND my place in my village church where I quickly found a strong connection with Jesus and that remains today when I am healing. During this time I was shown stages of my future through vivid dreams that were frightening. These dreams have all come true and is how I was eventually guided to meeting Tina Pavlou, who taught me Angelic Reiki and Theta healing. In this process I was able to take my gifts with which I had been blessed and was shown how to do what I had come here to do.

TWO YEARS prior to this meeting with Tina I had lost my brother Ross, he had been an addict since the age of 15 finally taking his life at the age of 42. I was very close to my brother growing up but had felt I had lost him when he was 15. I wanted answers and searched for a clairvoyant which is how I found Tina. My past has been riddled with heartache, stillbirths, failed marriages, abuse in all forms and my heart was broken. The one and only thing that had always remained was my spirituality and my consciousness. This ability to instantly connect with this energy had left me frustrated at times as I felt thwarted in what it was I had been sent here to do. I am an empath and have now learnt how to be used by this to heal and empower other beings. I feel a strong connection with all that surrounds me and an instant ability to tune into their soul, communicate and heal.

IN 1974 UNICORNS were not as popular or talked about as they are now. I recall this particular night when I met one and it has remained with me my whole life. I was lying in bed frightened and I would close my eyes tightly to try and stop what I could see and sense. Then the unicorn came, taking me higher and higher soaring away from this planet to the stars. It took me to a small metal fenced garden, to my left in the sky I saw angels. Later returning back to my body I realised I could call on my unicorn to take me away. It was after this amazing experience that angels and my unicorn would come whenever I wished. I grew up in a violent, abusive environment, something that I know I chose before coming here but that really didn't help. What did, was taking myself off out of my body whenever I wished and connecting with the creator, being with my unicorn, my angels and going into deep meditation. I was totally unaware that I was healing myself and being guided. I later discovered that this was Theta.

. . .

IN 2007 I was guided to a course that I took over 3 days, The Landmark Forum. After years of pain, my whole life being riddled with one heartbreak after another, I had been searching my whole life for something that I had no idea was about to be discovered. It was logical to me and spoke to my spirituality profoundly, so I wanted to master being a human being and find like-minded people that loved life and this amazing planet. So, when I discovered the Forum it literally blew my mind and I knew it had been guided. It gave me the ability to strengthen myself and prepare me for the future to do what I came to do, to heal, inspire and empower through my guides and healers from other planes.

I HAVE SPENT the last 12 years healing myself, peeling back the various layers rather like an onion, going deep into my soul and my spirituality, opening my heart and learning from and about all that is and has been in my life, also my deep understanding and deep connection with the planes of the spirit world. Combining the two and being consciously awakened and attuned. The guided path has been realised and is being shown to me every moment that I tune into it. It's a natural experience full of lightness and joy. It is my quest to spread this across the universe, to share my gifts with everything, which reminds me of my children.

MY FIRST CHILD, who I did not think was possible after two stillbirths, Eleanor and Lucy. Made everything possible again. He was sent with an ability and a gift. I still smile at the memory of him trying to climb his golden chord as he described it. My second child was also strongly connected and would spend time playing with his sister Eleanor from spirit and my mother would visit him and give him butterflies. I was later blessed with a daughter, a gentle soul that has most definitely been here before. Both my boys are crystal rainbow children labelled in these times as ADHD or likewise.

Despite the many painful experiences I chose for this lifetime I have been guided and gifted with the ability to manifest and bring abundance into lives. This often is something that is seen as a positive however what I have learnt is that we can manifest both negative and positive. I have now mastered how to have the positive and have caused a huge number of miracles and gorgeous, joyful manifestation into my life. I have spent the last 2 years travelling, during this time I have been guided through my Angelic Reiki and Theta healing to heal everywhere and everything that allows me to. In particular the sea, the corals, the fish, the plants, the trees and animals. I intend mastering this and will be adding this to my holistic treatment menu along the way.

So, what do I offer on my menu? Which is rather apt because I am a retired head chef, as well as a Singer, Model and Healer. Today I am guided to heal through Angelic Reiki, Theta, Massage and Auricular Acupuncture whilst tuning into all that is shown to communicate with you. Whether that be a lost loved one in spirit or guidance in your life as it is now. Giving you healing, healing on all levels whether it be past lives or right now. To heal ailments, disease and illnesses. Bringing abundance, love, light and joy to you heart.

Some sharing from 2 friends:

Kerry has an energy, an insight, a spiritual connection that enables her to connect with people not only on a spiritual level but on a physical/psychological level. I have experienced this not in a healing session as such but in a general conversation which flowed very naturally; great insight was obviously seen into who I was spiritually and psychologically. This was given to me and posed questions which made me think deeply and come to realisations about myself that enabled me to move forward with less emotional pain.

THIS WAS A VERY powerful type of healing and quite unique. I feel it is the love and compassion she has to help her fellow man, and all the skills that she has learnt and acquired through her life and how she combines them that has enabled her to be a unique, effective and very powerful healer.

MY WONDERFUL JOURNEY through life with Kerry began two years ago and I have been fortunate enough to accompany her on her travels and witnessed the way she embraces and loves life. She is serenity personified when at one with nature and; with her natural, spiritual gifts enhanced by training, it is a wonder for me to see how she approaches life's hurdles and stumbling blocks. Issues that would exasperate and be over analysed by most people are dealt with by Kerry in a meditative and contemplative way which reduces the challenge faced to its most simplistic view and, whilst the perfect solution may not be found, the issue can be dealt with in a calm, rational manner with all the pressure of panic and despair removed.

I HAVE EXPERIENCED THE CALMING, relaxing results of Kerry's Reiki Healing and am learning daily how Kerry's gifts are able to help other people if they allow her to. I know Kerry to be a caring, loving mother and it is a privilege to see how her children are flourishing under her nurturing and guidance. I believe the spirituality she shares with them has resulted in the beautiful, open way they live as a family. I would not have had the professional success I have enjoyed over the last two years had it not been for Kerry's support, advice and guidance.

Thank you, Kerry xxx

My quest and charter for my life is to Empower, Inspire and to be the Guidance to where dreams come true. To assist through my ability to bring healing down from the spiritual healers. To bring Peace and Ease to this planet and everything in it.

# ABOUT THE AUTHOR

## KERRY SHUTTLEWORTH

Kerry Shuttleworth was Born in 1970 in a small Village on the South Coast of England .

Kerry is currently an Angelic Reiki Master, Psychic Clairvoyant, Auricular Acupuncturist, Massage Therapist and Theta Healer Practitioner. She is also a current participant and senior Graduate of Landmark Education.

Kerry's past careers and experiences have included being a Head Chef, Actor and Singer, Model ,Adventurer and Explorer.

Kerry is a mother of 3, her passion now lies in her Healing and Psychic abilities which have been there since early childhood and which she now chooses to fully express. It was her connection to the Spirit World that has enabled her to survive the various darkness pain and loss that have been part of her life's journey.

**Contact**
Kerryshuttleworthhealing@gmail.com
https://kerryshuttleworthhealing.com/

# LAURA MASON

*I*t was February 2008 and I was in my final year of university studying for a business degree in Wales. I was sitting in my room feeling stuck in anxiety, depression and desperation. I felt like there was no hope. That nothing would change.

SOME OF THE feelings were mine, but some were feelings I unconsciously picked up from other people. I had become very attuned to other people's feelings, thoughts and pain at a young age. I often absorbed other people's pain and emotions in my own body. This resulted in me suffering from exhaustion, physical pain and poor gut health. I felt stuck in emotional sludge, and saw no way to get out.

EVENTUALLY, I got fed up with feeling like I was trudging through life like a zombie. I went to a doctor to see if he could help me. He put me on anti-depressants and anti-anxiety medication, but nothing changed. I still wasn't living, I was just going through the motions.

Ultimately, the medication just made me worse. I got so tired, I could barely get out of bed for university. I put on a stone and a half of extra weight. I was tired of living.

THEN ONE DAY a close friend of mine who I was house sharing with gave me a book to read, "The Secret." It's a book based on the law of attraction. I had never heard of it before, but I decided to give it a read.

I FOUND THE BOOK FASCINATING. I had my doubts whether it really worked. But I decided I would give it a go, I had nothing to lose. The book suggested starting with manifesting something small. I decided I would manifest for a rose. I set my intention and asked the universe to bring me a red rose. I cultivated a positive feeling that I already had the rose.

THREE DAYS LATER, I was walking down the road to my part time job and there in front of me on the road was a red rose. I felt so excited. Maybe there is something in this, I thought. Maybe the law of attraction really does work. This thrilling new discovery inspired me to learn more about the law of attraction and how it works. I spent hours on the internet learning about it.

I MADE a manifestation list of how I would like my life to be. I created a vision board. I came across different methods to help me to actualise my manifestations faster. One powerful technique was the Silva Mind Method, a meditation process that helps a person enter into an alpha brain wave. In this state of meditation, it's possible to reprogram limiting subconscious beliefs into positive empowering beliefs.

Strongly held beliefs can bring manifestations into reality at a rapid pace.

I BEGAN to practice this method of meditation. As my old programming was released, I tapped into innate abilities that I had on a much deeper level. Angels, spirit guides and ascended masters revealed themselves to me.

ONE NIGHT I was lying in bed. A light filled my room. I felt scared, but also excited. What would happen next? The white light, I somehow knew, was Christs' Consciousness. It stood in front of me and asked me to go out into the world and spread the light. I didn't know what to think. I just accepted it. The light entered into my body. I was scared, but I let it in. It felt like a new knowledge, or new way of knowing, came in.

ANOTHER TIME, I spontaneously astral travelled. One minute I was lying in my bed. The next, I became aware that although I was in my physical body, my spiritual body was rising above my bed. I went on a journey to my mum's house. My spirit floated through the rooms. On another occasion, I was lying on my bed in London and my consciousness shot through the dark sky. It was pitch black, like I was travelling through a tunnel at the speed of light. At first, I didn't know what to do. I was taken down into a room in Ireland where my partner was, for work. I could see and hear him clearly in the room speaking with a friend.

BEFORE I KNEW it I was back in my bed. The experience only lasted about two minutes. The next day I told him about my experience. He confirmed that he was indeed in that room having that very conversation at that time. I had remotely viewed him. I thought, "Wow, this is amazing."

MY EXPERIENCES IGNITED a passion to pursue the spiritual path and all things metaphysical. I became fascinated with crystals and healing. A whole new extraordinary world opened up to me. I felt so excited to share with people this new-found knowledge and experience of how the universe works. I began to share it with my family and friends. I soon discovered that many of them were not open to these new ideas.

ONE NIGHT, when I was staying with a family member, huge lights appeared in front of me. I recognised these lights. They were angelic beings. I had seen them before. They began to communicate with me.

I SAID to my relative excitedly, "Can you see them?"

He said, "See what?" "The angels," I said. "No," he replied. He looked at me like I was crazy. A lot of friends and family members couldn't comprehend where I was coming from. As my sensitivity to other people's thoughts and feelings became more heightened, I could sense some of these people questioning my sanity. It hurt my feelings.

AS MY VIBRATION RAISED, most of these people drifted away. Others, I withdrew from. It was painful to be around them when I was so aware of their feelings and thoughts about my new-found "spirituality." One family member even suggested I go to see a priest for help. This was really painful for me. In hindsight, I can see these people were acting from love. They were frightened for me and wanted to help.

. . .

I BECAME MORE DISCERNING about who to share my spiritual journey with, for fear of being judged. I was also scared of being looked at like I was a crazy person. My guides continued to accompany me on my spiritual journey. I would meditate regularly. I would see spirits who had passed but still remained near their loved ones. Light bulbs would suddenly blow, which scared me. I found out later that when a person's energy gets stronger, electrical objects and electronics can go haywire.

I MANIFESTED things on my manifesting list as if by magic, like tickets to a Madonna concert. Then one day, I started to experience headaches. This lead me on the path to seek help to heal it. I came across a healer in Wales, where I was studying, and went to him for my first-ever healing session. I remember driving up to his home and passing through a foggy forest before arriving at what looked like a chicken farm. I wasn't sure what to expect. On one hand I was filled with excitement and on the other I was filled with fear. I thought to myself, "What am I letting myself in for?" I wondered if it was even safe for me to be visiting a man who lived in the middle of the countryside in Wales. Then I thought back to all of the wonderful testimonials I had read about this healer.

AS I APPROACHED HIS HOME, I was greeted by a woman who I discovered to be his wife. She seemed nice. This made me feel safer and more comfortable. Then I met my healer. He was a middle-aged man who wore a white coat like a doctor. Let's call him John.

HE LED me into a healing room and asked me a number of questions. He seemed like a kind man. To begin the healing process, he performed a ritual to clean my aura using sage and a white feather. This was all very new to me and I found it intriguing.

. . .

HE LAY me down on a massage table and surrounded me with crystals. He performed hands-on healing around my feet, my shoulders, and my chakras. I felt myself dropping into a state of deep relaxation. I could see angels standing around me healing me. It was lovely. The final part of the healing consisted of him using an energy healing technique to train my cells with feelings that I had never felt before - feelings such as safety, security and joy.

JOHN EXPLAINED that sometimes we don't develop certain feeling when we're growing up. For example, if a child grew up in a home that was unsafe and unstable she may never develop the feeling of safety in her body. Even in later years when she is safe, she won't be able to feel safe and can't recognise when she is, in fact, safe. I didn't immediately feel anything after the healing session. It was two days later that upon waking I felt a feeling that I never had before. It was the feeling of joy, and it felt amazing.

THE FEELING WAS SO good that I wanted more. I continued to see John on a regular basis. The more clearing I received, the more I opened up spiritually and intuitively. I would have premonitions, where I would see things in my dreams before they happened. It was freaky, but cool. I was amazed to have such a heightened awareness but it could be tough and painful at times. I remember one time lying on my bed feeling massive pains in my chest. I felt like I was possibility having a heart attack and feared I would die. This lasted a short while. I later discovered a close relative of mine had a heart attack. It turned out I was experiencing the heart attack at the same time as him. When I discovered this, it brought me back to when I was fifteen and I experienced a pain my aunt felt when she was losing her baby. It was horrific. I could physically feel the same pain she was feeling, even though we were not in the same country.

I CONTINUED GOING to see healers: shamans, colour therapists and spiritual healers. I did physical cleanses to rid my body and my mind of toxins.

I CAME to realise that one of the reasons I was so aware of and attuned to other people's feelings, thoughts and emotions was because I had experienced physical and emotional abuse in earlier years. I learned to read what other people needed and wanted. If I could tune into what their needs and wants were and meet them, there would be a much better chance that I would be left alone. Maybe even taken care of. It was a way that I learned to ensure my survival. It was unthinkable to think of what may have happened if I did not do this.

UNFORTUNATELY, by using this survival behaviour, I lost touch with myself, meaning that, I couldn't discern the difference between my wants, needs, feelings and thoughts - and other people's wants, needs, feelings and thoughts. I had become like a sponge, constantly absorbing other people's feelings and emotions.

I HAD BEGUN my journey in a state of anxiety, confusion and depression. I couldn't disentangle my thoughts, feelings, beliefs - even identity - from those of other people. I didn't really know who I was. And I wanted to find out.

As I CONTINUED on my healing path, old painful feelings came up. Feelings that I found really difficult to deal with, like the desperation of my teenage years when I would binge and purge. I would eat and eat when I felt bad, only to puke it all up a few minutes later. Then I would be filled with shame and wracked with guilt. The binge-and-purge cycle felt like going around on a merry-go-round with no way out.

IN LOOKING BACK, I see these behaviours were symptomatic of the hatred I felt towards myself. It was an unconscious way to feel I had some control of myself and my life.

I HAD LEARNED to hate myself. I guess on some level I felt there must be something wrong with me. I must be worthless.

OVER THE NEXT FEW YEARS, I trained in a number of different methods of energy healing and intuitive healing in an effort to heal myself. I received many great healings. And I facilitated many profound healings on my clients. I also met many wonderful healers who helped me along my way.

I FOUND that I was getting so far with the healing and couldn't get any further than a certain point. Then one day when I was on a course in America I met a wonderful lady and healer who helped me immensely. She helped me realize that one reason I had not received healing on a deeper level was due to emotional and physical trauma experienced in my younger years. The traumas affected my life on many levels.

I DISCOVERED that when a person experiences this degree of trauma they often have aspects of their psyche that do not receive healing.

Often, parts of a person can be frozen in the old traumatic experiences, which can hinder the healing process. Other aspects of them may resist healing. They may consciously desire to heal, but they could resist the healing because parts of them fear the healer. Or, perhaps parts of them hide because they do not trust anyone to help or heal them.

THIS DISCOVERY INSPIRED me to pursue a degree in psychotherapy.

My psychotherapy studies opened a new world for me. They taught me so much, but also deeply challenged me. The work made me look at my life deeply and evaluate it and myself. It opened up my shadow self, which I had to work through.

AS PART of my training I was required to attend a minimum of 50 hours of psychotherapy, as these courses naturally bring up issues for everyone which need to be worked through.

I FOUND a psychotherapist who specialised in trauma. I attended more than 200 sessions while pursuing my degree. They loosened the emotional lid on things I had forgotten about. I had to look at a lot of old painful feelings, limiting belief systems and behavioural patterns such as people-pleasing and self-sacrifice.

THANKFULLY, I had some magical tools in my tool box that I could use to change my limiting beliefs very fast and release the pain associated with them. In my previous healing trainings, I learned how to connect to Divine energy through a hypnotic state and change limiting belief systems in a matter of minutes. This can clear years of pain with ease.

. . .

Now, I had a deeper understanding of how the psyche works. I could use this along with the tools I had learned in my trainings to heal myself and my clients on a deeper level.

My psychotherapy sessions taught me the importance of the relationship between the therapist and the client. I learned how it is vital to have a connection with a therapist who is empathetic, listens well, and validate my feelings while at the same time challenging me. This in itself created massive healing for me.

As I began to understand things - and myself - more clearly, I seemed to be able to accept healing from other healers on a deeper level. Looking back, I now see that part of the reason I could heal only to a limited extent was because aspects of myself refused to allow healing for many different reasons, mainly associated with survival.

When I look back at things from a universal perspective, I clearly see that part of my journey was to learn to heal myself, I could also learn to guide and support other people in healing themselves. On a soul level, I had chosen to go through these experiences to put me on the path to self-love and, eventually, wholeness.

Today I have a successful international practice. I travel the world conducting workshops, teaching , and working with clients. I love to travel, experience new cultures, meet new people and embark on new adventures.

I live together with my husband in a loving, supportive relationship. I also enjoy spending time with my cherished friends. I live in the magic of co-creating my reality and life every day, and relish in the joy, excitement, and enchantment it brings.

I HAVE DEVELOPED my own Therapy called the Mason Method.

YOU CAN DOWNLOAD your free healing meditation at www.lauramason.co.uk"

# ABOUT THE AUTHOR

## LAURA MASON

**Author Bio: Laura Mason**

Laura Mason BA hons began her healing journey over a decade ago. Back then she was stuck in anxiety, depression and desperation. She felt like there was no hope. She would often absorb other people's pains and emotions into her own body. This resulted in her suffering from exhaustion, physical pain and poor gut health. She felt stuck in an emotional sludge and saw no way to get out. Things became so bad that she tried anti-depressants and anti-anxiety medication, but nothing changed. She wasn't living. She was just going through the motions. This was the pain that led her down the spiritual path of healing and self-love.

She had a difficult upbringing with complex family dynamics. She had many mountains to climb, and trauma to heal, to be where she is today.

Today life is very different for her. She is a psychotherapist, a healer and a spiritual teacher. She has a successful international business. She is based in London and she teaches and practices both locally and worldwide, working with students and clients in-person and virtually. She works with an array of clients; from those who want to achieve wholeness and healing, to those who want to become even more empowered through limitless possibilities.

Her psychotherapy and integrative counselling training includes; child psychology, sociology, trauma, addiction, couples therapy, and family dynamics. She has done extensive training in many energy and intuitive healing modalities. She has created her own healing methodology. The Mason method. She travels the world conducting workshops, teaching, and working with clients. She loves to travel, experience new cultures, meet new people, take risks, and embark on new adventures. Laura specialises in healing childhood trauma, relationships and family relationships.

She lives together with her life partner in a loving, supportive relationship. She also enjoys spending time with her cherished friends. She lives in the magic of co-creating her reality and life every day, and relishes in the joy, excitement, and enchantment it brings.

**Contact**
    Email: Laurathetahealing@gmail.com
    Website: www.lauramason.co.uk

          [f] facebook.com/laura.mason.315

# LISA O'CONNELL

## SERENDIPITOUS 11:11

*I* had appeared to be operating under an illusion or a facade that was only a partial representation of the truth. In a bid to display only the good things about people or situations I encountered on my journey through life.

I SEEMED to be slightly out of touch with that which was true or in accordance with reality or fact, because surely life couldn't all be unicorns and rainbows. Could it?

I HAD ALWAYS BEEN FASCINATED by something much greater than anything else I could imagine. The phenomenon of the creation of the Cosmos. I had invested years staring at the night stars the world over, knowing they were a true reflection of the light inside of me. I had always been able to find such stillness in the grandeur of the Universe. Being able to feel the serenity in nature and coming to the realisation that we are nature. There is no separation.

. . .

I BEGAN TRAVELLING the vast distance of the globe because I am drawn to explore the wild oceans, majestic waterfalls, peaks and troughs of mountain ranges and to walk barefoot on the shores of exotic beaches feeling the sand between my toes, whilst allowing myself enormous pleasure in admiring the swaying palms and crystal-clear waters that surround me. On each journey leaving behind nothing but my footprints and echoes of laughter.

WHY? Because it is my birth right. Why are we given this beautiful thing called life on this incredible planet, if not to enjoy every minute of it we are gifted.

MY BELOVED grandad Bill had once said to me 'that yesterday is history, tomorrow is a mystery and today is a gift and that's why we call it the present'. I learned to enjoy life from an early age living in the moment and focused on being in control of my own destiny. Thankfully I was able to recognise the intuition of my higher self, giving me the ability to identify both my positive and negative emotions and the effect they had on my life.

AND SO, I began mapping out my own karma.

SETTING INTENTIONS, chanting mantras, enrolling on more courses because knowledge is power. I learned Thai yoga massage, Usui and Angelic reiki healing, Tina Pavlou being my phenomenal guide and master. I began working with crystals and meditating and finally when I felt ready, I became a yoga teacher. I envisioned my future doing my part to pass on the wisdom I was gaining and to participate in honouring the Cosmos.

. . .

BUT ABOVE ANYTHING else I longed to open a yoga retreat on the magical Greek island of Corfu. An island steeped in history and once ruled by the British, the Ottomans and the Venetians. All leaving their own unique imprint. An island engulfed in olive trees. It's cobble-stoned streets lined with brightly coloured buildings and ancient window facades, enveloped in bougainvillea of vivid pinks and purples. It's dramatic coastline cascading into the turquoise waters of the Ionian Sea. An island shaped like a mermaid. My Greek paradise!

I SAW IT SO VIVIDLY, that I knew it would one day to be a reality. All I had to do was set the intention and manifest my thoughts. I started to believe that I had already accomplished my goals. As much as I knew they would come to me, I never set a deadline as I felt I would not be trusting in the Universe enough if I presented it with a time frame. So, I entrusted it to all unfold organically. I'm not saying it has all been plain sailing. Far from it in fact, but faith always keeps me going. You see, the Universe sees and hears everything, so if we are true it will thank us by honouring us with that which we need in life, but not always with what we want. However, sometimes what we need and what we want, can turn out to be the exact same thing!

MY DIRECTION in life changed at precisely 12.11pm on Sunday 3rd April 1994 When at twenty-three years old I found myself the proud owner of a six pounds eight-ounce baby girl.

MY DAD DERIVES from an Irish Catholic family descending from Knocknagoshel in County Kerry. I wanted to give my baby an Irish name in honour of dad's heritage. Saoscha Montana O'Connell was named. Saoscha is derived from Saoirse meaning freedom. This, more than anything was what I wished for my child through life. Complete freedom to be whoever or whatever her heart desired. I would support her decisions as my parents had always done with myself and my brother Simon.

THAT DAY I made her a promise to guide her through life with just the essentials! Love, laughter, compassion and inspiration. And to show her from where wonder, strength and courage are born.

HER DAD WAS GONE by then, never to be seen again and I was a single mum.

MY HEART YEARNED for our freedom so passionately that I felt guided to explore unknown lands with my child. A calling from far away that resonated within my soul. I exposed my inherent spirituality seeking the knowledge to experience even more reflection of our vast cosmos. I imagined new possibilities for us after learning previous lessons from painful experiences. Life could indeed have been a giant ball of confusion if I had allowed it, but it all depends on how you choose to look at things. I allowed my perception to change from that day because I knew it was impossible to form any sort of relationship going forward without honesty. After all, nothing can be built on broken foundations.

I TOOK control of our future and strove forward saying yes to each great opportunity that presented itself. By the time Saoscha had reached fourteen years old, she had kicked her beloved football on the shores of forty-three countries and she was learning the trials and tribulations of a liberated life. Saoscha knew from an early age to always speak the truth no matter the consequence. We must always seek the truth as it's essential in creating a balanced life. Occasionally though, those scales over balance and we are left hanging on for dear life. It's during these times we just need to hold on, enjoy the ride and learn!

It was 24 December 2004 and as I sat on the beach in Koh Samui, Thailand. I was unable to stop thinking of my friends James and Philippa in Khao Lak further north. They had been on a live aboard boat, diving for a week and had just disembarked with friends on their honeymoon. They rented beach huts next door to each other overlooking the sea.

For the most part I dislike mobile phones but sometimes they are literally life savers! This was one of those days that I found myself happy to own one. I couldn't stop calling them and nagging them to leave there. After a multitude of calls they started to get annoyed with me. But I really wanted them to leave Khao Lak and come to Koh Samui. I didn't know why, just that they couldn't stay there. Intuition? Sixth sense? Crazy stalker friend with behavioural issues? Maybe all three, but they finally relented and said goodbye to their friends.

Christmas day was memorable, we enjoyed a BBQ on the beach with great company, over twenty of us that day, all together from Corfu.

As the sun began to set the mood changed to a much more sombre affair, and I don't refer to the company, but the weather. It was full moon, the wind was fierce, and the tide had completely disappeared. We had spent many a Christmas on that particular beach but there was something unfamiliar about that night. Something slightly sinister. Little did we know what was literally around the corner.

. . .

IT WAS LATE when we went to bed and early when we rose. We had gone deep into the island to visit elephants. When we emerged later, I had sixteen missed calls from my parents. My heart sank!

I WAS ABOUT to call mum when my phone rang. I answered "Hello mummy". A voice of hysteria at the end of the phone was screaming "Oh my god you are alive, what about the earthquake? "What earthquake mum?" "What about the tsunami?" Mum questioned. "What tsunami?"

IT WAS a little after 8.30 am on 26 December 2004. The morning of one of the biggest devastations in the world.

AN EARTHQUAKE STRUCK which generated a disastrous tsunami devastating fourteen countries, killing nearly 228,000 people. Here we were in Thailand amidst utter devastation in total bewilderment. We were all safe! We made our way back to our bungalows in silence unaware of quite how serious this catastrophe was, which was unfolding at that present moment.

PHILIPPA TRIED to contact her friends in Khao Lak. The phones were dead and tragically their bodies were never found. It is with pure gratitude that I thank the universe for keeping my friends and I safe on that fateful day. I had begged them to leave that bungalow. Khao Lak turned out to be the worst place hit in Thailand. There are some people in life you have a deeper connection with than others. An understanding of, or a knowing. I have always had this with them. Philippa fondly refers to me as her ginger witchy.

. . .

SOME EXPERIENCES WILL NEVER LEAVE you. That day certainly made me aware of my own mortality and that of those around me. Life is so fragile and that is exactly why we need to live each day as if it's our last, because one day, in the blink of an eye it just will be!

I HAD TRIED to ignore the signs for years because I am logical and for most parts realistic. However, I saw, I felt, and I knew things and so I slowly began to accept my path as it should be. I found myself being guided by messages and numbers constantly.

ON THE 11TH December 2008 I awoke with a knowing feeling that I would see my old friend Rich for the first time in years. I was living with my dear friend Lisa, and I spoke of my dream. She knows me well so wasn't surprised at my certainty of it happening that day.

I THOUGHT I kept hearing his voice, but as I scoured the sea of people all bustling through the busy German Christmas market in central Birmingham, I was unable to find him. No ordinary morning, Spirit and Don't give up by Chicane played relentlessly through my little travel speakers all day long on repeat.

I HAD WORKED the Christmas markets for years, selling crystals from a wooden cabin immersed in deities of beautiful quartz, amethyst, jade and malachite. Himalayan salt crystal lamps, Carnelian, Obsidian, so much vibrancy and wonderful energy encompassing me. Hundreds of agate wind chimes hanging from the ceiling all dancing and singing from the arctic winds blowing through the side of the hut. Incessant freezing cold days outside under multiple layers of clothes. The smell of bratwurst and beer unavoidable. I was once more surrounded by old friends and familiarities. Oh, how I loved those six weeks of each year!

ON THIS DAY we had decided to stay late after work in my kindred sister Lynne's hut. Seven of us in a space just about big enough for two small people. Candles flickered through the crystal tea light holders. Everything inside illuminated by the ever-changing colours of the LED selenite lamps. The sound of laughter and trojan ska exploding into the outside world through the cabin's wooden panels, mixed with the smell of red wine and nag champa.

AT AROUND 11PM we said our goodbyes for the night. We always finished at 9pm and that extra two hours meant our normal nightly walk home was no longer available. We found ourselves taking an unfamiliar route back. As I stepped from the pavement, I checked my phone. The time was 11.11pm.

"I WAS SO ADAMANT I was going to see Rich today" I said to Lisa. As I brought my gaze back from the road to eye level, I began to smile like a Cheshire cat. "And there he is" I said to Lisa. We started giggling. I had known it!

As I WALKED over to greet my old friend a cloud of smoke exploded in my face as he exhaled and exclaimed "I knew that was you bab, even before I saw your face. I felt it all day. I knew I was going to see you" in his strong Brummie accent.

IT HAD BEEN a while since we had last been in each other's company but on this day the planets had aligned for this meeting between old friends. The connection had been established but the reason unknown.

IT WAS PRETTY MUCH from this moment that my spiritual journey took its own leap of faith.

THE MESSAGES CAME FAST. So many messages. So much confusion. Was I making it up? How did I suddenly know so much? The dreams, the feelings, the visions, absolutely consumed my entire being at that time of my life. It scared me as I couldn't find the off switch. I spent that winter in India and Thailand trying to make sense of it all.

THE FOLLOWING SUMMER I was back in Corfu. One night I began to feel unwell. I clutched my leg as the pain became stronger. Thundering through me like a rail road train and finally stopping at my heart centre. I couldn't get my breath, I was gasping for air, gripped by the tightness in my chest. Then all was calm, and I drifted off to sleep.

AS SOON AS I awoke the next morning, I remembered my experience and Rich had been present in my dreams so there must be a connection, I thought. The messages had to be for Rich or why the chance meeting? I called him. "Listen mate we need to talk. I'm getting messages. Who is M and W, and someone needs to get white lilies today. Please call and ask your mum now. Who is the big S?" A barrage of questions he did not know the answers to when put on the spot. I keep seeing the letter S over and over and an aeroplane. I told him it had felt like a blood clot in my leg travelling to my heart. There was a long pause. "my brother Scott died recently of a blood clot when he got off of a plane" The tears were flowing, and the connection was established!

M AND W WERE REVEALED, Scott's wife and daughter. Maisie and Wendy. When he called his mum Pauline, she had been on the way to the florist with Maisie to buy Wendy flowers. It was her birthday. They had been discussing what flowers to buy. The phone call arrived about the white lilies, so the choice was made for them.

SCOTT HAD ALWAYS GIFTED white lilies to his wife on her birthday. This was to be her first birthday without her beloved husband and yet she still received those flowers. The same flowers they had on their wedding day. Those white lilies were significant!

LATER THAT NIGHT I received a call from Rich, the time was 11.11pm. I had mentioned for him to watch out for butterflies during the evening as they would be significant, and that he would feel Scott's presence when the butterflies appear. Maisie had been alone in her room and emerged with four pictures she had been painting. Four beautiful brightly coloured butterflies. One on each picture. Scott's young daughter then gave his mum, dad, brother and wife each a picture with their very own butterfly "Wow bab, you really are a witch, that has just completely blown me away."

IT HAD BLOWN me away too, but somehow, I knew. I still tell him things now that I could not possibly know. But I always know, and he always knows that I know!

WE WOULD STAY in touch through the years, me often trying to help him out of his darkness.

.   .   .

THE CONNECTION to 11:11 were always apparent between us.

SO FAST FORWARD TO 11.08.18. Rich was making an impromptu weekend trip to Corfu to catch up with old friends. He had messaged me to book him a room for two nights. The hotel was full, they had just one room available.

IT WASN'T until I was on my way there to greet him, that I laughed to myself and thought "I bet he is in room 11". Upon my arrival he was waiting in reception. He questioned if I had anything to do with the room number? "No, it was the only room they had left, why are you in room 11?"

"ADD an extra one bab and you would indeed be correct. I'm in room 111 the very same room that has butterflies on the wall."

RICH HAD BEEN battling through life since losing Scott, feeling angry with the sudden loss of his big brother. He chose to live his life in and out of toxic relationships, his demons often making an appearance. Punishing himself because of his loss. The empty Scott shaped void forever present.

BUT THAT WEEKEND IN CORFU, he would indeed truly see the light within him. He finally understood that despite the distance between their worlds, his dear big brother Scott will always be right by his side to guide him. They will always be connected. He had been given so much proof that it was impossible for him to deny.

. . .

WE HAVE EXPERIENCED an abundance of profound moments together through the years which could only have been orchestrated from above. So many in fact, they need their own book! All further proof that the Universe knows what it's doing, and if we just open our eyes and see the bigger picture it's easy to make sense of reality. However, at times we also need to remember to close our eyes and be still, because we don't need our eyes to look within us. And this is imperative in understanding the essence of our foundation.

I WOULD OFTEN TELL Rich "When you live with an attitude of gratitude, you reside in an energy that can create miracles." He finally chose to reside within that energy and is now starting his own children's clothing brand called FIND YOUR SAVIOUR. Funnily enough it has an amazing spiritual story behind it!

I HAD DISLIKED goodbyes from a very young age. I would become emotional when leaving someone I loved. So, you can imagine that funerals are not exactly my favourite thing.

IN 2016 A VERY SPECIAL family I have known since a teenager had suffered the loss of their beloved mum, the incredible lady Jo Doyle. This amazing soul passed at 4.17 in the afternoon after losing her battle with cancer. Her funeral took place on 26 July. It was a beautiful service bursting at the seams with people in attendance to show their appreciation of the effect she had on their lives and to thank her for the four wonderful children she had gifted to the world and of whom we are all so fond.

AT SOME POINT of the evening I was driving my dear friend Gemma and her husband Matt home. Gemma is Jo's eldest daughter. The distress and pain in my beautiful friends' heart were so apparent. We all sobbed the whole car journey back. It was a VERY poignant moment in life. I can't really explain it, but I felt Gemma's pain that day.

FOR ME THERE was something more profound about mama Jo's funeral, and I was no stranger to funerals. With the loss of friends and family to me over time through suicide, accidents or sickness being incredibly high.

THE ENTIRE DURATION of that day, I had a dreaded feeling constantly of it preparing me for something emerging very soon in my life. I didn't know what, but I certainly knew it was for me.

JUST FIVE DAYS later my dad Tony began to feel unwell. Short of breath. He had a rash all over his body.

IT WAS SO UNLIKE HIM, a strong golf playing man of seventy-three so full of life whom suddenly was incapacitated to the sofa. Numerous doctor's appointments, scans and tests but nothing seemed apparent to either his GP or the local hospital, during those first two weeks.

BY THE FIFTEENTH of August and four visits to the doctor and hospital we descended upon A&E. The hours passed, eventually we saw a junior doctor who told us he would not be going home. I pushed for answers and he was finally admitted on to a ward. We had been waiting there with him struggling to breathe unaided and in desperate need of oxygen for over ten hours. I left that night knowing he had a type of Lymphoma. Not because I was told by anyone, but I just knew.

．　．　．

THEN SUDDENLY THE realisation of maybe losing my dad was staring me in the face. Not my wonderful dad. My go to person. He had always had my back, even when he vehemently disagreed with my choices, he would still stand my ground and support me. My heart, my guide, my inspiration, my hero. I wasn't ready. I felt my heart breaking. I had never been acquainted with such a vast emptiness before. Oh God I wished I was wrong.

TWO DAYS later my worst fears were confirmed, and he was moved to the Macmillan ward.

HE HAD BEEN DIAGNOSED with Angioimmunoblastic T cell Lymphoma a rare and aggressive type of non-Hodgkin's Lymphoma. It was stage four, but the doctors still gave us some hope.

WE WOULD SPEND our days in the Macmillan garden. Dad loved this beautiful little sanctuary. Some days he could walk there unaided, some days we had to take him in his wheelchair, He had marked his favourite spot from day one and we would sit for hours laughing and talking fondly of old memories. They were wonderful days to cherish. I had been traveling for over twenty years, but right now when this disease had turned our world upside down, I was living in England and able to be with him all day, every day. How blessed I am!

WE WOULD PRACTISE gentle yoga and before long, the nurses would start to join in from behind the glass doors of the chemo room. It became a regular thing. I had been talking about doing a yoga for cancer course for a while, so I made it my mission. Within five months I had completed it at Guy's hospital Cancer centre in London. Again, on to pastures new!

Now my dad had never believed in a lot of the same things I do. I believe in spirit, I believe in numerology and I have faith. Not in any religion but I have faith in the universe. I receive pennies from heaven. I have lost count of the times white feathers have landed on me. My friends will agree that my whole life has been spent falling in shit, yet I still end up smelling of roses. I suppose people would call me lucky, but I disagree.

So, I must believe in the fact that despite me leaving different places at different times every day I arrived with my dad at the hospital at precisely 11.11am those first eight days. Of course, 11.11 is subject to our own interpretation but for me it's a sign of being protected by our angels and makes us aware of their presence and guidance. It's merely a nudge from a spirit to stop and recognise that moment in time. A clear message from the universe telling us to be conscious and aware. An energetic doorway opening where spiritual growth is available. 11.11 asks us to tune into the love and synchronistic guidance always available to us.

Dad had a comfortable four weeks in hospital until his first round of chemotherapy, after which he was allowed home. I worried terribly about him becoming neutropenic. We all sat in mum and dad's garden, the sun was shining, and he was glowing. His skin looked bright and he appeared so much younger than his actual age. I had not seen him look so well in years. He looked great!

I had to leave the next day, as after many years of searching we had found the perfect land to buy in Corfu and the time had come to sign the papers. It was a short trip of just three days. I didn't want to leave dad, but he told me not to worry and I spoke to him every day.

OUR LAST DAY and the papers were signed. We were now the legal owners of a mountain with incredible sea views on two acres of land in Corfu, overlooking the most beautiful emerald green lake set deep in nature. Things were finally starting to happen. All my hopes and dreams were becoming a reality. This was one of the best days of my life just about to take a complete U-turn. It ended up being one of the worst days of my life!

AS OUR PLANE finally came to a standstill at Stansted airport. I took my phone out to call mum.

GARRY HAD a look of concern on his face. Mum had messaged to say that dad had been rushed into hospital. He had neutropenia and they were taking him to ICU. We drove at what seemed like the speed of light to the hospital. My family were all in the waiting room when we arrived, but the doctors didn't let us stay long as they needed to perform tests.

I WAS up with the songbirds the next morning and as I got in the car and switched on the radio, the song playing was 'Don't you worry child' by Swedish house mafia. The words "my father said don't you worry child, see heavens got a plan for you, don't you worry, don't you worry now" repeating over.

WHEN EVERYONE WAS PRESENT, the doctors came to say they needed to put dad on a life support machine for a few days. We were given a short time with him before he slept. We all assumed he would wake up as the doctors had said he would. We just needed to be patient.

ON THE 20TH SEPTEMBER 2016, I felt his time was close. I set up camp on ICU and surrounded him with crystals to ease his transition. I never left his side for a minute. I got to spend his last night in this life with him, for which I am eternally grateful. This was now the best night of my life about to turn into the worst day of my life!

21ST SEPTEMBER. The 25th anniversary of my Grandads death. My dad's dad. We were told that dad had deteriorated so much that they must switch off the machines. We were left to say our goodbyes. The hours passed, all of us at his bedside. All his favourite songs playing on shuffle. At 4.17 in the afternoon my parents favourite song, ironically, 'I want to live' by John Denver started to play. Dad was ready to take his final breath and surrender his soul to the light.

LIFE HAD JUST CHANGED FOREVER!

23RD SEPTEMBER ARRIVED IN A BLUR. We had an appointment at the funeral directors. I said to the family. "They will probably offer us 11am on 11th October. After leaving the room to call the crematorium the funeral director emerged once more to offer us a date. The 11th October. I nudged my sister Kerry to check the clock on the wall. The time was 11.11. We all just glanced at each other.

"11AM?" I questioned. Her response was that the funeral would be at twelve, but they would be bringing dad's body to the house for the final time at eleven. Well of course they were. Why would I have expected anything else? He arrived home that final time at 11.11 on the 11<sup>th</sup> just to prove a point.

24TH SEP ARRIVED, and the family had arranged to meet at the florist to order dads flowers. We all chose what we wanted and paid. We were just about to leave when I decided I needed more flowers just from me!

"I NEED SUNFLOWERS" I told the florist. "how many stems?" she replied. "Eleven" my response. "Well that's a bit precise, why eleven?" I began to explain the connection to 11.11. The conversation piqued the interest of the other staff and they all came over to see where the story was heading. I began to explain its significance and told them of dad's passing at the time my parents favourite song began playing, a song by John Denver. At that very moment Saoscha said "wow listen".

John Denver had begun to play through the radio in the florist. We all stood in silence. The florist pointed out the digital clock on the wall behind us. The time was 11.11!

For a man that hadn't believed in spirit he was sure getting his messages across loud and clear.

IN THE CAR on the way home I said to Saoscha "I'm going to order another eleven sunflowers. I need another eleven sunflowers." "God mum don't be silly, then you will have twenty-two. Eleven is fine mum" No! I wanted another eleven and I vowed to order them as soon as I got home. The thing is though. Sometimes the things we need in life can literally materialise immediately.

As I PULLED the car onto the drive a cardboard box stood tall against the front door. I had not been home for days. I thought the package was for someone else, but it was addressed to me.

I OPENED it and pulled out the contents. A bouquet of sunflowers. I proceeded to place the sunflowers inside a vase. 8, 9, 10, 11. No way! I was just stressing in the car about getting another eleven sunflowers for dad. But they were not meant for dad, they were meant for me!

MY BELIEF in the universe is sincere. However, are my beliefs creating my experiences or do my experiences create my beliefs?

THE FAMILY WERE MEETING at the registry office in the afternoon to register dad's death. I, in the meantime would go to the hospital to pick up the death certificate. I had an appointment at 1pm. I was never this organised but was clearly being guided by my dad Tony the perfectionist. Wanting everything in order with his spread sheet in hand, dotting all the I's and crossing all the T's just as he had done in life.

I GOT in my car and put Eva Cassidy on. My favourite song in the world. Songbird, originally by Fleetwood Mac. I sang those words through my tears like my life depended on them. "For you, there'll be no crying. For you the sun will be shining, and the songbirds keep singing like they know the score and I love you, I love you, I love you like never before."

AS I WAITED outside patient liaison to receive the death certificate the door was opened from the inside. A familiar face smiled at me. It was dad's doctor. She hugged me and offered her condolences and told me to take a seat and she would be back soon with the paperwork. She entered that waiting room at 1.11 and handed the death certificate over. The signs were constant during the first nine days of dad passing.

BACK IN MY car I continued to play Songbird at full volume all the way to Rochester. Saoscha was like, "Seriously mum, enough now!" I told her I wanted it played at Grandads funeral. I was going to ask the others when we met.

AFTER LEAVING the registry office we went to a little tea shop over-looking Rochester Cathedral. It was a gloriously sunny day. There were two tables outside on the street basking in the sunshine. There were three chairs at each table and there were five of us.

AT ONE TABLE was seated a man alone. Headphones on, his head swaying from side to side in time with his music, a huge smile on his face, his eyes closed. I thought it best not to disturb his moment, but I wanted the two unused chairs at his table. Oh, the dilemma! I slowly walked over and tapped his knee. "I'm really sorry to bother you but are you using these chairs. Would you mind if I take them please?"

HIS EYES OPENED, the smile still fixed to his face. He gently nodded and said, "Of course sweetheart, help yourself."

I TOOK the chairs to our table and we began to discuss the funeral. I mentioned Songbird, but as much as I love Eva Cassidy it had to be the Fleetwood Mac version. They are my favourite group on the planet. This song is said to have held the band together during difficult times. This song made them realise how much love they shared between them and what they had been through together. The current situation our family found ourselves in. The songwriter had once said that this song was a gift to her from the angels. My dad was now an angel and I wanted this song played for him.

THE LAST TIME I had seen Fleetwood Mac in concert perform song-bird had been the 11<sup>th</sup> October, the date of dad's impending funeral. The connection was there. The guy at the other table was still smiling and I needed to know what he was listening to as he looked so happy and peaceful. I once more stood up to disturb the gentleman's peace, again tapping his knee. " Sorry, me again, sorry to be a pain but you look so content there I just want to know what you are listening to?" "Oh, it's from way before your time my love, it's someone called Eva Cassidy." "Which song?" I asked already knowing the answer. "Song-bird" his reply. "My mum just passed away, it was her favourite song. It makes me smile as it reminds me of her." I burst into tears, hugged and thanked him for making my day and once more returned to my family.

RIGHT THEN, as I had been for the previous five weeks. I was still in the presence of the same four witnesses. For years my nearest and dearest had categorized me slightly mad for my beliefs, but some-times, even sceptics are unable to deny the messages staring them so blatantly in the face on a regular basis! Our loved ones maybe gone from sight, but spiritually they are always there, right by our side.

THE DATE IS 11.11.2018. 2+0+1+8=11. So, as I start to write this final paragraph the time is 11.11.11.11.11. (That was intentional)

· · ·

ALL THOSE YEARS of manifestation now so apparent. The life I have visualized so many times I am now living! For years I have focused all my energy on moving back to Corfu and building a yoga retreat with my partner Garry. He has believed in me enough empowering me to follow my vision.

So, I find myself once more living in Greece. We are fifteen days in, and work has begun on the yoga retreat.

I WAS PUSHED to be here right now by a stray dog that stayed by my side all afternoon on my birthday last month. I had run a yoga retreat in Corfu that week and there had been a last-minute glitch with the accommodation. There was a stray dog living in the garden of the new villas. The yoga girls all loved her and fed her, and she was showered with affection for those five days. I felt so sad for the dog, but I couldn't take her. I lived in England! That night I stayed home with friends. My Saoscha was in England but I wished for a Saoscha hug. My mind tormented with thoughts of that poor dog.

JUST BEFORE MIDNIGHT as my birthday was ending, the front door flew open and someone shouted "surprise" and there she was. I burst into tears as my darling Saoscha and her beautiful girlfriend Cheyenne had flown in to surprise me. I got that Saoscha hug I had longed for earlier. Sometimes a wish is enough!

THE NEXT MORNING, a big group of friends were meeting for my birthday breakfast together. We ate, then headed to the beach. Within seconds the dog appeared and began throwing her best yoga moves in the exact spot we had practised yoga every morning at sunrise those previous days.

· · ·

FRIENDS STARTED TELLING me I should keep her. After all, yesterday was my birthday and she could be my gift. The yoga dog. She was named Luna because that day there was a brand-new moon. Just lately though, I am beginning to wonder if Luna is short for Lunatic?

THE LAST THING I wanted was a dog in Corfu when I lived in England, but her eyes looked deep into your soul.

WE TRIED to coax her from the beach, but she was so scared. Lisa and I left for the pet shop to buy her essentials and would go and pick her up later. After all she had been there a week. When we got back, she had disappeared.

WE SEARCHED that area for two whole days. I was beside myself. We went to the dog shelter and drove around for hours looking for her. I cried a lot those two days. I was showing everyone pictures of her and said to call me if they saw her. Lisa reassured me that if she were to be mine, she would come back at the time she was meant to. I of all people knew this to be true but It didn't stop me worrying. I already loved her.

ONE MONTH AGO TODAY, at 11.11am on 11th October exactly two years since my dad's funeral, I received a call from a local fisherman. He had found the dog and she was eating his lunch on the beach and could I go and collect her. She happily came with us that time. After a few days, I left her with my friend Trevor and flew back to England. Garry and I got the cats in the car. One train, two boats and five countries later we arrived in Greece, leaving everything else behind for that stray dog.

I LIKE to think that I rescued Luna that day, but the reality of it is, I am now living my dream in Corfu. She rescued me that day and gave me the life I had envisioned for so long. She gave me a reason to take that leap of faith! She needed me, and I needed her. The Universe changed our hotel booking at the last minute because she was waiting for me at their villas in another part of town. Ready to give us both our happy ever after!

THESE ARE JUST some of many synchronicities in my life and why I will always have faith in the universe. Signs and messages are always apparent.

NOTHING IS IMPOSSIBLE, not even those difficult paths we face on our journey. Because if you believe you deserve it, the universe will serve it.

So, as I lay here illuminated under the hue of what could be either a sunrise or a sunset in my Greek paradise. I contemplate my life of utter fulfilment drenched in the smell of Serendipity and wet dog!

# ABOUT THE AUTHOR

## LISA O'CONNELL

Lisa O'Connell is a red haired, sunflower obsessed, barefoot hippy. With a bohemian lifestyle, the soul of a gypsy and a penchant for Greek delight. Her trusted side kick Andrea likes to refer to it as a Gift from the Gods. It's like Turkish delight but made by Greeks and better!

Leaving school at sixteen, she was someone that had always felt the urge to wander both mentally and physically. Exposing herself to many lifestyles, cultures and ever-changing situations. She was for want of a better word a big part IRRESPONSIBLE! Yet acknowledging her sixth sense and trusting her intuition, she galloped though life like a purple whirlwind of love and laughter mixed with a hint of sunflowers.

After attaining her travel and tourism diplomas at college, she worked for various travel companies, as a holiday rep and air cabin crew amidst an abundance of other positions until her early twenties when she found herself working on the Greek island of Corfu, making henna tattoos on the beach and selling clothes and silver jewellery from India and Thailand. Allowing her the excuse to travel frequently for more supplies. She also owned a mechanical rodeo bull in a holiday resort nightclub. She would tell customers "Give me your money and I'll give you the best ride of your holiday. The louder you scream the faster we go."

Since this time, Lisa has also been selling holidays online all over the world. The last five years predominantly specialising in Thailand and Greece, for which she has won awards. Who wouldn't wish to book their holiday with someone so passionate and knowledgeable about travel? She has remained self-employed for the last twenty-six years and still travels at the drop of a hat.

She had shown an interest in things of the supernatural from early on and had a longing to discover the stuff that intrigued her. She began to meditate and practise yoga and did her first reiki course at twenty-four. By her early thirties she was helping cancer survivors after becoming a cosmetic and medical tattooist training in Harley Street, London. Before finally working alongside doctors and surgeons in Greece giving women back their eyebrows and nipples after cancer treatments and breast reconstruction surgery. She would mostly offer these treatments for free to her clients who were at the end of a long fraught journey and had been unable to work due to their illness. But the law of karma or the bank of mum and dad would normally prevail to balance the equation in some way. She has appeared in Greek national newspapers with her work.

Lisa says what she means and means what she says and will remain in pole position to accept the abundance of opportunities that life has to offer.

Lisa also works as a yoga teacher from her tipi overlooking a tranquil secluded emerald lake in Tsilaria, Corfu. Her mission is to have a yoga retreat 'SERENDIPITY BY THE LAKE' up and running soon. Watch this space.

Lisa's qualifications include but are not limited to

- Diploma of excellence in SPMU
- Diploma in Medical tattooing
- Advanced SPMU techniques
- Third and fourth Master degree of Angelic reiki
- Usui reiki system of natural healing. One, two and masters.
- Level 3 Anatomy and physiology
- Thai yoga massage. (The Union of Thai traditional medicine society)
- Level 3 Diploma in teaching yoga (QCF) teaching hatha , yin and yoga nidra
- Post graduate diploma in yoga for those affected by cancer and their carers
- Aerial yoga teaching training course (Active IQ)

Lisa believes the world is a book and those who do not travel read only the first page!

Her favourite quote being 'Travel is the only thing we can buy that makes us richer.'

CONTACT
Email lisacorfu@hotmail.com
Lisa.o'connell@ite.travel
https://www.facebook.com/Independent-Travel-Experts-by-Lisa-OConnell

WEBSITE
www.serendipitybythelake.com
http://www.independenttravelexperts.co.uk/
http://www.independenttravelexperts.co.uk/store-information/?store_id=309

# LINDA R. BIRCH

*I* was terribly homesick and frustrated with my situation. I had been living in the southeast coastal area of England for about three months, crowded into a small terraced house with my husbands' parents and three dogs, while waiting impatiently for our house to complete contracts so we could move into our own space. I missed my kids, who are grown but a big part of my life, I missed my friends and I missed my home in California. The problem was I no longer had a home. We had sold our 4-bedroom, 2-car garage home of 18 years, given away just about everything we owned and moved across the world so that my husband, Garry, could spend more time with his ailing mother, while she could still recognize him.

WITH ALL GOOD intentions we spent 6 months packing, preparing, obtaining Visas, as well as a passport for our little dog, and set out to completely change our life, naively unprepared for the difficulties awaiting us. Tempers flared, tears were shed, and the long back garden was paced in frustration. I needed to get out! I needed a place of my own, and most of all I needed a support system to get through what was happening. I needed a spiritual tribe.

I WAS ALREADY an experienced energy healer, an intuitive for as long as I can remember, as well as a degreed and certified astrologer. I did not expect to start over and set up a practice in the UK since our time would be focused on helping my mother-in-law with her house, garden and life in general as she descended into dementia. What I did want was a place for spiritual connection, with people who spoke my language, a comfortable place to fill my soul.

ONE AFTERNOON GARRY returned from town excited to tell me about someone he had met. While in a café he overheard a man and woman discussing astrology. Alerted, he leaned over, introduced himself as the spouse of an astrologer and asked if he could have me get in touch with them, since I was new to this country and knew only his family. The man agreed and gave his phone number, which Garry eagerly passed along to me, commenting "What are the odds of that happening?". Surprised and delighted I called the number, briefly introduced myself and my astrological background, and made a date to meet for coffee.

WHEN WEDNESDAY CAME Garry and I took our seats at a table in the tiny vegan café and ordered tea and coffee while we waited. In walked a man in jeans and sweatshirt, around 40 years old who looked around warily, spotted my husband and moved to our table. He was rather serious as I smiled and introduced myself. I would like to say we fell into easy conversation, but it was rather stilted and awkward, especially for him. I had the distinct impression he didn't trust people easily. However, I continued our conversation about our astrological mutual interest, what our major chart indicators are and how we were being affected by the latest planetary transits. He relaxed some and before leaving we made arrangements to meet the following week. Soon we were meeting to talk every week and becoming friends.

DURING ONE OF our meetings he mentioned a spiritual center north of us in one the many wooded areas of Kent. My husband and I took an afternoon to go and visit the center after investigating it online. The location was beautiful, and the list of classes offered looked interesting. I met a nice gentleman manning the store counter, asked a few questions and decided to return for a drop-in class on Psychic Development. Nervously driving the 40 minutes to the center that Friday, I joined some 8 other students, mostly mature people like myself, sitting in a wide circle of folding chairs in a large room with dimmed lighting. In whisked the owner of the center, a woman of middle-age who sat unsmiling in the lead chair and went straight into the start of class without so much as a 'hello'.

I WAS TAKEN ABACK by the brusqueness of her style but carried on following instructions and participating as best I could. After all I had come to learn and brush up on my skills that had been largely ignored during the upheaval of our move to England. I attended only two of those classes and both times felt rather like an outsider. I wanted to be welcomed and made to feel at home. This was not the place for me. However, before I left class, I picked up a brochure which had more information about treatments and classes on offer. Some were being taught by other teachers and outside experts. I was particularly drawn to a class they had held at the center the previous spring called Angelic Reiki. I could feel my heart center pulling me towards it, though I had never heard of it before.

BACK AT THE family home where we were staying, I researched this healing modality on the Angelic Reiki Association website. I did not learn as much as I wanted from their description but felt an inexplicable pull to it. I tried to find a teacher in the area I was staying, but to no avail. There was a picture of a pretty blonde woman named Tina that drew my interest, on the list of teachers in Kent. However, when looking at a map, I saw that she was an hours' drive from my location. I was a new driver in the UK, nervous to drive 10 minutes let alone an hour toward unfamiliar territory.

SINCE I WAS SEARCHING for my new tribe, I had actively cleared out my Facebook page of negative messages, political posts and 'friends' who did not serve my highest vibrations. I searched and joined an array of pages on Light, Angels, Healing, Love and anything else I could find that was uplifting. I needed all the help I could get to lift me out of the depression and desperation I had been feeling. One of those pages was "Angel Wings of Dover" (which has since changed its' name). I saw that Marcia, who ran that page, was writing about giving Angelic Reiki healings. I quickly messaged her asking where she learned it. She excitedly wrote back "You have to go to my amazing teacher Tina Pavlou in Ramsgate!". Ah, the synchronicities. Tina was the very woman I had spotted on the association website! Since I am well indoctrinated into the understanding that there are no coincidences, I knew I was being guided.

I CONTACTED Tina by text and she wrote back that she would contact me after she returned from a retreat. A few days later we traded information and I was signed up for the next Angelic Reiki levels 1 & 2 workshop. At Tinas' suggestion I put a plea on her page for a carpool ride to class hoping there might be someone else coming from my area. Marcia popped up with the offer of a ride from Dover, so I only had to drive halfway and ride the rest with her and one other student.

Little did I know how these ladies would change my life and become my dear friends.

NEAR THE END of August 2017, I drove off into the unknown, phone GPS leading the way. I found Marcias' house set on a sloped street and parked directly across as Marcia popped out of her front door waving me over while talking on her mobile phone. I climbed into the back seat of her car and we were off, flying through zigzag roads heading further uphill to pickup Michelle. On our ride to Ramsgate I listened in the back while the other two chatted animatedly. I have a bit of a problem understanding the various English accents, so I didn't hear everything they talked about, but I did learn that they have known each other for many years.

WE ARRIVED AT OUR DESTINATION, walked along the pavement and down another path running between two houses. There in the back was a school yard on the right and on the left a small nondescript one-story building. Inside was a foyer with a small kitchen on the side where several women were greeting each other with cheek kisses, squeezing in to choose their tea or coffee. Through the main double doors ahead was a chapel like space without pews, but with an assortment of chairs placed in a circle. The dais, or stage, at the front was draped in heavy purple curtains, the sides of the room lined with small highly placed windows and various spiritual and religious pictures sprinkled in between. The energy inside was nice, welcoming, relaxing, even while the incoming women, and one man, noisily greeted and chatted with each other. Once again, I felt out of place, but then Tina Pavlou appeared before me with a huge smile and sparkling eyes to welcome me with a lovely hug.

WE ALL TOOK an available seat at random, noting that each chair had an angel oracle card on its seat and a photocopy of a large symbol on the floor underneath. Each of us had a different card, but some of the symbols on the floor matched others. Tina explained that where you chose to sit was the perfect place and the message you receive on the card is meant for you. Then she went around the circle having us introduce ourselves and give a brief statement on who we are, where we're from and what brought us to this class. When Tina came around to me, she put her hands together at her heart, nodded her head and told me she was honored to have me there. I was speechless. Why would she say that, I wondered? I had been feeling small, insignificant, out of place in this country, but I felt myself lifting a bit as she looked into my eyes.

As THE COURSE began and Tina gave us our first attunement to the Archangels, she repeated a series of words, symbolic words I had never heard before. My ego mind was scoffing saying "what have I gotten myself into now?", but I stayed silent. Then I started to feel the energy being generated by the attunement, subtle at first and then building in intensity all around me. I relaxed back into my chair and let it wash over me. Ahhhh, the bliss of Spirit. It had been awhile since I'd felt that, and I'd missed it.

THEN TINA TALKED to us about her experiences and why she is known as the Angel Lady. What I remember most is that she warned us in detail about resistance that could arise in our minds. Our ego. I laughed because that was exactly what my mind did, trying to distract me. That is the last time my mind tried to interfere during an Angelic Reiki class. Thereafter it seemed like a weekend submerged in bliss. I loved it!

PRACTICING this healing method on the people I was paired with proved a little bit of a challenge for me. I am an experienced healer, but this was something different. I found my mind trying to direct the healing to what I was used to seeing and doing. Pulling back and remembering to channel rather than do it myself took some focus and, of course, practice. But it was so worth it when I was able to let go and allow the Angels to do the work. The healing energy coming through is so powerful and profound, there are no words that describe the feeling of floating, the joyful light that you become.

WHEN THE WEEKEND came to a close, certificates were distributed, my first from a spiritual type of class. I had been gifted with my healing abilities many years ago and had not learned it from this kind of training. I found myself feeling very proud of that certificate made out in my name. But I really wanted more of the healing with Angels, especially because I was feeling like my joyful, fun self again. So, I signed up immediately for the next set of classes, the Masters, which would be held the following month.

DURING THE FIRST set of classes we had 3 or 4 ladies who assisted Tina. They had taken Angelic Reiki 1 & 2 a few months earlier and were very anxious for the start of the next course. I observed this rambunctious crew as they giggled, laughed, disrupted a little bit, then ran around preparing our tea and coffee during our breaks. They were a delight, and obviously knew each other well. It appeared I was the only student that wasn't known or connected to another in some way. Still feeling like an outsider, we all gathered at the end of September for 3 days of Angelic Reiki levels 3 & 4. This was a large group and was the first Master's class that Tina taught.

IMPOSSIBLE AS IT SEEMED, The Masters classes were better in every way: More fun, more healing, more blissful. We discovered a vortex of energy was being created in the middle of our circle and on breaks I liked to stand in the vortex and float on that elevated vibration. It caught on quickly and others were doing likewise, giggling like school girls when feeling lightheaded with the intense energy. We learned many different techniques that weekend and worked with several different partners, which allowed us to get to know each other a bit. We could also plainly see the changes we were displaying from day to day. We were growing and glowing!

AT THE END of the workshop we were told that although technically we could teach Angelic Reiki now, it was strongly suggested that we wait a year and assist at future classes to gain insight and experience. So, in early November I showed up, driving all the way by myself for the first time, to assist with a very large Angelic Reiki 1 & 2 class. I learned so much from watching Tina and the students that weekend. Joined by a couple of other alumni to assist, it was here that I started to feel more accepted, more a part of the group that was developing, the "Chicklets and Roosters".

BEFORE WE LEFT on the last day, Michelle asked me if I was going to take the Theta Healing Basic class, which Tina would begin teaching in January. I didn't feel the same pull towards it that I had with Angelic Reiki and I was concerned about where the money would come from, since my husband hadn't found a job in the UK yet. I told her "No, I don't think so", but she immediately countered with "Yes, you are. I've seen you there with us"! That surprised me and had me reconsidering over the next two months.

I REMEMBER at one of the Angelic Reiki classes, Tina had said that daydreaming is a more powerful manifesting method than intense focus. I would imagine because you are then in a relaxed state of flow and not forcing it. So, one day on the long drive back from Ramsgate after class, I was in a very relaxed high vibe state and was letting my mind daydream about the perfect job for my husband, seeing all the different aspects and conditions he desired. Then I sent it up and let it go. This was around early November and within days he started getting calls for interviews after hearing nothing for months. Within a week or two Garry interviewed with three companies and was deciding between two offers. Naturally the one he accepted had everything we had talked about having in his perfect job, the very daydream I had for him. I still smile every time I remember this.

WINTER CAME EARLY and by the beginning of December I was learning to drive in sleet and snow flurries. Further classes were not scheduled until January and I was really feeling the cold. That was a problem because the cold aggravates my body with a variety of maladies, pain and tension. That season also brought up a problem for me in finding my place within my husbands' family dynamic. We thought I could take over his days of caring for his mother while he went to work. Unfortunately, one thing after another kept happening to sabotage that intention. First, I slipped on her narrow stairs, catching the rail to prevent a fall and wrenched my knee. Then, I sprained my right shoulder fending off one of my mother-in-law's over-enthusiastic larger dogs.

IT TOOK months and physical therapy to improve those injuries, during which I had difficulty driving and could not handle the care of my mother-in-law, her house or her dogs. In addition, I was having anxiety attacks and 3-day migraine headaches after spending an afternoon looking after her. Clearly my body and spirit were telling me not to do this, yet my inner rescuer and people-pleasing personality kept making me feel guilty if I didn't. Now don't get me wrong, I love my mother-in-law. In her right mind she is a loving, optimistic, creative and caring woman, a true pleasure to be with. However, the progression of Alzheimers' disease had taken away the woman I knew and loved.

THIS BECAME a huge lesson for me. I had spent most of my life diving in and fixing things in all aspects of my life. Now I was face to face with a situation I could not fix, and it was obviously hurting me. I had to let go, withdraw and release responsibility to my husband and his family. It wasn't mine to take on in the first place. As obvious as this sounds, at the time I felt stuck and unable to see a way out that felt right. All my worst emotions came flooding out: anger, blaming, frustration, shame, and finally helplessness. With the help of some dear friends, and long phone calls, I was finally able to step away and let the family figure it out. It turned out to be the best thing that could have happened. Now the siblings are all working together, making decisions and moving forward. They did not need me, and I needed to learn not to take on the karma of others.

ENTER JANUARY and I decided to take Theta Healing Basic. I had gone to the Introduction talk Tina gave and became very interested. More than that, Theta turned out to be the healing tool I desperately needed to clear away the beliefs and habits that were driving my life in directions I did not want to go.

SINCE THE CLASS would take 3 full days, I accepted Tinas' invitation to share a cottage in Broadstairs for the weekend, with a few students coming from a distance. This saved me a lot of time commuting back and forth from home as well as giving my still-healing body a break from the physicality of driving. We had a wonderful time in that lovely little house, where I met and shared a room with Leah, who was assisting Tina with teaching the class. She and I clicked together right away and would talk and laugh until exhaustion sent us to sleep. By the end of the Theta class, I not only had a new friend but felt I had finally found my 'Magic Wand'! Theta is the consciousness state that takes us directly to Creator/God space where literally all things are made possible!

I WAS SO EXCITED to develop this skill and practice more, and it does take a lot of practice. As I worked with it, I discovered my intuitive skill increasing exponentially and I trusted what I received, saw and heard, more so than with any other method. I was ecstatic! This was what I had been looking for, a way to trust my intuition and to heal myself and others with visible, confirmable results. What I did not expect was that this expansion of my consciousness would lead to more unusual connections.

A FEW DAYS after the Theta Healing workshop I was practicing going up to the 7th plane of existence. In the exercise I see myself in a bubble of light, streaking through the universe toward "The Light". I noticed each day that I had an escort flying with me, one on each side. Initially I thought they were angels, since I've had many high vibrational light beings, or angels, around me since my Angelic attunement the previous summer. This time I noticed they were blue in color. Thinking they were some of Archangel Michaels' legion protecting me, I continued on up to Creator space for my practice. When I brought myself back down into the universe, I saw the blue beings were waiting for me. As we flew, I looked at them and realized they were not angels but Extra-Terrestrials.

I COULD SEE what seemed like downy blue feathers on their humanoid shaped bodies. We stopped to hover above Earths' atmosphere and I looked into their eyes, noticing the shape of their faces and resemblance to birds. They felt gentle and kind as I asked them who they were and why they were with me. Communicating telepathically, I was shown that humans who are aware of them call these E.T.s Blue Avians, and they wished to share something with me. I asked them "Why me?" and they said, "Because you are ready". I did not fully understand this but listened as they guided me through a method of bringing Divine Source light through to Earth and to everyone and everything on Her.

I HAVE HAD several encounters with the Blue Avians since then, but lately only one of them comes and communicates with me. Without going into it too deeply, this highly evolved being and my Higher Self are friends on many levels and had devised a plan that included, and necessitated, my assistance. They wish to bring through a book of information from The Council of Light, of which they are a part. I am currently working as an oracle for them to bring this book into our dimension and time.

IN THE MEANTIME, I am very obviously in a human body, sorting through life and its' lovely dramas while straddling between this and the spirit world to which I connect so easily. In fact, I have been a channel/oracle since the late 1980s. But, because of repeated rejection by others and sabotaging myself with self-doubts, I had kept that part of myself very quiet and hidden. Only a few of my closest spiritual friends and a select few of my family knew about my ability.

So, here it was again, up in my face. "You are ready". I didn't feel ready, I still had so many doubts and fears that kept me held back from my potential. Thank goodness my guides and angels, Michelle included, guided me, pushed me really, into taking the continuing series of Theta Healing classes.

. . .

ALL THROUGH THE remains of winter, which included unexpected snowstorms in March, I alternated between taking classes in Theta and assisting at Angelic Reiki workshops. It was the best of both worlds being raised up by the high vibration Archangels and Ascended Masters, as well as developing the mental skills of Theta healing. In between we would gather for practice and healing shares. This truly has been some of the best times of my life. I felt uplifted, blissful and happy with what we were learning and experiencing, especially how we were all bonding so strongly together.

TINA ALWAYS TALKS about the sisterhood, but I didn't really get it for a while. I remember telling Tina at one point how I felt I did not quite fit in, and she turned to me exclaiming "It wouldn't be the same without you, Linda!". That shook me. I had not realized how accepted I was with the Chicklets. I started really paying attention and came to understand that I had seen myself as outside the group. I was part of it, but not within the "inner circle", and this was a pattern in my life to be cleared. Thank Goddess for Theta because that pattern and belief is leaving me, and I now feel fully a part of the tribe!

A FEW MORE DIFFICULT lessons popped up that spring. One was the upcoming trip "home" to California for a family wedding. I was excited to see my kids, as well as my brother and his family. However, as with many people, there were certain other members of my family, some whom I had not seen in many years, that I was more hesitant to meet. Ok, to be frank, I was frightened of getting my emotional buttons pushed again! I brought this up during one of the Theta classes to be resolved and also continued, on my own, to release the history and emotions attached to remembered and unremembered events. As a result, our trip home was wonderful and the wedding beautiful. I connected lovingly with most of my family, laughed and danced, and thoroughly enjoyed myself. I didn't react or feel pulled into any dramas. I felt free, happy and truly myself the entire time. I cannot express the incredible gratitude I have for Theta Healing, my angels and my tribe for helping me release my family "stuff" so I could sail through the event.

THE SECOND ISSUE came up in June while we Chicklets were on a retreat in Glastonbury, run by Tina. We had three fabulous days of sacred sites, workshops, delicious food and sisterhood. But, on three separate occasions that weekend, I found myself in the presence of men yelling angrily, pointing blame, at children in one case, and generally being public jerks. It pushed my buttons big time! I was instantly reminded of my (now deceased) father berating my mother or me and my siblings, publicly. My stomach was in knots and my temper was rising. I wanted so badly to get in their faces and put them in their place. But, "what good would that do, besides escalate the situation?" I reminded myself.

AFTER THE SECOND occurrence I was shaking with anger and needed an outlet but had become separated from my friends. I tried to walk it off, but my back ached, my feet hurt, and I was limping. I found Elizabeth sitting inside the Avebury pub and joined her for a cool drink and tried to calm my emotional storm. Unfortunately, nothing anyone could say would alleviate my distress. Hungry, tired, in pain and angry, I was not good company. Later that evening we had a workshop back at the ashram, a Unicorn attunement. I had done this with Maria Luisa before in Ramsgate, so I was looking forward to the lovely high vibe energy I remembered. What a surprise it was to experience so much more: The Unicorns healed me! They lifted away the trauma and memories that had pushed my anger buttons. I was freed! Oh, how blessed I felt.

.  .  .

I MUST NOTE HERE, if you don't believe in the existence of Unicorns, I invite you to see Maria Luisa for a Lemurian Unicorn attunement. Several people, including myself, were skeptical until they experienced their etheric pure light and enormous, yet gentle power.

ON THE LAST day of the Glastonbury retreat we were at the Chalice Well, gathered in the garden near a small waterfall. Tina was reading a lovely meditation to us when above my head a man started raising his voice, telling us "You can't be there, you can't do this here!". Tina tried to reason with him, but the man argued obstinately and got even louder. Interestingly, I checked in with myself and realized I was absolutely unaffected by the interruption. I was healed and had passed the test! Of course, Tina won in the end and got an apology from the manager. She is a powerhouse!

AS I LOOK BACK on the last year and a half, I am struck by the common themes I experienced: Finding a supportive place where I belonged; and releasing family related traumas. I am deeply and profoundly thankful for Tina and the Chicklets for guiding and supporting me through this healing journey. What Tina Pavlou has created and attracted are an amazing group of talented people who love and care for each other. Nearly every day we receive a message from someone in the group who needs help and we collectively respond, giving freely of our time, skills and intentions. I have come to understand what unity truly means, and I have seen that what we give out freely and lovingly to others comes back to us multiplied. We lift each other up and encourage each other to share our talents. With the opening of The Goddess Rooms in the fall of 2018 we now have a sanctuary to bring and develop our gifts. I am so very grateful to have a place to learn, grow and share mine.

# ABOUT THE AUTHOR

## LINDA R. BIRCH

Originally from the San Francisco Bay area of California, Linda now lives in a rural village in the southeast corner of England with her husband and little fur-baby (dog). She has 3 beautiful and talented grown up children and, so far, one granddaughter.

She is a lifelong intuitive/psychic, a healer, channel/oracle, astrologer and ordained minister. She has been gifted with the ability to "see" where there is a problem area in the body and address it with energy healing. Linda has performed healings on 100s, perhaps 1000s, of people over the years, offering help with emotional or physical pain wherever guided to do so. She has also worked with dozens of teens and young adults guiding, advising, reading their charts, giving them healings and hugs, and for some, a roof over their heads.

Lindas' background is varied, a Synchronized Swimming All-American in her teens, a Coach and Choreographer in her 20s, then corporate Accounting for more than 20 years. Meanwhile she embraced sobriety, studied Science of Mind and Law of Attraction, learned Meditation, led Channeling sessions, and attended Vibrational Massage school. When injury took her out of the office world and back home to heal, she took the opportunity to pursue her passion for Astrology by obtaining a Bachelor of Arts degree in Astrological Studies, at the then new Kepler College, while homeschooling her youngest daughter for several years. In 2017 she made the move with her husband to his native England where she was drawn to two more healing modalities. She has now added Angelic Reiki Master and Theta Healing Practitioner to her list of credentials.

Lindas' determination and resilience has seen her through several family crises including her own battle with stage-4 cancer. She credits a positive attitude and a great sense of humor for overcoming them all. At heart she is a nurturer and believes everyone has a right to be loved, heard, understood and accepted for who they are.

Currently Linda is studying the vibrational medicine of flower essences, teaching ascension astrology workshops, and writing her stories from 40 years of spiritual adventures, as well as transmitted material from higher sources.

Email: lindabirch2016@gmail.com

facebook.com/linda.birch.391

# LOUISE DEBLING

*L*ife is a beautiful blessing. Filled with many lessons. At least that's how I see it now.

AS A CHILD I was very shy, and very sensitive to what was happening around me. I had an imaginary friend that I truly believed was my guardian angel by my side, that would play, chat and give me confidence when needed.

FOR AS FAR BACK AS I can remember my first love was music, I used to play John Lennon 'Imagine' on my mums' record player [what a song and still today it holds something in my heart], when I wasn't listening to John I was rocking out to Michael Jackson and Whitney Houston. I'd always dreamt of becoming a singer, but I never thought I was actually any good, funnily enough my family now consider themselves blessed when I am rocking it out in the kitchen.

.   .   .

SCHOOL WASN'T my thing I had no interest in education/learning, I was a bit of a tomboy and I had more boyfriends than girlfriends. I was bullied regularly by boys and girls in my year and those above, I just hated being there. I left school with no GCSES and went into the world thinking I could treat "ADULT LIFE" the same way as school. Oh boy was I wrong!

I HAD a full-time boyfriend and no-clue what I wanted to do with my life. I decided to become a hairdresser, enrolled at college and got a job in a salon. I was still very shy when around lots of people and I was sad to find that the theme of bullying wasn't just at school, it followed me into my working life. Only 3 months into my new career I fell pregnant, I was overweight and suffered with high blood pressure, unable to work I was signed off. In September of 1996 my beautiful baby girl was born, being a young mum and living at home with my parents was hard. I was offered a house through the council and moved into it in January 1998; talk about new house, new baby! YES... I was pregnant again.

AT THIS POINT in my life I was very lonely, my weight had become out of control, I must have been 15 stone or more and I had awful OCD, emotionally suppressing all I felt. My second beautiful daughter was born in September 1998 I suffered with severe postnatal depression. I felt so lost, so disconnected, all my focus was on my children and not on myself; it's only now when I look back, I can see how much I suppressed everything, and I was literally eating my emotions away.

I DESPERATELY TRIED my best to keep my family together but lie after lie, being verbally abused and cheated on was killing me inside. Trying to hold my family together was taking its toll on me; little did I know I was pregnant with my 3rd child - Just 7 months into my pregnancy, my partner left me! Even though today, I see it as a thankful blessing, at the time I hit rock bottom, I cried all day every day for what seemed like an eternity, not knowing how I would cope on my own with 3 small children. Then one day I woke up and everything just felt different, new people started to show up in my life, I had many friends around me I started to feel good.

ONE SATURDAY NIGHT I woke up from my sleep in pain, my baby was on his way. Thinking I had loads of time, I started to prepare for the hospital, the pain got rapidly worse. I rang my mum who said she was on her way. With that I waddled to the toilet, as I came back down the stairs an awful pain came over me, I fell to the floor, my waters broke, and I looked down and thought OMG this is happening and I'm alone! With one push his head began to crown, I thought to myself I must listen to my body, as I didn't want to tear my insides after experiencing this with my first baby.

So, I started to pant and out he came straight to the floor, I scooped my baby up in my arms but there was no noise. I was so scared, I rocked him and shouted cry, cry!- With that thankfully, he gasped and cried. I heard this little voice come from upstairs, "mum". I shouted up to my girls to bring towels, my five and seven-year-old come running down with towels for me, I wrapped my baby up and told my seven-year-old to ring nanny. I sat on the floor on my knees for 45 minutes before the midwife arrived, it was just all so overwhelming. That evening when everyone had gone home, I lay on the sofa with my unnamed baby boy, I called him my little pooh bear. As I stroked his face, I thanked God that everything went ok, I promised that I would do my best to make our life easy.

IT'S AMAZING when we are in these situations how our body just knows what to do. In honor to myself and my children I enrolled back into college to finish my hairdressing degree.

A FEW MONTHS PASSED, and the weight was just falling off me, I started to like what I was seeing. At 24 years old I had gone from a size 22, and18 stone to a size 16 in clothes. I now know I was emotionally depressed. I started smoking marijuana with my new friends in the evening, just to try and relax. I got very friendly with one in particular, little did I know I was heading for a relationship where I suffered mental, emotional, physical, and sexual abuse. I hit rock bottom, drinking excessively, I also started taking drugs just to numb anything I was going through or feeling, just to get a high for a short amount of time. Very few people knew what I was going through and again I felt very much alone.

IN FEBRUARY 2004 I had the devastating news of my nan passing away, this was the first loss in my life and I didn't cope very well with it. Just 3 months later my other nan passed away, I spiraled down so deep and low, emotional overload had got the better of me! I remember hitting the worktops in my kitchen in anger, crying, I felt like my whole world had fallen apart, not knowing how to deal with all my emotions, all the pain was unreal, like a big whole in my heart! I miss my nan every day and I have been told many times by various healers/spiritualists readers that she works with me, guiding and assisting me along my journey, this always puts a smile on my face and sometimes I can even feel her presence.

I REMEMBER VERY WELL straight after attending my nans funeral, my partner telling me to stop crying, and him pushing me to the sofa, grabbing my hands, hitting me with them and telling me to stop, of course this did not help me. This relationship was one of the hardest things I ever went through, and even harder to get out of.

ONE OF MY dear friends came to visit me from Hastings it was summertime 2005, we had such a laugh, as she left to go home, she said to me you're welcome at mine anytime. This was like a light bulb going off in my head, somewhere for me to go, take my children and get away. 'I said I may well take you up on that', and I did! I packed my car up and off we went. Just 24 hours later he turned up at the door, I had no idea how he knew I was there. On our way home, I knew there had to be an easier way to get out of this relationship, I prayed for help. Somewhere out of nowhere this courage, this strength was there, right when I needed it the most.

I THANKED God for this courage and also my sister, she was like my rock always being there for me holding my hand and keeping me strong just when I needed it, who knows what would've happened if I had stayed with this man.

A WEEK later I went to visit my friend, I needed to get away, I just wanted to feel safe, I was searching for security. My friend's partner had one of his friends over, he was nice, he had guided me to my friend's house the last time I was down, after getting a little lost. We all had a laugh together, it was much needed, as life had been so hard for so long. To laugh and feel free felt so good, we became friends and there was definitely a connection between us. In just one month, he and his daughter had moved in with us, we had lots of laughter, lots of fun, he made me feel safe and secure. He gave me a feeling of being at home, very caring, very loving. But I wasn't used to this and I started questioning why I deserved this, it's crazy how we question things when they are good!

. . .

THINGS WEREN'T easy being a step family, but we had each other's back, I felt so supported but I was still drinking, unconsciously not dealing with anything that I had been through. Drinking 6 bottles of wine most evenings, it was my way out of dealing with anything!

I DON'T KNOW how I did it really, I felt like this black cloud was over me and I felt so angry. I didn't understand how I could have one partner the way he was, and then another so completely different.

ONE SATURDAY MORNING I woke up feeling awful, the floodgates had opened. I was sitting on the sofa crying and crying and crying, my loving partner just held me not knowing what to do. A few days later, after an appointment at the doctors where I did a questionnaire they told me I had depression. They gave me tablets and told me to come back in 4 weeks, I was on a high dose of anti-depressant for some years.

I WALKED AWAY from that doctor thinking those tablets were going to solve everything, save me, set me free from all I had been feeling. Month after month being put on a higher dosage because nothing was helping me, I just didn't want to be alive, all I could think about was just ending it all! All along these tablets were making me worse, suppressing my emotions more than before! Obviously, now I see that a mix of alcohol and anti-depressant tablets don't exactly go together!

NOW I UNDERSTAND we feel depressed because we have many emotions going through our body that we struggle to deal with, the doctors put people on tablets that suppress our emotions even more.

That's why the dosage keeps getting raised or they change you to a new tablet because they don't work anymore, but the real problem isn't being dealt with. Like how to understand and deal with these emotions, identifying how you feel, whether it be anxiety, sadness, anger, fear and so on. When we are in pain we take, or we are given drugs to suppress that pain, when people have a disease, we give them medication to suppress the symptoms of the disease. When in reality these symptoms are the body telling you something is wrong. The imbalances we suffer from are what manifest as disease, the biggest imbalance that we suffer from is emotional baggage, trapped emotions.

THESE ENERGIES that stay with us after traumatic emotional events that we experience. Identifying the emotion takes the power away from feeling this way, asking 'yourself why am I feeling this way?' If anything, this has taught me to listen to myself, my body and understand it's ok to feel this way, to just take a deep breath, re-centering myself in my heart.

WE ARE SO LUCKY TODAY, as there are many healing modalities that can help us, rather than us just taking tablets. We are not born depressed, it is developed from situational factors, and environmental triggers, and a lack of understanding that it's ok to feel. I've learnt that emotions build up because we have been taught to resist things that don't feel good and we don't always know where to look for answers, but the answers are inside of us because the feelings are from inside of us.

I MEAN if you had just been through a great ordeal how do you expect to feel? I started to have weekly counselling sessions, as much as these sessions may have helped some people they just didn't help me. I am so so blessed to have had a partner that put up with all I threw at him, I was short tempered, argumentative and aggressive. In some instances, some people would have called me a bit of a psycho, I really was in a dark, dark place.

ONE DAY I woke up and said **no!** No more I knew there had to be a different way and I put my tablets in the bin. **I do not advise** this to anyone! Seek your doctors' advice and come off the tablets in the appropriate way. I honestly felt worse on these tablets, suppressing all that I needed to feel in order for me to heal. I stopped drinking obsessively and started seeking other alternatives. I went to a weekly meeting group of people that were suffering with depression, I learnt so much and it helped me to deal with everyday life.

IN AUGUST of 2009 my partner and I married, it was a beautiful yet a somewhat stressful event. We were lucky to get away on a honeymoon, seeing as we had 5 children at home! We were very blessed to have friends that looked after them for us, being a step parent wasn't easy not just from my point of view but my husbands too. We always tried our best but sometimes it just wasn't enough, at times we forgot the children had feelings too and needed our attention. In gaining understanding of this, I often felt like I wasn't the best mum, and I know we all make mistakes. I love my children and step children very much and thank them for blessing my life.

IN OCTOBER 2010 my husband and I had our first baby together and our family felt complete. Just five months later we had an unexpected gift of falling pregnant again, we didn't expect this, but we were happy anyway. After a week or so of finding out, I started to bleed, this was very unusual for me. I had never experienced this before, so I contacted the hospital and they sent me for a scan. They couldn't find a baby, so I was sent to another ward where they did bloods and a pregnancy test, it came back positive.

THEY SAID the baby was too small to be detected with the scan, and they sent me home. A week or more went past and I hadn't heard anything, until one Saturday morning the hospital rang, and asked me to go in with an overnight bag, as they didn't know how long I would be in for. I was so scared, I had another scan and they found the baby in my left fallopian tube, they told me I would have to go for an operation, as this was very dangerous.

AFTER MY OPERATION the doctor came around to see me, he said to me they were so sorry for leaving me for so long and that I'd had a pint of blood in my stomach. If I had been left any longer, I would have died, in complete shock I cried! Still to this day it baffles me how someone should feel about this, as it's a baby that didn't make it to your womb to grow and be nurtured. It's not a miscarriage but still you have lost a baby and a part of your body was taken away. The feelings that I felt are indescribable and my heart goes out to all those that have lost babies.

AS THE KIDS were getting older and started to get in touch with their emotions. I truly believe their Dad leaving them at such a young age, had a big effect on them. My husband's children didn't have it easy with their mum either, we were dealing with a house full of emotional children. It was hard, when we only wanted to do right by them, but we didn't have the support around us to help through this tough time. My second daughter had gone to spend a couple of weeks with her dad, he didn't have his own place he was living with friends, just around the corner. I was ok with this as I could go around whenever I wanted.

. . .

MY ELDEST DAUGHTER came home from school one day and somehow an argument occurred, she told me she was going to live with her dad, she packed a bag and off she went to him. I was heartbroken not knowing what to do, her dad and I sat down, we spoke about what was right at that time for the girls. I allowed the children to stay with him, as they were clearly looking to rekindle the relationship they once had with him.

VERY QUICKLY HE got himself a flat this was even harder for me, as I knew my children were doing what they wanted with no parent guiding them. We fought hard for the children and this was on going for a good few months. My husband was due to go and work in London employed as a security officer at the London Olympics 2012, this year was probably my most challenging year ever. Even though my depression was sort of under control, all that was happening around me had pushed me to drinking again. I had my son, my baby girl and my step daughter at home with me whilst my husband was working 12 to 16-hour days. Not having him by my side was hard, he was my rock, I would drive up to London one day a week to see him, yet it wasn't enough.

I COUNTED the days until he would be home but after the Olympics, they had asked him to join a dedicated team and stay until the end of September. I didn't want him to, it crushed me inside, yet I was so proud of him. He said to me that he would only do it with my support and offered to come home if I needed him to. I knew this was a life-long dream of his to be working at the Olympics, so I swallowed my feelings and said, "No you stay you do what you need to do". While really this was all a lesson, one I didn't cope with too well I can look back now and thank God for getting me through these hard times.

When my husband got back that September, I felt like my right arm was back, my strength had been given back to me. We fought tooth and nail to get our children back.

With the help of social services my second youngest daughter was brought back to us just before Christmas, yet my eldest daughter went to live with her boyfriend and his family. A lot went on far much to write for this chapter anyway.

In November of 2012 I was at a Christmas Fair, I was selling kids toys, cups, and nic nac things. A lady walked up to me, she introduced herself as TINA THE ANGEL LADY, she told me she was doing readings for people, this sparked something in me, I was very interested. I remember before she walked away, she said to me, not to take life so seriously, my heart sunk, my eyes welled up, she was so right! Within a few months I had booked a reading with Tina, I had a broken wrist at the time of seeing Tina and she gave me some healing after my reading. It wasn't long after that I started seeing Tina on a regular basis for healing sessions, we used to do EFT (Tapping) on you tube after our Reiki session, I really looked up to Tina and thought she was amazing.

Reiki truly helped me start my healing process, and I am grateful to Tina for coming into my life right when it was most needed. I was seeing Tina fortnightly for Reiki sessions and it was the best thing I ever did, investing in myself in this way. Some weeks I would walk away feeling so connected, with so much love in my heart and other weeks I would walk away feeling a lot of emotions. I always felt like Tina was there for me, sometimes we would just have a chat and a hot lemon water together, she was like the big sister I never had, someone that understood me. I was grateful for that because it can be a lonely road, if we don't have people in our lives that understand us.

I JUST WASN'T happy in Margate, I always felt like I was seeking something else. I had regular clients with my hairdressing business, but life was calling me to go in a new direction. We started to look to move to Hastings, East Sussex, I had a few friends there, so it felt right. One of my friends worked in Asda and she got me a job interview, working as an Asda ace, it wasn't working for Asda like I wanted, but I thought 'I am starting off where I want to be.'

I TRAVELLED up and I got the job as an Asda ace, I was in a little bit of a panic, as we hadn't yet moved to Hastings! My friend kindly offered for me to stay with her and that's what I did for 6 months, travelling home twice a week and still doing my hairdressing in Margate. I loved my job, but I wanted to be working on the other side as a checkout operative, as soon as the position become available, I applied for the job, and I got it and within 6 months we got a house transfer.

AFTER MOVING into our new house and making it our own, I started to learn Reiki, my plan was to become a Reiki master, travel around the world healing and teaching other light seekers. Traveling is a big passion of mine!

AFTER A YEAR I LEFT ASDA, being an empath was really quite draining working on the checkouts. My husband invested in me to start my own business, selling kids clothes, toys and much more but I had itchy feet. It just didn't feel right, so after a short amount of time I sold all the stock. I got hardly anything compared to what my husband had invested. But I really enjoyed giving people a bargain ha-ha. I then went on to do my security guard training, my husband had started up his own business after being at the Olympics. I thought it would be good so that I could help him when needed. Even though I enjoyed helping him out, I knew it wasn't my path and it didn't make me happy.

I WAS STILL SEEKING my path and what felt right to me. I got myself a little job in a sandwich bar and gosh that wasn't right for me either I was only there for 2 short months, it was Christmas time and I was happy to just concentrate on being with my family.

I AM VERY BLESSED to this day to have an amazing supportive husband, I am always seeking new things to learn, thing to get my teeth into, and healing myself at a deeper level. I received an amazing Christmas gift from my husband, he got me Tony Robbins Unleash The Power Within ticket. I attended the event at the excel in May 2017.

I FELT VERY proud of myself for traveling all that way on my own, as driving on the motorway wasn't something I enjoyed, all those lorries used to make me feel anxious. I was also feeling very anxious about being with thousands of people. I had met a beautiful lady online just before the event and we had been chatting. We planned to meet for a coffee, we spent every day together at the event learning lots about each other as well as ourselves. We walked over hot coals, we danced, we hi-fived, we hugged strangers and we got out of our comfort zone.

STILL TO THIS day we are friends, talk about how the universe has your back, the right people and situations have always come into my life right when they are needed. Tony Robbins was amazing, the whole event is life changing, I can recommend it to anyone looking for change in their life.

AFTER THE EVENT it left me feeling so high, I was seeking the next thing and I wanted to go on a retreat. So, I put the question out there and Tina messaged me she said she was holding a Goddess retreat in Glastonbury in September, I booked in! September soon came around, the energies in Glastonbury are truly amazing, it knocked me off my feet! The retreat was phenomenal, the workshops we did and being back in Tina's company was just so exciting. I had so much gratitude for Tina, it was Tina who had helped me on my healing journey, everything felt so right.

AFTER THE RETREAT, I was in a bit of a mess, all the spiritual work we had done had put me into a healing crisis as I sat on the sofa crying, I thought to myself "no" I cannot go through this again. Tina kindly offered for me to go and assist at her Usui Reiki II workshop [I had done my Usui Reiki attunement a few years before in Hastings] I travelled down to Margate, I received some healing and it felt amazing to be helping Tina after all she had done for me, I knew this was my path!

EVERYTHING FELT RIGHT and even though I was going through some sort of healing crisis, I felt good. My true path had shown itself to me, the door was open and in just a few months I had become an Angelic Reiki Practitioner as well as an EFT (Tapping) Practitioner. Angelic Reiki is a beautiful high vibration and a very powerful healing modality.

IN 2018 I did my Angelic Reiki Masters course it was after this course that I started seeing spirits, angels and orbs around me, not long after I started my Theta Healing Practitioner journey, all of these healing modalities have helped me grow and become more connected. Being a part of a sisterhood has been a beautiful experience, something that I wasn't used to being a part of. I now have many sisters I can call upon, knowing we have each other's back is truly inspiring. Learning with Tina has been a blessing to my life, she is filled with love and likes to share that with everyone. She has come a long way in the six years I have known her, she inspires me to continue to work on myself, and also me being a seeker of life's true bliss. I now know it's not about the destination it's about enjoying the journey on the way.

**Once you say yes to yourself**
**The universe will bring everything to you**

In April of 2018 I was so lucky to be chosen to become a Crew member for Tony Robbins, being of service to 13,000 people was truly breathtaking in itself, so life changing, it felt so good to give other people a unique experience knowing how I felt the first time I attended, I knew I could give positive words of wisdom from my own experience. I'd like to think I touched many hearts, giving back to other people even if it is just a kind word, can mean so much to a person as we never know what someone is going through.

I LAUNCHED my healing business in November 2017 and have added to my services over the year, I love the energy of Reiki and enjoy giving my clients a unique healing session.

EVEN THOUGH I haven't gone into depth with my life I can now look back with love in my heart and I thank God for all the lessons learnt, all the people that were there for me, the people that were not, I thank you - I wouldn't be who I am today without all of you. I now let go with more ease, as things come to the surface for me to look at, to feel, and to let it go.

OUR LIFE PURPOSE is to love one another, help one another on this plain of existence, and have fun along the way. I wish someone had of told me all those years ago to listen to myself, to trust my intuition. When we need answers to go within, as there you will find all you need to know! No two people will go through the same thing in life, when we get really good at listening to ourselves, we will stop seeking for answers outside, and live life in bliss and be grateful for the lessons that we've learnt along the way.

LOVE & Light

# ABOUT THE AUTHOR

## LOUISE TILBURY

Louise Tilbury was born in Margate on the 2nd of August 1979 she is a Daughter, Sister, Mother, Wife and nana she has 4 beautiful children, 2 step children and 2 grandsons and is proud to be alive in this world.

Louise loves to take walks in the woods and just being surrounded by and encompassed in nature, she often sits looking out at sea envisioning all there is in the world to explore, having a big passion for traveling the world and seeing its beauty it stills her heart and enlightens her soul.

Louise also loves listening to music, swimming, dancing and singing she always dreamed of becoming a singer and even though she never thought she was any good it's never stopped her from breaking out into song whenever she feels the urge. Louise also loves to watch romantic films, always being someone that falls in love with love itself, she gets teared up when watching a happy romantic film. Louise has been empathic from a young age but never really understood this until adult life, always taking on other people's emotions she now understands that she had many gifts from a young age and is now remembering as she steps more and more into enlightenment, reawakening all she has inside.

Louise has an NVQ Level 2 in Hairdressing, is a Usui Reiki Practitioner, Angelic Reiki Master, EFT (Emotional Freedom Technique) Practitioner and a Theta Practitioner

Louise started her self-Healing journey in 2013 after many years of not knowing her true path, her spiritual journey showed itself to her in 2017 after attending a Goddess retreat in Glastonbury when the doors were opened to her spiritual path she carried on walking towards the light. Following this she then became a part of a sisterhood something she never envisioned not having had many friends that were girls! she now embraces her 'sisters' with open arms, and relishes in the loyalty and the love, she enjoys every get together they have.

Louise fully submerged herself into her healing business in 2017 after becoming a Usui Reiki II Practitioner in 2016 she then went on to add more Healing Modalities to help herself and her clients. Her business has grown somewhat in the past year and she loves giving her clients a unique healing experience.

Website: https://www.freedom-healing.uk/

facebook.com/FreedomHealinguk

instagram.com/freedomhealing_lou

# MARCIA STAPLES

*I* am just about to embark on the biggest decision of my life and I'm waiting patiently for the transition to occur. Everything I have ever known is about to be turned upside down and I'm putting my trust wholly into the universe. Life is now amazing, having stepped back onto my spiritual pathway at the beginning of 2017, when I met Tina Pavlou 'The Angel Lady'. I've always known I have a spiritual calling but up until then life always got in the way.

At 40 years old having endured numerous traumatic events and a somewhat difficult upbringing, I decided it was my time, I decided that this life needed to be lived for me. I needed to work on myself to become the best version of me. I knew that life had much more to offer than the craziness, the fear and the constraints of my own body. Having this realisation has enabled me to do the work to become my true authentic self.

The day I contacted Tina, I was somewhere between a rock and a hard place. Feeling totally submerged into the depths of my soul; trying to untangle the ever-weaving webs of fear, despair and frustration. Not being able to function properly as a human being, I tried to come up for air and was seeking a little guidance from the powers that be. Knowing I couldn't carry on with emptiness, that I often attempted to fill or expected others to fill, I had a deep void within that always needed that something, I just didn't know what that something was.

RIDDLED with fear and reaching the tipping point of my life, I had a few healing treatments to address this from local healers and began working on myself. I was in the worst relationship of my life and didn't understand how I ended up there knowing how pure I was inside. My relationships were getting worse and shorter. I even started to think I shouldn't be in a relationship, that I should be on my own forever. In fact, I remember thinking if this is the best I've had from my life then I'm happy with my lot. Although I did drugs for years and partied hard being a DJ before this, at least I'd had a laugh along the way, and to be fair I did have the best house parties.

LEAVING that life of drugs behind and all the so-called friends and partner that came with it, I was now at a cross roads, it was DO or DIE. Carry on almost killing myself trying to fit in with what everyone else was doing or break away and continue taking the very thing that was keeping me alive - wheatgrass shots! and the knowledge that something else, and something bigger was out there.

MANY A NIGHT back at mine we were all so wasted and completely off our tits, this went on for hours going into the early hours of the morning, in fact sometimes it even carried on the following day and into the weekends. I remember sitting in the bathroom so many times, being so ill from doing so many drugs. Completely losing myself in the ecstasy tablets so my body could rest and I didn't have to give a shit about anyone or anything, acting the fool and saying things no one else dared to say. Snorting the next line to wake me up from the pills, drinking more alcohol to take the edge off the coke, mixing cocaine with alcohol to produce an even stronger drug, it was a vicious circle. Hugging the toilet not knowing my arse from my elbow but feeling so empty and sick from the concoction of the previous night. Sneaking up to my bedroom at 6am hoping they wouldn't notice downstairs that I'd gone, making me stay up longer if I was caught. Laying in bed feeling my heartbeat pounding out of my chest, totally wired knowing I'd gone too far again.

LISTENING to the party carrying on without me, hoping for some kind of cuddle or reassurance as I detached more from this world. Eyeing up the Valium I kept for a rainy day in case I couldn't get to sleep. Downers were not something I'd usually do, but this also became a habit, so I could switch off at bedtime. And now I had the added worry of what the Valium was going to do as it slowed my heartbeat down knowing the drugs had sped it up. Those moments in-between wondering if something bad would happen but just wanting to go to sleep and hopefully wake up out of this nightmare. Not knowing if I would wake up or even care if I didn't, at least it would be over and I'd had a good time. This was my lot and I couldn't see it getting any better than this.

DOING ALL this and being as spiritual as I am had its downside. I would leave myself wide open to whatever was out there and saw spirits quite clearly, more clearly than my waking day. It became my party trick and people would say not to talk to me, as the emotion I provoked ended in streams of sorry tears. To me, I was only talking to them and listening to them, as they shared stuff they'd never talked about before and even though it was at parties I knew I had a calling to help people. I would always be accused of being too deep and too serious which became more and more apparent. Things got so bad about seeing things and feeling entities in my house from all these parties and taking on people's 'stuff' that a friend of mine had to shut me down and clear my house spiritually. When I say shut me down, I mean I could not feel a thing after that and didn't see anything either for about 4 years. I came out of that relationship, broke away from all my friends and ditched the DJ lifestyle I had been accustomed to for around 15 years on and off. I had only attracted relationships where the other person was also on drugs, and there I was saying goodbye to everything I knew.

DURING THAT 4 years of being shut down I had two more relationships but this time no drugs were involved, which felt much harder and with worse lessons to learn. I went from the frying pan into the fire and that's when I ended up in the worst relationship of my life. I should have known from the beginning now I look back, but at the time I suppose I attracted what was already programmed into me from an earlier age. Three months into this relationship the physical abuse started and within 6 months I was being strangled and accused of cheating as I was talking to my ex before that. I was accused of being narcissistic because I was answering her back in a horrible tone, not wanting to entertain her ridiculous behaviour, it came across like I didn't care about her.

NOT KNOWING if I was coming or going the violence got worse, so did the panic attacks when it happened. My behaviour changed trying to defend myself, I spoke less to family members and only had one friend left to talk to, but even then, I didn't explain everything that was going on, I was ashamed and embarrassed it was happening to me. Plus, I'd seen a family member go through all this before in one of their marriages so I couldn't really talk to them either, I knew they would tell me to leave but I just couldn't. I was stuck there wishing, hoping and praying something would change. It never does though once the violence starts, so I was left with only one option, to observe and monitor.

By the fifth time of being strangled and over a year into the relationship, I was thrown against my front room wall and for a moment I saw stars, my head felt like it had been smashed and my skull split in two, the impact was unimaginable. I remember dropping down to the floor in shock and out of breath then out of nowhere getting back up and punching her in the face to make her stop. She was stunned that I had finally hit her back and I insisted that was enough, so we agreed that was enough, or was it? I turned around to compose myself and whack! there she was again, hitting me from behind. I just wanted it to stop and out of complete fear that I would die, I got up again and knocked her to the floor where I continued to hit her head on the floor five times shouting "Are you going to stop now? I told you not carry this on!" And there I was lowering myself, becoming everything she was accusing me of. I ended up with post-concussion syndrome that affected my life dramatically.

Although this was enough to leave I was stuck in a relationship where I would fall for the 'sorry' afterwards, hoping she had changed and still wanting things to get better. By this point I think I lost all respect for her and couldn't really see a way out, I really didn't know how I was going to get rid of her as she wouldn't leave me alone. Constant phone calls and text messages, if I ignored them she would turn up on my door step. Still accusing me of cheating and finding the odd photo on facebook from my past gave her ammunition to believe I was doing things behind her back; She literally thought a car pulling up out side was my ex planting love letters under the plant pots.

Nearly everyday she would trigger and make life hell. It got so bad that I ended up cheating on her, I believed she would never want me again, at least that way I would be rid of her forever, right? but after time she claimed she loved me so much that even cheating didn't put her off. Now I really had become everything she had accused me of and I knew this was not love.

If you loved someone you wouldn't go around treating them like that, that goes for me too. I had become an arsehole, I didn't even recognise myself. What the hell was I doing, thinking it was ok to have just one nice day with this person when the rest of the week was so horrible. Turns out she had been cheated on in every relationship before me and was projecting her 'stuff' onto me, she thought I was going to do the same thing and even though I swore until I was blue in the face I would never cheat, I ended up doing exactly that.

Life had now got too much, I couldn't even get back on an aeroplane after years of being scared because I was so afraid to travel. I couldn't use public transport because I didn't trust people with my life; I didn't like being a passenger in a car because I wasn't in control. Fear was everywhere, and now scared to get into another relationship in case I really was a narcissistic cheating arsehole. I got back in touch with my friend who shut me down, I explained that he did a good job, as I didn't have anything bothering me for years. He asked if I would like it lifted and I said yes. As soon as he did the flood gates opened like everything had been waiting all this time for me to open back up.

So, my quest continued to work on myself through these sessions with the local healers and my reason for going was to get back on an aeroplane and face my fear of flying, I had been abroad several times before, but I was now riddled with fear and it was getting worse. After about two months of going 1-2 times per week I started feeling a bit better. I remember visiting family and leaving there wanting to use symbols which I could only think were Reiki symbols when I was attuned back in 2000. I studied up to the second level in Usui Reiki, along with psychic classes too but life got in the way and that was the end of any attunements or courses. I asked the two people who were working on me where I could redo my Usui Reiki and they both gave me names.

As soon as I heard one of them say 'Tina Pavlou the Angel Lady' I stopped her in her tracks and said "YES" that's the one. I could literally feel it was meant to be and continued to grab her details. The very next day I contacted Tina on facebook and asked if she taught Reiki and when was the next class. I explained that I had already been attuned to level 2 and she replied to say that level 3 was being taught the day after. You just couldn't make it up, before I knew it, I was booked in taking my level 3 Usui Reiki and picked up exactly where I'd left off all those years ago. It was almost as if fate had grabbed me by the short and curlies', urging me to go on and take this course, to change my life.

During that class I was downloaded with unconditional love and was amazed at this feeling of love that I'd had for the first time in my life. How was it possible to feel a feeling that was missing this whole time? I was so surprised, shocked, speechless, a little emotional to say the least. The day after the level 3, I was allowed to resit my level 2 and wanted to be reattuned with my new teacher anyway, plus it had been so long, it was good to recap. A month and a half later I was learning Angelic Reiki which I'd never heard of before but, knowing what Usui Reiki did for me, I was in. Little did I know how much this was going to blow my head off. Being attuned to the highest vibration on the planet and working with Angels, Ascended masters and

Galactic beings was just totally off the scale and the most amazing experience, not only to work with a teacher who works from pure love, but also to find like-minded people to share our journeys with.

BY THIS POINT I had left the abusive relationship knowing I was worth more. I did all my crying in the relationship, so it was easy to walk away in the end, I never looked back. Leaving there realising you can't help people who won't help themselves, thinking I wasn't even qualified to deal with what that relationship presented to me. Knowing all those lessons were over and I didn't need to keep repeating them. This was a massive shift and that void started to fill from the inside, from a place of love.

BEING a lesbian since my early 20's I didn't really have a gay scene or hang around with gay people, so I started chatting to girls online 'as you do', to see if anyone was up for a bit of fun with no ties. I just wanted to be gay and have fun around gay people. This wasn't working out very well though as my vibration had lifted so much from the attunements that what I was seeking before did not match what I was looking for now. After a few months I decided to stop looking and just be happy with me, knowing no matter how long it would take, I was happy to be on my own even if it was for the rest of my life. If, I was looking for someone she would be someone who I could grow and evolve with, to travel this pathway together. She'd also have to be older than me as all my previous female relationships had been younger. I knew deep down I would meet a woman through this new pathway and she'd have blonde hair and just left it at that.

LITERALLY A WEEK LATER, one of the women I was talking to at classes, was looking much more radiant than usual. It was weird because I had shut all other avenues down but for some reason I was still talking to this woman. She had been on holiday in the summer and we were chatting lots on facebook, so much so that we were almost missing each other. When she came back I dropped her daughter off who was also doing courses with Tina and as I was saying goodbye from the car she caught my eye. She went indoors then came back out with her sausage, yes 'Martin' her sausage dog, but, it was the way she stood there and held herself, dropping her barriers to reveal her tenderness and charm. I remember thinking 'wow' how cute does she look, I felt an instant pull and was instantaneously intrigued. There she was, my beautiful Olivia glistening in the midsummer evening not knowing she had just shown me everything I needed to see for another chance at love.

WE SPOKE lots after that and we even met up. I invited her along on a road trip I had for work, well she kind of hinted to come along and usually I'd say no because I'm happy doing road trips by myself but for some reason the invitation went out. She willingly agreed to our journey and off we went together. The whole time her arm was resting along the back of my driver's seat, leaving herself completely open and revealing her body language which was totally into me. Picking up on the signals, she made it so easy to talk to her, I could feel myself being sucked in by the love she was oozing across the seats. It was so nice to meet someone with an open heart and mind even though I had no idea where all this was going. I tried to play it cool as she had never had a girlfriend before, as far as I knew, and was technically still married with 4 children.

WE CONTINUED to meet up everyday after that and our connection was inextricable, we became inseparable. It was apparent that we were falling in love from the get go by the way we were looking and touching each other. By the end of the first week I couldn't even eat my food or concentrate on anything I was doing. 'Bang!' I was falling for her and didn't even realise. Over the next few weeks we fell in love and were given lots of psychic messages. I was shown that I would love her until her last dying breath and she was given our wedding date. I also remember a psychic reading from Tina some months before saying about marriage and how I would be loved like I've never been loved before. It seemed to me that my life had changed for the better. And here it was, the new love I had found for myself had been mirrored and matched by my new partner. Everything was flowing instead of being arduous. I knew she was the one when I became the best version of myself around her. She is beautiful, she is my Olivia.

FROM THERE, Olivia started doing courses and between us we did our Angelic Reiki Masters levels 3&4 which enabled us to become teachers in it. We also started learning Theta Healing with Tina and working with 'Creator of all that is' from the 7th plane of existence which is the highest place to work from. The miracles we witnessed not only on ourselves but with each other in classes was totally mind blowing. We were changing, shifting and removing limiting beliefs that held us back, even delving into past lives having brought them forward into this life. To actually go back and resolve a past life to free you up in this life is a miracle in itself. Obviously, you would have to believe in reincarnation to grasp this concept and you'd also have to have some kind of belief that there is a higher power or energy source out there, regardless of what you'd like to call it. Some people call this God, Divine Source, Allah, Buddha, however, we are all talking about an energy much greater than us humans. After all, everything is energy which inevitably makes us all one.

As THE COURSES went on and the classes grew we all became really close and formed a sisterhood. The most amazing and beautiful beings coming together, baring our souls in front of each other is nothing more than a stroke of genius. Having each other's backs is one of the most loving things I've ever been a part of. There is so much love, kindness and a willingness to help each other and its all done with 100% pure love and light. How lucky are we to have such a knowledgeable and trustworthy teacher, who has done the work on herself, which enables her to share her gifts and insights for our highest best. I've also been on the most amazing retreats to Glastonbury arranged by Tina, and the sisterhood just grew and grew.

WITH MY NEW VIBRATION, my new partner and my new circle of friends, things were finally starting to look up. I was being loved like I'd never been loved before, I was loving like I'd never loved and I was losing everything that no longer served me. Doing the 'the work' was paying off.

OLIVIA and I went off to do EFT & Matrix Re-imprinting which brought a different dynamic to the table. We learnt that we are programmed from a very young age and that everything happens to us before we're 7 years old. This is because of a decision we made about the world that day we were traumatised or something happened to us. Once we make that decision it becomes part of our energy field which is like an invisible layer around our body. All our programmes sit in this energy field and the universe matches it by giving us exactly what we want, good or bad. For example, if you were looking for garden equipment online but you already had a lawnmower and you typed 'I don't want lawnmowers' into Google, what do you think comes up?

THAT'S RIGHT, a shed load of lawnmowers. This also applies to our thoughts. If we go around thinking 'I don't want that' and 'I don't want this' where do you think those thoughts are stored? Yes, right again, in our energy field where the universe says "as you wish" Do you see how our negative thoughts are being manifested on a daily basis. The universe doesn't know words like 'I don't want' exactly the same as Google doesn't. We can be the world's best manifester but if you have limiting beliefs and programmes that are deep seated, then it can feel like nothing ever goes right until you change them.

HAVE you been attracting the same thing all these years? The same partner? The same old friends? The same boss? The same money problems? Then ask yourself where it comes from because life doesn't happen to you, it responds to you.

TAKE MY ABUSIVE RELATIONSHIP, it doesn't mean I'm a nasty or horrible person; it means that somewhere in my energy field I was carrying the vibration of domestic and physical abuse or violence. Now I can either take that as gospel and think well that's just life, it's just one of those things that happened to me, I hate her for what she's done, I wish her really bad luck, or, I can do the work on myself and find out where it came from to find resolution and move on; By doing this it would have changed the energy in my energy field around my body and thus attracting something different, something better for my life.

GROWING up with my three younger brothers, we were all smacked and quite hard too. If we were really naughty we'd even get the slipper, what with that and sleeping on the bathroom floor, the odd night in the porch and even being locked in our bedrooms you can see how a program or belief could have been formed. Not only is this seen as physical abuse these days but it's quite normal now from our generation to think that a clip around the ear was ok, it didn't do me any harm and made me the person I am today, but, if you actually go back and ask that 'younger you' how you felt about the abuse or trauma that happened in your life, you'll be surprised how you feel about it. If your reply is "I'm fine about it" then that tells me you have become accustomed to it, that you have already told yourself it was ok what happened, or you've buried it so far down that it's been filed and stored in your body which in turn could be the start of an illness or disease.

Also, when answering you are replying from the front part of your brain; your consciousness mind so it's not a true reply. Using these modalities, you close your eyes and bypass your conscious mind which enables us to access the back part of our brain; the sub-consciousness where all our memories are stored and where the real magic happens when we do 'the work'.

The care givers in my life were not making me feel safe, wanted or loved. I don't remember being brought up with love and cuddles and although this may have happened when I was a baby, I would have been far too young to remember this. I do remember playing board games, colouring lots and going on holidays in the UK as a family so it wasn't all bad.

In a session going back to these events and finding what beliefs I formed that day, I started to realise that maybe the younger me wasn't ok. She wasn't ok that she was smacked, she was so scared that she used to wet the bed until she was 10 years old. She didn't like being locked in her room feeling trapped, lonely and isolated. What did this teach me, It taught me that love was abuse; which meant I attracted abusive relationships as an adult, that I must be seen and not heard; which meant I couldn't speak my truth as an adult, it taught me to be on my own; which made me too independent, that I didn't need anyone else and pushed people away as an adult, but most of all it taught me that this was not love. It was just old programs running that my parents didn't know how to look at either, let alone shift it from their bodies, so for that I make allowances because they didn't know any different.

I DON'T BLAME my abusive relationship either because that was in my energy field and she turned up to teach me what it was that I needed to do, to work on myself, to be my most authentic self, so for that I thank her. Through the darkest times and finding everything I didn't want, has enabled me to find everything that I do want. By taking responsibility and not blaming others is just part of the healing process. To really go back and nurture your younger self is priceless, doing inner child work is probably one of the most powerful things you could ever do for yourself. It's the best investment you'll ever make and boy it's so worth it.

I CHOSE before coming back to earth that I would be the one in my family to stop these programs being passed down from generation to generation. It hasn't been easy trying to repair my relationships with family members over the years, nor did I find it easy to be a mum to my beautiful daughter, but what I do know, is that I will do anything to stop this happening to my daughter's children and my great grand-children so we can light up the path for future generations to enjoy and live in a world where peace on earth exists. It is coming, but it will take time as more and more people wake up and raise the vibration of the planet.

ONE OF THE hardest things I've found doing this work; which I was nowhere near prepared for, is that not everyone wants to get better, that's including some of my own family. Watching people with a serious illness or disease playing out their old programs and wanting to keep them, not knowing it's serving them somehow, even when pointed out to them they are too scared to let them go. Think about it; if you have been on benefits for a long time or most of your life, getting better means you may lose your financial back up, it may even mean you'll have to go out and get a job. What about the lady who got cancer when her husband cheated on her, if she lets that go then it means she's forgiven him for what he did, but on a subconscious level she wants him to pay by looking after her for the rest of her life. If she gets better he won't look after her anymore and where is the Karma in that?

AND WHAT ABOUT the man who has a life-threatening illness that has people fussing over him day and night, chauffeuring him around to and from hospital and when offered healing he refuses because he'll lose his identity. People become defined by their illness, lost and trapped in a constant cycle of lost identity. Having had it so long that he wouldn't know who he'd be without it. This has been a massive lesson for me as a healer because I always wondered why people were unable or didn't want to get better. It's been hard knowing if they didn't sort it out in this life then they'd have to come back and do it all again anyway, however, everyone has their own journey in this life and it's not up to me to tell them what to do. I'm only here to guide and give people who want to be helped the tools to help themselves.

OLIVIA and I have recently opened our new business called Fluid Minds where we can now give back to others and help them along their way by offering an array of modalities like Angelic Reiki Healing, Theta Healing, Crystal Healing, EFT & Matrix re-imprinting, Access consciousness 'The Bars', Sound Healing and much more to come. Learning all these have given us a much wider scope on the world and how we work and function as humans. One of the things I have noticed from all this work is, what ever you want to work on is just an aspect of ourselves and not who we are today.

WE SOMETIMES TRY to live in our grown-up adult body but end up looking at the world through the eyes of our inner child when we were hurt, abandoned or abused which triggers us in our adult life. We then react to these triggers and lose sight of where we are going and what we're supposed to be doing. By going back, we can rescue and save our inner child and be the parent we never had. By calling forward the part of you that is ill, depressed, bereaved and so on... you are speaking directly to the aspect of yourself that's holding all this 'stuff'.

TOGETHER WE FEEL the mental health crises is mostly down to our emotional needs not being met as children, this is not taught in schools and in most cases, not being taught at home either. Going to counsellors and taking anti-depressants is simply not working, it's about time we stood up and helped ourselves. We would like to give people the tools to be able to do this themselves and function as human beings on a much higher vibration than what they've ever been used to before. Its starts 'here', it starts 'now' and it starts with 'you'. What will *you* do to change your energy fields and live the life you've always wanted?

SO HERE I am slowly shutting down my self-employed dog business of 5 years being a full-time breeder, re-homer and psychologist, selling my home that I've had a mortgage on for the last 9 years and even selling my 2014 plate Zafira that I purchased 2 years ago. All these things were started when I was on a much lower vibration and it no longer serves me in my new life. I simply cannot be trapped to the house anymore, it causes cabin fever and makes me feel stressed, I can't even relax in my own home. Getting paid 2-3 times a year makes this financially a very difficult job, especially when mother nature plays her part when bitches don't come into season on time.

I'VE ALSO EXPERIENCED puppies dying in the litter this last year which has never happened before and is totally disheartening. It would appear that the universe has others ideas for me and its time I surrendered to help others, now being on a higher vibration I understand my job and that way of life is morally wrong. I have been living in fear my whole life and although I'm only 42 now in 2018, I'm about to embark on the biggest decision of my life and waiting patiently for the transition to occur.

# ABOUT THE AUTHOR

## MARCIA STAPLES

Marcia Staples is currently transitioning from the 'Matrix' way of life into her new spiritual pathway leaving behind everything she's ever known. Having full trust that the universe has her back, she has just left her job as a successful dog breeder, re-homer and psychologist of crossbreed doodles in Dover, South East England. She has turned her hand to many things in her lifetime to include being a DJ which developed into a mobile disco business.

Marcia is in a same sex relationship with Olivia who is the love of her life, allowing her to be the best version of herself. Marcia also has a 23-year-old daughter who has flown the nest, however, is still yet to realise the potential of her own spiritual gifts.

Marcia stepped back onto her spiritual pathway in her early 40's after 17 years. She pretty much picked up where she left off and is now working as a natural healing channel that encompasses love from 100% pure light, she works with beings from all realms through the creator of all that is. Through pure determination and a passion for helping people, she has become a Usui & Angelic Reiki Master Healer & Teacher, Advanced EFT & Matrix & Past Life Re-imprinting practitioner, Theta Healer, Crystal Healer, Access Consciousness 'The Bars' and a Sound Therapy practitioner.

Marcia specialises in finding the deep-rooted issues that have become our beliefs from childhood, the programs that we walk around with playing out in our everyday lives. Having experienced the darkest depths of her own soul growing up, bad relationships, carrying trauma and living in complete fear she has made friends with her shadow side. This has enabled her to help and empower others, giving them the tools to help themselves. Doing the work on herself through courses and self-development has enabled her to lift her energy, functioning on a much higher vibration leaving behind everything that no longer serves her.

Marcia is very proud and excited to be alive at a time when the consciousness of the planet is shifting and rising. It really is time to get ready for something big, something magical and something long overdue. Let's move into the 'New Earth' together as one and embrace the Goddess energy to help balance and restore our masculine world. Let's bring peace on Earth as we know it because after all, we are HUMAN KIND!

Not everyone will wake… will you?

Contact details
   Email: marcia.staples@sky.com
   Website: https://www.fluidminds.co.uk

 facebook.com/marcia.staples

# MICHELLE SIMMONS TARIMO

*W*hether you call it a healing journey, a spiritual path, or the pathway to enlightenment, my own journey began in the April of 2002 when my Mum told me she had trained to be a Reiki Usui Master. I recall pulling a face before replying sharply, *"a what?"* in a scornful tone. I had never heard of Reiki. I was totally sceptical of the whole concept and giggled whilst she sat me down and placed her 'healing hands' on me. I can't say I felt a huge amount that first time, probably because I was (as I now know) blocking myself. I had no idea that this was the first, tentative step for me onto my own spiritual pathway. Shortly after my first treatment and a several more sessions my Mum trained me to level 1 and level 2 in Usui Reiki. I tinkered with it for a few years, healing my friends and the odd family member but I wasn't particularly passionate about it or committed to it. I am a very passionate person and will sing from the rooftops about something I believe in, but I decided that Reiki wasn't really for me. Instead I carried on living the 'fabulous' (eye roll at myself writing this) life I had already designed for myself.

· · ·

LOOKING BACK, my life at that time was far from happy although to anyone looking in from the outside, I had it all! I honestly thought I was living life to the full, aged 24, working as a Store Manager at a leading travel agent. I had been a travel agent since I was 16, being promoted into management at just 18 years of age and running my own store shortly after. I was always on foreign holidays, mostly 5 star all-inclusive breaks in Europe or the Caribbean and living in a house overlooking Dover, the castle and the channel. I was in a long-term relationship with an amazing, kind, gentle, loving, funny, man as my fiancé and had the most fantastic stepson. I had a multitude of friends and partied…. hard…. very hard…. I would dance all night at raves and nightclubs then onto the after parties then roll home some-times not until the Sunday night or even Monday morning. I would drink vast amounts of alcohol and took a lot of drugs…. I never injected anything (that always seemed too hardcore for me and I didn't like needles, or I may well have tried in all honesty!) I was a wild child of the highest magnitude and prided myself on being THE life and soul of the party…. or so I thought….

ALMOST EVERYTHING I WAS DOING, pushing myself to be the BEST store manager, the most outgoing and outrageous party girl in town was a mask for the demons I was carrying inside me. Everything I did was my way of dealing with (as best as I could) a decade of sexual abuse that began when I was just 3years old. Until recently, whenever the subject of childhood or first memories came up in conversation, the same vision would flash through my mind. I would immediately be transported back to being 3 years of age and in my Mums bed. She wasn't there, but somebody else was…. and he was masturbating…. I could feel the vibration and shaking as he was doing it next to me. I asked him what he was doing and that's where that all began. The abuse didn't stop until I was around 13 years of age when I finally told my Mum what had been happening during an outburst of anger. I was standing in the kitchen, angry and making a cup of tea. I was working on a family tree for an English assignment and I had refused to put this particular man in it, favouring my deceased, alcoholic, physically abusive, biological father instead.

My Dad had died through alcohol when I was 9 years old, I hadn't seen him since I was very young. I remember looking for his death certificate as I didn't believe he was dead and being very distraught when I finally found it. I thought he was my last chance at getting away from what was happening to me at home so when he died I felt like there was no escape.

My Mum, of course, didn't understand why, so an argument started, and it was at that point I blew the whistle on what had been happening. The abuser had already told me he would kill me and my mum if I ever told anyone our 'secret' and that he wanted to be able to do what he did to me even when I was grown up and married.

As a child I believed every word and thought I was protecting both Mum and myself by keeping quiet. I would sit in the living room cuddled up with her on the sofa looking at him on the chair opposite me wishing I had a gun to shoot him. I had also seen a film where a girl hid a knife under her pillow, so she could stab the person that was raping her when he pinned her down in her bed and I would daydream about doing the same.

I didn't think about what would happen after I told my Mum what was going on because I had never intended on telling her, but when I did it then all went a bit crazy.... Police at the house, people close to me crying, many questions being asked, my head was spinning.... I got through the Police interview the following morning in a safe house in Kent and went back to school that afternoon.

No-ONE KNEW how to deal with me or what to say to me, teachers, family or friends.... Many stayed away. I wish they hadn't, I felt incredibly alone and the belief that I had to do everything myself was signed and sealed. He went to prison for his crimes against me, no-one else was prepared to stand up and say it had happened to them although I knew it had as I could remember some of it. I guess I expected from that point that the suffering would finally be over, it really wasn't, and people close to me made decisions that would take many more years for me to understand why.

THE WEEK after my 16th birthday, I collected up my GCSE results, moved out of the family home, started two jobs, had a number of boyfriends and started to party hard. Of course, what goes up must come down and the harder I partied the closer I came to pushing it too far. I had a number of experiences where my sanity and life were at risk. But it was my way of dealing with the situation and the over-whelming feelings of confusion and anger.

AT THE AGE of 18 I had to live with him again temporarily. He was out of prison by then. I would lock myself in my room at night and I had nightmares full of him getting in to my bed and doing it again. Thankfully not too long after that he was removed from my life for good. But the damage was done, and I had an awful lot of anger directed at quite a few people close to me, and also anger with myself. I had counselling for years but apart from one group counselling session with a number of other girls I didn't really get much from it, only irritation about having to sit opposite someone with a notebook nodding and asking me questions as I was expected to relive what had happened over and over again. I was determined to deal with the emotions I carried, I knew I was very strong, but I didn't know where to start. I know among others, Mum was desperate to help me somehow, but I was far too angry at her, and the world to trust her or anyone else again. When I look back on that chapter of my life it's almost like it all happened to someone else.

FOR YEARS I enjoyed the same things....exotic holidays, partying, and an abundant amount of money to spend on an obscene amount of clothes and shoes. My relationship fell apart with my fiancé, so I threw myself into meaningless sex with people and carried on partying hard. In December of 2009 predictably it all went bang. I was signed off work with 'severe reactive depression and anxiety' and I had a complete breakdown. My mum was amazing and was now the ONLY person whom I really told what was going on in my head.... her and the doctor anyway....but I had made up my mind and I wanted to go to the light. I felt like I had no fight left in any part of my body. I wasn't sad about dying, but I was certain I couldn't deal with the injustices of the world, the injustice of what had happened to me and those around me. I wanted to be with the Angels. In a place of peace and light. My mind was made up. I didn't want to fight or be strong anymore...

LUCKILY FOR ME a very close friend of mine took me on a road trip in May 2010.... to Amsterdam and Berlin. I barely spoke to him some days, but I did take my first angel book by Diana Cooper with me and started to read....... She set small tasks for the day..... I remember the first was to treat the next person you meet as if they were an angel. The next was to smile at every person you make eye contact with. PERFECT! I didn't need to talk to anyone ha-ha! Another was to imagine you have golden roots growing from bottom of your feet going down to the centre of the earth and back up again as you took every step – like a walking meditation. I was enjoying it. Towards the end of our trip we went to Bloemandaal beach outside of Amsterdam .

THE BEACH WENT on for as far as you could see, I loved it there. Whilst walking to the beach I said out loud "I can't do this anymore, please, if Angels do exist come and help me now" I sat down on the beautiful beach, close to the shore, the sun shining down on me and listened to a pod cast about meditating and working on your base chakra. Whilst I was doing that my friend interrupted me with a phone call from my mum with some amazing news and that I was at last finally free from one of the shackles that had kept me so unhappy.

I ASKED my travelling companion to drive me home to collect my tent, so I could come back to Bloemandaal and stay for a while. It was the perfect escape from the world I needed. I spent the next month in my tent alone, apart from one night when a guy I had met in Thailand came over from London for the night to hang out. I read so many books, mostly Diana Cooper books and books about angels, ate nuts and the odd breakfast at the café across the road when I could afford it, drank herbal tea, walked for hours and hours on the beach and sampled some of Amsterdam's finest homegrown herb!

IT WAS whilst I was there, I made a decision. I was going to go to Africa. I had always thought I could never work with children that had been abused as it would stir up too many pent-up emotions for me (I would soon discover it helped me empathise with what they were going through) I felt a real pull to go to Africa as soon as possible, so I packed up my tent and booked my ticket to Dover that day. I dragged my tent and belongings all the way to Amsterdam coach station, I remember them being insanely heavy, but I didn't have the money for a taxi so caught buses and trains to the coach office.

. . .

WHEN I GOT to the coach office they had booked me on the wrong coach and my coach had left hours before.... luckily, I was able to prove this wasn't my fault, but the decision rested with the coach driver as it was full. I had no money left at all so threatened to pitch my tent in the office if they didn't take me and sat and prayed for the angels to help me....they heard me and luckily I had a seat and off I went home.

I ARRIVED BACK into Dover on my 32nd birthday where my mum met me at hideous o'clock in the morning at the port with a birthday cake and stack of birthday cards. 6 weeks later I watched her fall to her knees with worry as I jumped onto a train to Heathrow, London and flew to Tanzania to volunteer for a children's project for a few months.

I landed at Kilimanjaro airport early August 2010, utterly exhausted and very apprehensive about what to expect, but also filled with excitement. The moment I stepped off the plane I felt like I had arrived home.... I was shown to my tent, which I shared with 2 other girls in the gardens of a hostel. The toilets were forever flooding, the shower was more of a dribble, only sometimes hot and the electricity was intermittent. There were snakes, spiders and bugs SO huge I saw one flying through the air carrying a dead tarantula. The first morning I was shown a breakfast room where there was rat faeces in my coffee cup (I called it the rat room after that) the bread was intensely dry, and you could hardly read the label on the pot of jam as it was covered in ants.

THIS WAS ALL VERY different from the 5-star luxury I had become accustomed to. I knew it was time to put my big girl pants on.... so off

I went to a village called Mabogini around 20/30 minutes' drive away from the town of Moshi where I was living, on a small minibus designed for no more than 10 people (I counted 35 people and a goat one day) and met 40 little girls at a project called Kilimanjaro Young Girls in Need, KYGN.

I DIDN'T SPEAK a word of Swahili and was shown a classroom with 15 little ladies who didn't speak a word of English. The small classroom had no amenities at all. The children all sat on the dusty concrete floor and I had one third of a piece of chalk shared with another 2 teachers, one of whom would just disappear home whenever she felt like it. I realised almost immediately I was going to stay there for more than a few months…. I had no idea it would be nearly 5 years. I was promoted very quickly to an assistant project director, I absolutely LOVED being there, I experienced so much, witnessing the most heart-breaking stories of abuse of all kinds which these children had been through and were still living – daily. I loved them so so much and did everything I could to light up their worlds in any way possible, starting off with taking in 10 litres of water a day just so the children could have a drink.

IT WASN'T all sunshine and smiles…. Far from it but my experiences there confirmed my belief in God …. I always had referred to him as source until that point – I just didn't feel comfortable saying God but the first time was 4 months after I arrived (I was meant to have flown home the month before) and I was sat at a water springs meditating, my head slumped forward and I wanted to know how I was going to stay there, was I meant to stay there etc; I was crying and in a bit of a state…. I felt my head being pushed up by a beautiful bright light and I heard the words "There is no need to worry, you are meant to be here" they weren't my words or my thoughts – so whose where they? I knew. It was the Creator/God/Jah/Allah. I was more than a little blown away and sure enough a pathway opened up with the help from one of my close friends who I had no idea would be part of the sisterhood I am blessed to be in now and I stayed for nearly 5 years.

In June 2011 I met a Tanzanian herbalist healer or shaman as some may call him – I am still not entirely sure what he is…. but in August 2011 we carried out an amazing sunrise meditation together and I wrote a letter full of LOVE to the person who had sexually abused for me so long. I called in Archangel Michael to help me – Shabani confirmed I had 4 angels around me at that time with Archangel Michael blowing light into me…. that was precisely what I had visualised. I fell asleep after writing the letter and woke up a while later with 2 white feathers right next to me. I felt FREE, the freest I had ever felt and thought I was healed…. hmmmmm nice thought ha-ha!

5 days later I was attacked …. I was robbed, cut open with a panga (local sharp tool) and repeatedly told I was going to be killed…. I was in a taxi with another girl who was being attacked on the back seat. My friend and I had been set up. The registered taxi had driven us to a secluded spot, so we could be robbed and beaten. I know they were intending to rape us too, as afterwards we found out it had happened to 5 sets of girls across Tanzania and all the others had been raped…. My friend got away, but I was thrown back into the taxi AFTER they had robbed me and driven off at speed. I remember keep screaming "NO" whilst the attacker was beating me from behind, the taxi driver just looking intently at the road ahead.

Then I heard a voice again. CRYSTAL CLEAR AND LOUD. "Get out of the taxi now!" So, I opened the door and threw myself out onto the road and ran. I was covered in blood and hysterical, I wasn't really sure where I was running to, but I ran….. I passed some of my belongings on the floor and stopped to pick them up, at this point the reverse lights came on and the taxi came to get me again.... All the houses around me where in gated communities, I spotted a security guard and screamed at him to let me in to safety.... He chose not to, but thankfully a lovely old Tanzanian lady had heard my screams and she literally dragged me into her garden and slammed the gate shut, just as the taxi pulled up beside her house. It then sped off and I was able to call friends for help.

OBVIOUSLY, I sustained a number of injuries that night, mostly from throwing myself out of the car and it took a few weeks for me to be able to walk properly, and it was even longer to heal emotionally from the event. My faith was well and truly rocked, I felt really angry I had only enjoyed 5 days of freedom before I knew I would have to forgive again ! But my mind kept going back to that voice.... and when Shabani appeared a couple of months later at my door (I had started to slip back into a depression so had increased my anti-depressants and stopped answering people who were wanting to help me through it), with a leg of goat, a bottle of konyagi (an awful tasting local drink that puts more than hairs on your chest), a packet of cigarettes and huge cuddle I broke down and spoke my truth.

I WAS SO VERY ANGRY. I felt immense anger towards the attackers, not for robbing me, I understood that - but for the level of violence they used. I was angry at myself for not being more aware, angry at people in the UK who had been vocal about their fears of something like this happening to me, and mostly I was angry at God for letting it happen. He was meant to be my mate now! I had openly been saying I believed in God for the first time in my life and this is how my faith was repaid? (told you I was angry) Everything came flooding out. Shabani was used to my outbursts, by now he had become a close friend.... so, he tuned into the situation and asked if I'd had any travel plans in the

WHEN THE GODDESS CALLS

weeks after the attack.... I did.... I had been planning on going to a festival in Kenya on my own as no-one else wanted to go.

I WASN'T FAZED by making the 5–7-hour coach journey on my own so it didn't occur to me it could have been so dangerous. Silly really as interestingly I had repeated this same mantra every day for months until I was attacked "I am divinely guided and protected by a special guardian angel at all times" In reality I KNEW east Africa was unsafe. My mantra had come from FEAR I came to realise this years later.... more on that later! Shabani told me the creator had stepped in because if I had travelled to the festival I would have been in far far greater danger. I understood but I couldn't face going through having to forgive again so soon.... so I tried to put it behind me and carry on with my life there.

FAST FORWARD TO 2015 and after a heart-breaking decision to leave the 200+ beautiful children, my amazing village of Mbokomu where I had adored living and all my Tanzanian friends, I returned to the UK. With the amazing support of people worldwide the KYGN had moved to a new site, a new school had been built with a library, safe house, a number of classrooms and enough room for over 200 children to attend. I had done everything I could to help and now it was my time to look after my family......

BY NOW I HAD A HUSBAND, an almost one-year old daughter and another little one growing inside me. I took a while a settle but eventually I did. I had changed so much, I realised materialistic things did not excite me in the way they had before, I had grown to love a much simpler life, moving away from synthetic toxins that are used in and around many homes and on our bodies and children's bodies. I was questioning everything in my life in a way I hadn't before.

· · ·

ABOUT A YEAR after my second daughter was born, I started to look around for meditation groups, I knew I needed to get back into meditating but I wasn't sure where to start. I had no idea what was waiting for me around the corner but my life was about to change significantly again….it had to….I was gripped by a constant feeling of fear. Fear of no money, fear of my husband not being allowed to stay in this country, fear of my husband cheating on me, fear of my children getting sick if I did or didn't chose to vaccinate, fear of drowning, fear of car accidents, fear of ridicule, fear of losing all my friends, fear of my life never getting any better than it was but the most crippling fear I walked around with daily was that people were going to sexually abuse my children.

I ALREADY KNEW at that stage in my life that the power of the mind meant you could draw events to you, manifesting them, and I was petrified that my thoughts and visions of them being sexually abused and hurt were going to come true and it would be all my fault. But I couldn't control it which made me torture myself even more. What if I manifested it? I would never forgive myself. I was constantly suspicious, particularly as my eldest daughter approached the age of 3 years, when the abuse had started with me, checking her underwear regularly, panicking if she ever had any form of discharge or sign of infection. I had gotten thrush many times as a child, of course due to the interference, so the first time my eldest daughter had suspected thrush I went into a panic and felt completely overwhelmed with fear. I couldn't share this with anyone although, I did confide a little in a close friend who had also been abused, she understood but neither of us knew what to do about it.

I HAD BEEN SEEING pictures of a friend doing Angelic Reiki courses and from what I could see she was flying. I knew she had been through her own traumas and I could see how happy she was. I was immediately excited…. Angelic Reiki? I had never heard of this before but oooooooooooo yes please! So, I went along and met Tina Pavlou for a Reiki share night. The very second I met her I felt her love. Real love. She literally welcomed me into her arms and heart. I remember her cuddling me and I felt like I was going to fall over?!?! I felt safe for the first time in a very very long time, maybe for the first time in my life. I immediately trusted her implicitly and meeting her ignited something within me that was going to change everything about my life.

Now I have known her for nearly 2 years she is not only the hardest working healer I know, constantly pushing us as a group to heal more, release more, learn more, but she is also my best friend and soul sister. She is one of the few people who challenges me, and I allow it and I like it…. most of the time…. when I have stopped sulking anyway.

To begin with I put all sorts of barriers in the way of my progression. When asked if I wanted to learn Angelic Reiki I had a number of excuses as to why I couldn't (I now know this as resistance!)…. "I can't afford it, I don't have the time, who will look after my children etc" but it all fell into place…. And in August of 2017 I completed my First and Second degree in Angelic Reiki and I felt on top of the world. A week later the next big changes happened. I had been asking the Angels to bring me definitive proof of wrong doing against me for a while. Only now was I ready to listen and it was presented to me in undeniable black and white evidence. I had finally woken up and realised as I was raising my vibration, I had to be single. Sheesh.

No-one has ever said healing is easy! Obviously as I sat with my head in my hands as my family slept, I didn't know how I was going to do it, when, where, but I knew it had to be immediate. Very late that night I contacted the same sister who had taken me to Angelic Reiki for the first time and told her what I had found. She sent me angels and amazingly as I lay with my family that night, I felt peaceful and happy. I felt the presence of the angels; their wings were wrapped around me and I was lifted off the bed and held in love. I had the biggest smile on my face and I knew this was the beginning of the rest of my life and it was going to be amazing.

AMAZING IS one word of many I can use to describe what has happened to me over the last 2 years. I have set up my own Earth Mama page on Facebook, so I can help others learn how we can love our Mother Earth more, love ourselves more by reducing toxins and to inspire people to begin their own healing journey and assist those who are awakening or have awoken. I have started to write my own childrens meditations and hosting them which I adore, I have attained my Angelic Reiki Master Degree and participated in several Theta Healing courses, working hard to release and heal trauma, releasing debilitating fears that I had put so much focus on I was attracting them into my life, clearing blocks and being witness to some phenomenal healings, whilst manifesting and creating the beautiful life I now know I truly deserve, for me and my beautiful light seeking children.

MY FIRST MEMORY no longer makes me feel sick after an amazing EFT, Matrix re-imprinting session with one of my soul sisters, I no longer put a barricade at the front door every night, my children will not have to heal traumas or beliefs I would have passed onto them.....Isn't that awesome! On more than one occasion I have been brought to my knees and wanted to stop whichever course I have been sat in....but I always finish absolutely elated and so grateful of what we are able to achieve during our classes. I love raising my vibration and healing another part of me every time I work on myself, not to mention how honoured I am to be part of many other people's healing journeys around me.

A HUGE PART of this journey is the sisterhood I am now so blessed to be part of. The sisters I have raise each other up, we truly love each other and have the ultimate respect and loyalty for each other. I honestly never knew sisterhoods like ours existed. I had always felt intimidated by the girls who appeared to have it all, with their perfectly preened appearances and lives whilst I seemed to go against what everyone thought a woman/wife/mother should do and look like.... but I know it just wasn't my crowd.... I didn't feel like I was fitting in because I didn't!

I AM my true self with my sisters, I am safe to speak my truth without ridicule because I know it is met with LOVE. Obviously, there are some I am so insanely close to I feel like we are one at times, but seriously my heart is full of love and gratitude for all of them. I know they have my back and I have theirs. Just like the universe.

ONE OF THE biggest changes for me is that I no longer live my life in fear. I cannot tell you how free that makes me feel, even as I write this. Worrying as much as I did was exhausting! I am learning to step into my true power and realise my self-worth. I know I will continue to work on myself until I draw my last breath in this lifetime, and I hope to inspire others to do the same. Although some of those who have been closest to me for many years do not necessarily understand why or how I do what I now do, they don't need to – this is my journey and I am striving to be the best possible version of myself not only for me but for my beautiful girls. We all deserve the highest and best. And I am leading us 3 girls there.

. . .

I AM NOW ready to do what I came here to do. To continue to bring love and light to this beautiful world we live in, to continue to work hard to heal myself and heal others until the time comes when I am ready to move on. My soul has had some tough lessons, more than some, less than many, all of which I have the ultimate gratitude for but now, I am ready.

# ABOUT THE AUTHOR

## MICHELLE SIMMONS TARIMO

Michelle is a 40 year old former travel agent in the South East of Kent. Now she is a full time single mother to two beautiful little girls and is an Angelic Reiki Master, Theta Healing Practitioner and founder of Earth Mama, committed to assisting others on their transformational healing journey.

Like many people she has faced a series of somewhat distressing events throughout her life, although her drive and determination to heal and help others heal is very apparent.

Her passion for healing has been driven by a lifetime of abuse and self-abuse using alcohol, drugs and food as a shield to hide what lay beneath them.

As a young girl she had been particularly impacted by the pictures and news stories of the many children in Romanian orphanages and at a young age made up her mind she would go and help orphaned children when she was an adult.

After a breakdown in her early 30's and whilst suicidal, her mother asked her what she wanted to do other than end her life. She felt she had to go and help children in Africa. A few weeks later she went to the Kilimanjaro region with the intention of helping the children there in any way she could. She didn't have much in the way of money to help financially, but with an overwhelming feeling of love and empathy for the children, she knew she had to stay to do everything she could. Shortly after her arrival she realised she was also looking for answers as to why she had suffered so much, how she could heal from those wounds and who could help her do it.

After 5 years volunteering in Tanzania and a marriage breakdown she finally started to hear the answers she was ready to hear.

With the help of her Mentor, Tina Pavlou and new found sisterhood, Michelle has been relentless in healing herself and unlocking her past so that she can live a life of freedom in her future.

My email is: michsimmons2003@yahoo.co.uk

Facebook Group Earth Mama ID is https://www.facebook.com/groups/1343798679054703/

facebook.com/michelle.simmons.1401

# NATALIE BRADLEY

*T*here is a great saying; "I am not what you think I am, you, are what you think I am." Now, I had to read that a couple of times to get my head around it and you may have to do the same. Once you can understand this, life becomes a lot less painful.

MOST OF MY life I have felt like I don't belong, or didn't fit in with certain crowds. The moment I realised that it was actually those people who didn't fit into my world; my whole life changed!

MY LIFE IS one big playground; with things that only happen to other people, happening to me every day! I make people feel normal and that suits me just fine.

EVEN AS I sit hear typing this out after being told to take half an hour in complete silence with no distractions, turn your phone off and get lost in the writing, I find myself sat in the busiest airport in the world;

Dubai. As I sit here with my laptop on my lap, typing away after having the most incredible holiday with best friends and my family, my deadline is in 2 days! So, in true Bradders style I will just get it done in what ever conditions life gives me, but I can promise you I will always give it 100%.

I WAS BORN and raised in the South East of England in a town called Margate in Kent, where I lived until the age of 33 when I emigrated to Perth, Western Australia, where I live today with my husband of 16 years the amazing Wozza and our blessings; our 3 beautiful children, Summer, India and Ashton.

IT WAS NEVER my dream to move away to another country, it was Daddy bear's, but I knew that I wanted my children to live in a world where the sun was out for most of the year, they could live an outdoor life and experience things and have opportunities that they may not necessarily have where I was born.

EVEN WHEN I applied for our visas, I still never really believed this was happening but in the back of my mind I remember an amazing clair-voyant reader 20 years ago telling me that I would meet the love of my life on water, I would move overseas and get to the top of a company beginning with 'A'.

WELL, amazing lady, I met Wozza while working on the ferries, we moved to Australia and I am a Vice President with Arbonne, so my friend, you were spot on!

FROM A VERY EARLY age I always felt that something was not quite right, from the awkward feeling of being in a room full of people I am 'supposed' to fit in with and feeling like the odd one out, to sitting at the dinner table listening to negativity and judgements on other people's life choices. That feeling in my tummy was telling me that this is not the way I want to live my life and I now know this to be my gut feeling or intuition.

I GREW up doing exactly what I was told to do, go to school then college, get an education and then get a job. This is always tricky when you still don't know what you want to do with your life, I'm not sure if I ever will know, but what I did know for sure was that I didn't want to slave away for someone else for the rest of my life, being robbed of my freedom and choices, and that mindset is what has brought me to where I am today.

FROM THE RIPE old age of 11, I started working and earning my own money, from having a paper round to being waitress and chamber maid at the Ivyside Hotel in Westgate on sea, to B&Q and working in my Aunties sweet shop in Birchington. I left school and had a belief that I 'should' follow in my mum's footsteps to please my parents and become a nurse, well it became clear very quickly when I did my work experience in a Maternity ward, where I would get queasy and literally go green at the sight of hospital equipment, (let's not even mention needles!) that I was not born to be in the medical field.

I WENT to Canterbury College and studied Science and Health Studies (still trying to please) and when I graduated, I became a live in Nanny in the most beautiful part of the country, Aston Rowant in Oxfordshire. It was while working here that one of my besties growing up, Cheryl, passed away and this had a profound effect on my life and was a reminder that life really is too short.

. . .

I MOVED BACK to Kent and worked at a local factory that made toys and then in 1996 I began a job, onboard P&O Ferries - Dover to Calais, this w dramatically change the course of the rest of my life. It was onboard these ferries that I would meet the 2 most influential people who totally changed my life as I knew it, a very handsome guy called Warren, who totally gets me, understands me and loves me unconditionally - and a full of life (and then some!) lady called Tina.

I WENT on to marry that very handsome guy in 2002 on the beautiful Island of St Lucia and we started our own family. In 2009 we emigrated to Perth, Australia, with our 2 daughters and started our new life in the Lucky Country.

WE STARTED OUR LIFE AGAIN, leaving great incomes, our beautiful home we owned by the ocean, our friends and fur baby, Jackson. In contrast to our new life where we could not even get a mobile phone contract as we had no credit history here, having to rent a house and working such long hours to make ends meet. There had to be more to life than this?

WE WERE TOTALLY BLESSED with our 3rd child, a son, and it was while on Maternity leave that I realised I wanted my life to change. I wanted to have the choice to be more present with my children and Woz. I wanted to have more, so I could give more; not just financially but with experiences and whatever I could learn, so I could pass that knowledge on to others so they would benefit. It was then that I was given a skincare sample pack, that tiny gesture totally changed our lives, who would have thought it? Crazy as it sounds, I know! But its true, and 7 years later I have not looked back.

. . .

I QUIT my job whilst on maternity leave and started to grow an online business from my home, which has not only changed our financial situation but more so me as a person, it has taught me so many things, and things that I continue to learn and grow from every single day. I now have choices in my life. I choose when I work, who I work with and I have the choice of freedom.

IN 2013, two years after starting my Arbonne business, I had a light bulb moment while on conference in Las Vegas (gotta love Vegas and to be honest it was one of the reasons I joined the business) to go back to the UK and grow my business over there with the networks I had left behind. So, for 2 months I toured the UK growing my business. Whilst there, the wonderful and very persuasive Tina told me to attend a Reiki course she was conducting in Ramsgate. I was fully booked out but just knew that I had to clear the time to attend the course. I did, and this really began my spiritual journey that would become a huge part of my life.

I didn't really do anything with it at the time, I returned to Perth and carried on with my life, all the while becoming very much more aware of everything around me and tapping in more to my intuition.

IT TOOK me another 3 years to awaken fully and so I took my Reiki 1 again and then Reiki 2, and I went on to do Bars and chakra balancing and this really started my spiritual journey.

THEN, in 2018 Tina came over to teach Theta. Wow, just wow! This is a whole other level that I love exploring as it totally fascinates me. This, along with guidance and support from the incredible Tina, had helped me on my business journey and helped me be a better mum, wife, coach, mentor and leader to my team.

I WISH I had embraced my spiritual side a lot sooner in my life as I feel it would have lead me to a happier place a lot sooner. I would have understood a lot more and life would have made much more sense, so much earlier. However, I also understand that everything is exactly as it is meant to be, so I will take that and be super grateful that I even embraced it at all.

ONE OF THE points we were asked to cover in this book is, 'What did we learn from our early days in business?' I find that so difficult to answer as I believe that I am always learning everyday and never stop learning. One of my favourite quotes by Zig Ziglar sums it up, "You don't have to be great to start, but you have to start to be great."

THE BEST PIECE of advice I ever got has been from several different people, and it's just the same message over and over. 'Just keep being you and love you in spite of what life throws at you, there is only one you and only you can do 'you' the best!' After all, everyone else is already taken.

MY PURPOSE in this world is to inspire others to be who they want to be, and to achieve what ever they desire. If all else fails, I will continue to let my sitcom of a life make other people laugh and feel that actually, their life is quite normal!

THE HABITS in my life have had an immense impact on my success, more so than I ever really wanted to accept. Discipline has never been one of my strengths as I'm a 'go with the flow kinda girl' but to have what you truly desire in life there has to be some sort of a sacrifice, no matter how little or big, and let me tell you the sacrifices are so worth the rewards.

THE THOUGHT of any kind of personal development really did not float my boat to be honest with you and just how naive and silly was I to think I could create the kind of lifestyle I have always dreamt of by just doing what I had always done? Really Nat? Your mind is either your best friend or your worst enemy and sometimes it's both. You have a choice to either feed it junk or nourish it, and if I could give you one piece of advice, it is to choose the latter and make that sacrifice, I promise you, your future self will thank you for it. The quicker you choose to nourish your mind, the faster you will get what it is that you desire.

MY DAILY ROUTINE is something that is now a habit and not something I will change anytime soon. Yes, I get up early, (a huge sacrifice for me I can tell you!) this chick loves her sleep so you can imagine the moment you realise that's one of the first things to go. A morning routine of reading, journaling, affirmations and listening is something that has helped me grow into the person I am today.

I THANK Tina so much for not only giving me an opportunity to be a part of this amazing book, but for coming into my life and teaching me so much, not just about spiritual teachings; of which she is right up there in my opinion, but for showing me how to love and to be loved and to accept who I am and fall in love with that.

LIFE IS NOT about the number of things, people or possessions we collect along the way but the actual journey itself and the lessons we learn along the way and the memories we make. My wish is for my children to always have the best memories of their childhood and for them to know that I love them unconditionally with every fibre of my being.

If LIFE HAS TAUGHT me anything it is that our time around here on earth is short and none of us know what tomorrow will bring. So, save yourself a whole load of time and eliminate negative people out of your life who don't serve you anything but gut ache, do whatever it is you want to do with your life and do it with the people who fill you up, make you laugh and love you unconditionally.

I THANK my parents for the lessons and helping me become the woman I am today and the kind of parent I wish to be and for bringing me into this world, after all it was I who chose them.

WE ALL HAVE a choice in life, and I choose love.

# ABOUT THE AUTHOR

## NATALIE BRADLEY

Natalie Bradley is a fun-loving mentor to women and men in business and a successful business owner. Natalie started her online health and wellness business over 7 years ago, making it her mission to empower other men and women to do exactly the same. She is also a Reiki and Bars Practitioner and has a side hobby making personalized candles.

Natalie is passionate about showing people what is truly possible and that when you want to create a certain life you really can have it all and more.

Natalie always knew as a little girl she was different from the rest, and that her life was destined for something amazing and that feeling in her tummy was not one to be ignored.

Whenever she hits an obstacle in her life she firmly believes it is for a reason; to either teach her something or divert her in another direction, so she trusts in 'that feeling in her tummy' and feels her job is to walk the path that is already set out for her.

CONTACT

EMAIL: nataliebradley76@gmail.com

WEBSITE: www.nataliebradley.arbonne.com

LINKEDIN: https://www.linkedin.com/in/nataliebradleyarbonne/

f facebook.com/Nataliebradley

instagram.com/_nataliebradley_

# NICHOLA SPROSON

*H*ave you ever sat back, taken a look at your life and thought... "Wowzers, I created all of that!!!" If you haven't yet, or are not in a place to yet, don't worry! Up until a few years ago I hadn't either.

LIKE MOST PEOPLE, I did not understand that every decision you make, every thought that you have, every gut feeling you ignore, determines the reality that you live and it can change in an instant...if you just allow yourself to open your heart and let it!

LET me take you back to 2015. At nearly 34 years of age I looked like I had it made! On paper my life was great! I was on Maternity leave with my second son Finley. I had a 6 year career as a Police Constable, and my fiancé John was an engineer in the oil industry. With two 2 beautiful boys (Harrison then 3 years old and Finley just 1) our own 3 bedroom house in a lovely quiet location in Dover, Kent and we had just had our wedding day, a weekend long celebration on the top of a cliff in Ilfracombe, Devon with all of our closest friends and family...just perfect! Or so it should have been!!

THE FACT WAS I was so wrapped up in the reality that I thought I should be living, through the judgements of society and others; I failed to see that I had settled into a life that was not mine and that I was not happy living. I was miserable, full of anxiety and I felt trapped. I didn't think I deserved or was worth a life that was better. Feeling stuck, I carried on doing the only thing I knew how to do, push my feelings aside and playing out the role I had given myself, anxiety getting stronger with every push.

DURING THIS TIME my main focus was my career as I was due to return to work after 14 months off on Maternity Leave. If I am really honest with myself now, I have always wanted to help people, but the only reason I became a Police Constable was a last attempt at a good, strong, solid career with a good pension at the end of it - like society led me to believe I needed to have. Let's face it, if you are going to work doing the same job risking your own safety for others for 35 years of your life, you need a decent pension at least!

I WAS 27 years of age when I joined the Police force. I thought that this was it, I was in it for the long haul and there didn't seem like any other option for me, no going back...this was as good as it was going to get! What a crazy mindset to have, I honestly did not think that I would be able to retrain or pursue an alternative career...it was now too late.

BEING a Copper had its ups and downs and the "JOB", well it changes you as a person, it did me anyway. You put walls up, get hardened to the things that you see and deal with without even realising you have...you have to, it is part of the job, it becomes the 'norm' and I was ok with that. Life changes, most of the friends I had fell away and my behaviour changed, with a constant reminder that I was now a pillar of society there to uphold the law 24/7. I never quite got used to that especially since I had been quite the party girl before, but that's a different story. Ha!

To be honest I was pretty lucky and I had a great team of officers around me, all the Inspectors, Sergeants and colleagues I had within the Police all had a strong bond together and the laughs we had to get us through those long shifts makes you a family unit, I will be forever grateful to the support I had from every officer I ever had the pleasure of working with.

On reflection I was a good PC. I did my job and I did it well, but I never felt like I was an officer. It just was not me and I did not enjoy it. I much preferred to sit with the victims of crime and take statements than actually be out there, I don't actually like confrontation, seems so funny looking back that was my actual job for 7 years.

After having my first son Harrison, my whole perception of the Job changed again. I now had a little human being who depended on me, needed ME! Before, I didn't think about the dangers of the job, but they started to become more and more prevalent.

As a Police Constable you face many situations that you would never normally be in, in real life. You detach yourself from the reality of what is going on and if you do not deal with it mentally, it can bite you in the ass! This is what happened to me and was the start of my anxiety!

. . .

In 2014 I was in the report writing room at the station heavily pregnant with my 2nd child Finley. Some of my team were out assisting the Mental Health Team on a routine job. All of a sudden the radios in the office went crazy with shouts that there was a knife and officers were injured. Every available officer upped and left the office...except me!

I sat, hands on a moving stomach, listening to the radio not knowing the extent of the situation and wondering...what if that happened to me! Luckily even though some officers received stab wounds there were no major physical injuries and every officer that returned dealt with the situation with the usual banter...excitement over...next job.

Soon after that I went onto maternity leave forgetting about the incident, or so I thought.

Finley was born and all of a sudden life got crazy. With working in the oil industry, John was away...A LOT and I found myself trying to cope with having a 2 year old and a new-born on my own for the majority of the time. I was up to my neck in night feeds, day feeds, housework, nappies, baby puke (Finley did like to be sick) potty training and Harrison would not leave his brother alone, which meant I had to have one of the boys with me at all times. They could not be together out of my sight.

At this point in my life I had no knowledge about how the Universe works, the Law of Attraction, Angels, Divine Timing or Synchronicity. Now I know that I was majorly out of alignment with myself and my life's purpose and was about to get my butt kicked into gear by the Universe! Something magic happened and my life began to change, events began to unfold before me, and I was ready to listen. Don't get me wrong it gets messier before it gets better but sometimes it all has to come crashing down before you can build yourself back up.

MY YOUNGER SISTER Sarah joined a Network Marketing Company. I had absolutely no interest in the business at all but wanted to support her and help her any way I could. Over the next few months I watched and to my amazement she started to do things out of her comfort zone and looked like she was having fun. I met Sarah's upline 'Abigail Horne' and watched her story unfold with keen interest...I could do that! I had eight months left before I had to return to work and could build the business up when the boys were asleep giving me something to do in the evenings when John was away, and I was just sat in front of the TV wasting away.

WITH EXCITEMENT IN MY BELLY, New Year 2015 I started my own Network Marketing business...I had found the solution to all of my problems and was determined. All I could think of was if I could make enough money John could come home to work locally. I just wanted my family together.

IT WAS Abigail who first introduced me to The Secret Law of Attraction, and the idea that everything you think about you become. This made perfect sense to me and was the first time I started to think about everything as energy. How had I never come across this before? My mind started to open up and I started to see the possibilities I had available to me, and I was willing to work for them.

·  ·  ·

THE BUSINESS TOOK OVER! Every waking minute I would be watching or making training videos, networking or mentoring my small team of twenty. All I could focus on was getting higher up the ladder so I could get John home, and I didn't have to go back to the Police Force. This was about to drastically backfire;

I WAS all over social media showing people how happy I was and how great I was doing but inside I was a mess. Everything was going in slow motion, I stopped going to visit my friends and hardly left the house. By running my business I was fuelling my stress and anxiety, having mood swings and crying at the drop of a hat. When John was home, I made little or no time for us as a family, and I became frustrated and angry that he could not support me. But, how could he support me, I was obsessed and so closed off to what was going on around me that I retreated further inside myself.

BY THE TIME I was due to go back to work I was at breaking point. I was tired, stressed and the anxiety had well and truly kicked in. Even though my relationship with John was at an all-time low, and believe me we have had a few, I longed for him to work closer to home to be a family. But the thought of going back to work as a Police Officer, put me into overdrive. I was in the prison of my own mind and I didn't know how to get out.

FINALLY, I made the decision to go to the Doctor where I was asked if I wanted antidepressants or counselling. I chose both, I needed them.

I RETURNED to work as a Police Officer. Both my Inspector and Sergeant could not have supported me more in trying to integrate me back to work, easing me in very slowly and gently. I went back to the station on light duties, which for me meant working in the office and in civilian clothing (normal clothes). A month or so passed and it was decided that I would go into work still on light duties but in uniform so I could become accustomed to wearing it again. Unfortunately for me some wires were crossed and I was assigned a job out of the station straight away.

THIS INSTANTLY TRIGGERED major anxiety for me and on the way to my locker to pick up my airwaves (radio) I had my first ever panic attack. I dashed to the ladies locker room where I broke down crying, hardly able to breathe just pacing up and down. It was so scary. I had left my mobile phone up in the report writing room which was three floors up...I had to get upstairs. Not wanting to bump into anyone I took the stairs instead of the lift. I bumped into my friend who asked, "Are you okay?" This little sentence felt like the worst thing ever, I was not okay. Not being able to talk about it I dashed into the next toilets where I continued to pace up and down tried to catch my breath, with tears streaming down my face freaking out every time I caught a glimpse of myself in uniform in the mirror...who was this person looking back at me???

A COLLEAGUE CAME into the toilets and saw what an absolute state I was in and went and spoke to my Sergeant, who came into me and calmed me down enough for me to be come out of the toilets. It was then when the embarrassment of the whole ordeal kicked in. I was utterly mortified and felt so so stupid. We went to the canteen as I could not face going back into the office in fear of having another attack in front of my colleagues. It was decided that I was in not fit state to continue my shift and I left to go home. I didn't know it then, but I would never return to do another shift as a Police Constable ever again.

· · ·

AROUND THE SAME time my relationship with John broke down and we separated. I was now a single mum to two young boys, no career and a mortgage to pay. How had it come to this? Everything I had been fighting for, rightly or wrongly, I had lost. The split with John was not an easy one and lead to over a year of arguing and animosity between us. Totally broken I continued with my counselling and ended up having 11 sessions instead of the original 8. If I had not had those sessions, I don't think I would have had the strength to continue and know that deep down the relationship breakdown was for the best, for me, John and the boys, although it did not seem like it at the time.

BELIEVE it or not at this point my Network Marketing business was at its strongest and I was just about to hit my next promotion. But with the weight of the cost of what I had lost I just could not turn up for my business, I had burnt out. In the darkness of that time Abigail was my pillar of light. From the moment I met her she had seen something in me, a strength that I could not see. She believed in me when I did not believe in myself, and this was all I needed to know that I could do anything I put my mind to when the time was right. But now was not that time.

I DID NOT KNOW who I was? I did not like the person who stood in front of me, I did not recognise myself in the mirror. I had no self-confidence, no self-belief, no self-worth. Who was Nichola Sproson? I did not know. I had played the role for so long that I had completely shut down and lost myself along the way...I was numb and hated myself for what I had become and have never felt so alone. I had shut myself off from most of my friends and living in Dover, Kent, away from all of my family I had a very small support system. Not being able to pay the bills or put food on the table, I started to get myself into thousands of pounds worth of debt with my Dad. I went into denial, and into autopilot mode with the boys and although I retreated further into myself with despair, they were my focus my only joy in life. I had to get through this, I had to pull myself together for them. The question was "How?"

TIME FOR A BIT of Divine Intervention! I began to get thoughts pop into my head that I needed to have a card reading, something I had not done for a long time. I would not have said I was spiritual, but I believed there was something bigger and I was open to receiving guidance in any form. People started to randomly give me business cards of tarot readers, and I would see adverts in various places for different clairvoyants and mediums, but none felt right. The message "Write a Facebook post asking for local card readers" kept coming to me and I kept ignoring it. After a couple of weeks a friend wrote the exact message I was being told to write as her status. In the comments two mutual friends recommended the same person, a lady I had become connected with months before as I had approached her about my Network Marketing business. The penny dropped.

HER NAME WAS Tina Pavlou The Angel Lady. I don't know how I had totally missed this, I loved her positive energy and just thought she was a little crazy and super eccentric. I had no idea what an Angel Lady was or did, I just knew she was the one I needed to see and booked a reading for the following week. After the reading I was blown away, I had never experienced anything like it in my life. She knew things she could not have known and was so spot on it freaked me out a bit, in a good way. At the end of the reading she looked me in the eye and said "It's so nice to meet a true sister" and gave me the biggest hug you could imagine. Neither of us knew just how true those words were or of the sistership that was about to unfold.

· · ·

MY SPIRITUAL JOURNEY of transformation and self-healing had well and truly begun!

A COUPLE of days after my reading my life began to explode, as well as my head. Ha! Tina messaged me asking me if I needed some healing as I had just popped into her head. With no idea what 'healing' entailed I just said "Yes" and jumped into my car for the 30 minute drive to Ramsgate. On the way my Mum called to say that my sister Sarah had been rushed into hospital with internal bleeding after a hernia operation. I mentioned this to Tina on arrival an she casually said "Oh that's why you are here so we can send distance healing to your sister" I must admit I thought WTF but went along with it. Tina got me to lie down on the bed of her treatment room and she put on some meditation music. I could not tell you what happened as I was gone within seconds, flat out asleep. When the healing session finished, I came to and Tina said she had sent healing to my sister and that the Angels were with us. "Erm ok if you say so", was my first thought but at the same time I had a feeling that this was the truth.

As SOON AS I stepped my foot out of the door, I received a text from my mum to say that Sarah had just come out of surgery, she was in recovery and fine. What the hell had just happened and what the heck was that healing we just received...I hadn't even asked!!!

TURNS out that the Healing modality was called Usui Reiki and about to change my life forever. Reiki is a phrase the Japanese use for 'Universal Life Force Energy'. The practitioner channels this Universal Life Force Energy in a hands on healing in either a treatment of self-care or for a treatment of others. This energy raises your vibration clears your energy blocks, and enhances health across your physical, mental, emotional and spiritual wellbeing.

. . .

I KNEW this was what I was meant to do and signed up to learn Usui Reiki level 1&2 straight away, with Tina who is a Usui Reiki Master Teacher. I did the two day long courses back to back over a weekend in May 2016. Reiki 1 on the Saturday and Reiki 2 on the Sunday. This is not usual practice as there is a 21 day detoxing period after, but Tina felt this was the right path for me and I trusted her judgement. I trusted her from the moment I met her.

After this weekend my life exploded into change, I was not the same person I was before. I started to become very aware of the fact that everything happens for a reason, and that there is a higher power guiding, assisting and helping us if you only ask for it.

THE FIRST THING that happened was I got myself a Job and the synchronicity around it astounded me and confirmed what I had begun to open up to. My neighbour tagged me in (made me aware of) an advert on social media for an Admin position in an Estate Agents locally. It was perfect for me, 9:30am-1:30pm Monday to Friday which would allow me to do all the pick up and drop offs on the school run, and I had weekends off, so I did not have to worry about childcare for the boys. Now this is the mind-blowing part. Not only was it my perfect job for the time, it was Tina who had posted the Advert and was herself working in the Estate Agents during the day. I had no idea she had another job! You just couldn't make this shit up.

OVER THE NEXT five months up until Tina left the Estate Agents to pursue her career in the Metaphysical full time, I worked alongside her everyday sucking up the knowledge like a sponge during the working day, and at weekends assisting her teaching Usui Reiki classes, becoming a Usui Reiki Master myself in October 2016. I was working hard on healing myself, having Reiki swaps weekly to raise

273

my vibration and keep my energy clear. The higher my vibration got the more day to day life got easier to deal with, I came off the antidepressants and my anxiety vanished.

TO MY SURPRISE I noticed that I started to eat less and less meat, I just did not want it in my body anymore. I had been a big meat eater all of my life and I mean a big meat eater, I was a blue steak kinda girl, but by the time I had completed my Usui Reiki Masters I was Vegetarian. I was not expecting that but apparently it is pretty common for meat eaters to become veggie/vegan the more your vibration rises and the more conscious you become.

NOW THIS MIGHT ALL READ as nice and fluffy but believe you me healing and working through your energy blocks, brings up your shit. The deep rooted stuff you have kept buried inside you for years, it will come out. There is no hiding from it, but if you work through it and release it, the feeling after is just immense. This is what is commonly known as a 'Healing Crisis', as your body is going through a deep healing process. Believe you me they are not pretty, and the mood swings are pretty intense going from raging anger to a blubbering wreck on the floor in seconds. But when it's over you are like, what was that all about and you feel much lighter as your vibration raises higher and higher.

ALONGSIDE DEALING with Healing Crisis I noticed that the people around me started to show their true colours. I started to recognise what friendships were healthy for me and which were toxic. Amongst those who I regarded as my closest friends there were those who turned out to be people I could not trust and as much as it hurt like hell, and as hard as it was, I had to walk away from them and let them go, for myself. I was finally ready to step out of the victimhood, let go of the dramas of others and to put myself first.

In March 2017 I had a minor operation which needed rest and recovery time, so I went to stay at my Dads house with the boys for three weeks. Being back in my home town of Stoke-on-Trent surrounded and supported by my family I felt a shift happen within me...It was time to move home. I had been living in Dover for 13 years but now I was struggling, really feeling the weight of being a single parent. Not getting on with John I had hardly any support network to help with the boys and although I had a network of friends whom I met with during the day at weekends, I found myself alone most evenings once the boys had gone to bed. Our house had recently sold, and I made the decision to put my needs first and move to where I would be supported, and the boys would grow up surrounded by their cousins.

Nearly a year had passed since I had become a Usui Reiki Master when I learnt Angelic Reiki level 1&2 with Tina, who was now also an Angelic Reiki Master Teacher. I learnt how to channel Healing Energy from the Angelic Realms via Healing Angels, Archangels, Ascended Masters and Galactic Healers to promote powerful transformation and healing on the physical, mental and spiritual levels raising my vibration and consciousness towards Ascension. This was proper upping the game to next level of healing and exactly what I needed to assist me in the move back to Stoke.

I started to work more closely with the Angels asking for guidance and telling them out loud what I needed, and you know what I got it too, never once doubting that they wouldn't deliver. I visualised a 3 bedroom house in a quiet area with just a square lawn in the back garden so it was easy to maintain. Within a week of house hunting I found the house, it was the first and only house I viewed.

My next request was for a part time job, that I would enjoy doing with lovely people to work alongside. I received a voice in my head telling me to pop a status on social media asking if anyone knew of any part time work. This time I listened, and this is where the synchronicity comes in again. A friend who I met whilst working my Network Marketing business said she was recruiting and to send her a C.V. I did not know what the job was for, but I did know it was mine. A month later after I had the interview, I started my new part time job as a Customer Sales Officer in a bank whose ethics are in alignment with mine and an amazing team who all get on so well, there really is not a bad word spoken between anyone.

It was now August 2017, just two years since I had first gone to the doctors to receive antidepressants and counselling for anxiety, completely lost in myself - and now I was happy, healthy, supported and surrounded by family. Wow...what a turn around. In the same month I became an Angelic Reiki Master Level 3&4 and an Access Consciousness Bars Practitioner which essentially dissipates the electromagnetic charge that gets locked in our brains by the thoughts feelings and emotions that we have stored over time by lightly touching 32 points on your head.

Loaded with Healing tools I knew I wanted to eventually give back and help others to heal themselves the way I was doing, but I was not quite ready. One of the best pieces of advice I had ever been given was "You have to heal yourself first, before you can heal anyone else" and I did not feel healed enough in myself yet. I felt I had a long way to go and still struggled with self-worth and self-confidence issues.

. . .

I HAD BEEN Vegetarian for over a year now and I had naturally started to give up other animal related products, not drinking milk or having butter. I started to really look at my food and in New Year of 2018 an Integrative Nutrition Health Coaching Course came onto my radar and I began my studies with the Institute of Integrative Nutrition (IIN). This was a total curve ball, but I had never felt so aligned with what I was doing and the path that was unfolding before me.

EVEN WITH ALL of this learning I still had work to do on healing myself. I signed up to do Tina's next courses in Theta Healing. Theta is the purest healing energy. It teaches you how to go into a Theta meditative state and prayer to clear limiting beliefs and live with positive thoughts through Creator of all that is. It is through Theta that I have cleared and removed most of my limiting beliefs, have realised my self-worth, and come into balance with myself. I had done the groundwork, and now was the time to really dig deep and face my inner demons. It is through Theta that I realised Forgiveness is the most powerful and freeing tool you have in your box, not only for others but for yourself too. If you do not forgive you cannot move on and you stay stuck, it is as simple as that!

WHEN I SAID HEALING CRISIS' are not pretty...I meant it! From January when I took the Basic Theta Practitioner course to April when I completed the Dig Deeper Practitioner course with the Advanced course in the middle, I was in one continuous Healing Crisis...I was not easy to live with!! Fine one minute, in bed braking the next, joking around then snapping in frustration...all part of the healing process...you have to let it out!!!!

. . .

You see with all the healing I had done previously I was now in a space where I felt safe and strong enough to deal with past traumas that I had blocked from my memory and not told a sole...and Theta Healing sure was unlocking some big ones, but I could now view them from a space of learning and forgiveness for myself, instead of falling into the victimhood of knowing the truth...no matter how hard it is to see.

I am not going to go into specifics as I am not a victim and do not want to be treated as such. But for the sake of my friends and family reading this I will say that during my younger adult life where I have experimented with alcohol and drugs, there have been times where I was taken advantage of and even though that is not okay, I am, and I have forgiven them and more importantly myself...I have moved forward, I am no longer paralysed in those memories.

In Kent I now had a strong spiritual community. We have shared each other's secrets, laughed, cried, completely broke down, picked each other up and healed together. Tina through her knowledge and eagerness to help others heal had created a sisterhood so strong we consider each other family. And even though I now live in Stoke-on-Trent I never feel alone, and I am not...we have each other no matter where in the world we are.

I did not realise the full power of safety in the sisterhood until I was on one of Tina's Glastonbury retreats in June 2018. This is the retreat, the weekend where I had the most shifts personally with loving and accepting my body. For as long as I can remember I have always been self-conscious of my body, belly too wobbly, boobs too small, back too broad, legs too short and stumpy etc. This was the chatter I had in my head when I looked in the mirror or at a picture of myself...always criticizing.

TINA HAD ARRANGED for a private visit to the White Spring, a Temple built in a Victorian Well House at the bottom of Glastonbury Tor where the White Waters flow. The White Water is pure and has healing properties of calcite (The Red Waters flow opposite in the Chalice Well) Inside the sacred space of The White Spring, there are no windows the only light is from the hundreds of candles on the shrines. There are pools of healing White Water that you can bathe in and a full immersion pool. Everyone in the group had put on their swimming costumes/bikinis but I did not have any intention of getting in the water, so I didn't go prepared, but to my surprise I had the overwhelming feeling to bare all. I stripped down to my knickers and in I went, full immersion!!!

I HAD BEEN to the White Waters nine months prior, on one of Tina's previous retreats and had felt too self-conscious to do this! But there, in that Well surrounded by my soul sisters, hand in hand, chanting was the most connected and magical experience I have had...I didn't care that I was pretty much naked, I had never felt more liberated or alive.

THE VERY SAME weekend a soul sister Helen Porter, through her Divine Feminine Workshop taught me the most profound, life changing tool for me for my own body confidence. I am not sure whether my new nearly naked experience in the Well had woke my body up and brought it to attention or I was just now ready to change the way I felt about myself, how I viewed myself and most importantly how I spoke to myself.

· · ·

HELEN PLAYED a song "I am the light of my soul" Sirgun Kaur & Sat Darshan Singh. The words and music were so beautiful I was instantly moved. She said that if I played this song every day and danced naked to myself in the mirror I would have major shifts in the way I viewed my body. This resonated so much that as soon as I got home from the retreat...this is what I began to do! Every morning I danced naked while singing the words "I AM THE LIGHT OF MY SOUL, I AM BEAUTIFUL, I AM BOUNTIFUL, I AM BLISS, I AM, I AM" As hard and as weird as it was to do at the beginning, to my amazement it completely shattered the twisted image of my body that I had formed in my head...I looked nothing like what I thought I looked like!! I felt great and my confidence soared! I have done this practically every morning since!!

I STARTED to ask my body what it would like to wear and when I tried clothes on, if they looked bad, instead of my negative self-talk I switched my thinking to "Ah ok body so you're telling me that you don't want to wear this...ok let's try something else" And to my surprise at 37 years of age my body decided it looked good in a crop top showing my midriff...I am not toned by all means and have a mum tum but I don't care, I look and feel good just the way I am...what a difference 3 years makes!!

THE HEALING and empowerment journey is one that never ends, but right now I am a strong single woman, who knows who she is and loves herself and her body. I know what works for me, how to have balance in my life and to always trust my gut instinct. There are no negative influences in my life, instead I only have people who I can trust and build me up, with a sisterhood that is so strong it is a family.

IT IS NOW MARCH 2019, I have been on the most amazing journey of self-discovery and healing which will continue as I grow. I am a published co-author in two books an Alternative Holistic Healer and I have launched my own business as an Integrative Nutrition Health Coach empowering women to feel Balanced, Beautiful and Body Confident!

Wowzers, I created all of that!!!

Xxx

# ABOUT THE AUTHOR

## NICHOLA SPROSON

Who is Nichola Sproson??? This is the question that fuelled Nichola to look deep within and find out who she truly was. A healing journey of transformation, self-acceptance and self-love that would lead her to assist others on their own journeys of self-healing.

Nichola, is a mother of 2 young boys and an Integrative Nutrition Health Coach & an Alternative Holistic Healer in Stoke-on-Trent, Staffordshire. She is both a Usui Reiki Master and an Angelic Reiki Master and continues to expand her knowledge and self-healing quest through seeking out new modalities to add to her practice along the way, including Theta Healing Technique and Access Consciousness Bars and Suara Sound Healing. Although Nichola has always wanted to help others she firmly believes that "You can't help others to heal if you don't heal yourself first."

A Vegetarian for over 2 years, and a desire to heal from the inside out, Nichola realised she had little to no knowledge of health and nutrition. Aligning herself with the Institute of Integrative Nutrition she began her studies. Nichola knows that everyone is different, everyone has different needs, and no one knows you better than yourself. All the answers are within.

Nichola's mission is to empower other females to listen to their own bodies, work through any blocks and make small sustainable changes to heal themselves by themselves, so they feel  Balanced, Beautiful and Body Confident.

**Contact:**
Email - nicholasproson@gmail.com
Website - www.nicholasproson.co.uk
LinkedIn – www.linkedin.com/in/nicholasproson

[f] facebook.com/nsproson

# NINA WHITE

*M*y life has been a bumpy ride and I suppose you could say that spiritually I have lived most of my years in the dark. I lived my life as best as I could, and I had survived, but life was stressful, lonely and always seemed to be hard work. To everyone else, I was the life and soul of the party and enjoyed the company of others. I thought this was happiness, but it wasn't. I thought I needed people to fill that huge hole in my life. I hadn't learned to be happy in my own company and deep down inside was a very insecure and anxious little girl.

ALTHOUGH I HAVE ALWAYS BEEN aware of my spirituality, my real spiritual journey didn't really start until meeting Tina again a year ago. Until that point, life had just taken over and all those senses and weird feelings I had been experiencing were ignored. It frightened me to feel so different to everybody else at such a young age, so I pushed it away and hid from it. Of course, it would always bubble over and let me know it was there, but I just didn't know what it really was and how I could use it.

. . .

I HAD the gift of clairvoyance from a very young age. I would see the future in my dreams and I could just sense things, I knew where things were hidden, I knew who was coming to the door and I could tell good people from bad. If someone with a bad vibration came into the house, which was quite a regular occurrence as I grew up, I would pick up on it and react to it by misbehaving. I had always believed I was depressed and over sensitive from a very young age, but I now know I am an empath. I would pick up on people's sadness, loneliness and fear and take it on board.

IT USED to feel like I had a little black cloud above my head. I remember going shopping and seeing elderly people on their own and sense their pain and loneliness I was really affected by it. It affected the little girl I was and how I behaved. I was also very aware of the spirit of my Auntie Jennie. Jennie died of cancer in her twenties and she would visit me frequently throughout my life in dreams at poignant times. In later years, I developed "Clairsentience" abilities and could pick up on fragrances such as the lavender of my nan's talcum powder and the faint whiff of the whiskey that my grandad used to drink.

BUT AS I SAID, I pushed all of this aside and got on with my life. I had developed a kind of survival mode from a child from having to become independent at a very young age. I was able to shut off by bottling up my emotions. Life had made me strong, but I did not realise I needed to work through those experiences and release the pain to live a healthy and balanced life.

MY LIFE, without realising had become a constant battle of one stress to another, I was thriving on it as it was all I knew. I'd harboured fear, grief, hurt and pain. I'd let it ferment and fester inside of me, preventing me from moving forward and achieving my potential. I was hanging on to old beliefs that I wasn't good enough and that I was bad. I didn't know how to release any of this, I didn't know how to be mindful. I didn't have a safety blanket of love and protection. It was just me against the world. By not knowing how to deal with any of my problems I was just snowballing out of control and never managing myself properly.

I PERSONALLY BELIEVE ALL these stressful events happen for a reason, we either work though them and learn from them or we allow them to have a huge effect on who we are, who we become and ultimately on our health and wellbeing. Without release, these events shape our future and living a life on the edge in a constant state of fight or flight causes our bodies to be at unease, which may ultimately lead to disease, which in my case it did.

WE ALL EXPERIENCE stressful events throughout our lives. Hindsight has provided me with the ability to look back at the past to see where things went wrong. There are several events that I believe may have contributed to my health and wellbeing.

So, my story begins with my childhood.

I WAS RELATIVELY happy up until the divorce of my mother and father. But for as long as I can remember, I never felt loved. My mother lost her younger sister to cancer and I think she just gave up on life and being a parent. She started drinking and disappearing, leaving my sister and I alone most of the time. She completely cut off from us emotionally. She then moved us two hours away from my father and our family to embark upon a lifestyle of partying and drinking. My sister and I were neglected for many years and were deprived the love of a mother and normal family life. We never had any clean clothes or nice school uniform. We didn't have anything. We both had to endure some awful situations and watch my mother spiral downwards into a very bad place. We didn't see much of my father or the rest of our family. As I grew older, I started to rebel against this behaviour and the relationship between my mother and I began to break down further. My mother would play my sister and I off against each other, because my sister would be quiet, and she enjoyed turning us against each other. I would argue with my Mother constantly and in turn would be told how bad I was, that there was something wrong with me and how she didn't love me and hated me. She seemed to blame me for everything that went wrong, rather than blame herself. I can remember feeling a constant hurtful pain in my chest and I grew up feeling like there was something wrong with me.

I THINK my first experience of pure fear was aged 12, returning home from school one winters evening to find our flat completely empty. My mother had taken my sister and had left me behind. I was terrified. I did not know where to turn and our telephone only received incoming calls. I reversed the charges to my grandmother and told her what had happened. She told me if she had a pair of wings she would come and rescue me, then promised to call back. Shaking, frightened and alone and sat in the dark I had my first panic attack. I couldn't breathe, the room started to spin, and I didn't know what was happening to me. I felt so alone and sad. Then the telephone rang. It was my Dad. He told me to pack my things, to stay calm and that he had ordered me a taxi to drive me the two hours to his house in London.

So, I then went to live with my Dad. During those years I became extremely close to my paternal grandmother Betty and we would spend every weekend together. It was here that I experienced the real unconditional love that I never received from my mother. She truly loved me.

As I GREW OLDER, I needed my mother, so two years later I moved back but she hadn't changed. I was only there for financial reasons, as my father would pay her more maintenance money. She had met a very abusive partner who used to drink heavily and beat her. At times she would scream from behind the door to call the police, only to send them away and stay with him. It was a very unhealthy environment to be in and it wasn't long before things went downhill. I don't think either of them wanted a rebellious teenager reacting to their terrible behaviour under the same roof, so they became very nasty to me and at 14 years old, I finally ended up leaving home for good and putting myself into voluntary care. I lived with foster parents and there had the normality of a family life.

At 18 I left home to live in my first little bedsit. They were fun, new and exciting times and the independence was exhilarating. I soon met who I now refer to as my first love, at age 19. We were drawn to each other instantly. Our childhoods were similar, our personalities were exactly the same. We could make each other laugh just by looking at each other. It was a very deep connection and I truly believe Perry was my soul family. Although our intimate relationship dissipated, it was our friendship that remained solid throughout the years into adulthood and I loved him dearly. He was a huge part of my life and became like a family member, a brother, a confidant, a true friend. Just knowing he was in my life was reassuring to me. We didn't have a proper family, so we had to create our own and I know we were both an important part of each other's lives.

. . .

ROLL on twelve years and the both of us had grown older and had children. I was 33. I had just come back from a family holiday and I remember going up into the spare room to check my emails and there was one from one of Perry's friends telling me to call as he had some important news; but I just knew. I ran to the toilet to be sick before calling to hear the news that Perry had died of an accidental drug overdose. I felt the same pain again in my heart, the familiar rise of anxiety in my chest. I'd been left alone again! I was catatonic for two days. I could not function; the pain and shock were unbearable, and it took me many years for that grief to subside. I literally felt like a part of me died that day, like a little light went out. I still miss Perry, but I am reassured to know he is always with me.

ABOUT 3 MONTHS after his death, he visited me in a dream. It was so lucid. He sat at the end of my bed and I could have touched him. He told me not to worry about him, that heaven was amazing. He sat there talking to me for a few minutes and then he said goodbye. I then woke up and was filled with the most indescribable feeling of love. Every pore of my body tingled with love and I truly knew, he really had come to let me know he was ok, and this truly affirmed to me that there was more to this world, that there was an afterlife. I began to realise that all of those spiritual experiences I had as a child were real!

AT 21 I lost my grandmother to breast cancer, she was aged just 73. It was a short illness, but I was heartbroken as I loved her dearly. Again, the pain stayed with me like a dagger through my heart. My last memory of my grandmother was visiting her in hospital shortly after her diagnosis. She was yellow from jaundice but spritely and happy to see me. She had just got the hotel radio to play 'I just called to say I love you', something she'd always sing to me down the phone. Then she took my hand and told me how much she loved me. She died two months later. But I always feel her with me. Several months after this I found a lump in my own breast and was convinced I too had breast cancer, I had to undergo some surgery and removal of a benign lump, but this was to start a twenty year relationship with the breast clinic and a fear that stayed with me, that I would one day get cancer.

AT 31, I had a child and got married but it was a very unhappy marriage. We were two very different personalities. I was very suffocated and sad and knew I could not endure a life with this person. He was very cruel and unkind to me and frequently called me names and wouldn't speak to me for days on end. It was miserable and although I wanted the perfect life and family for my son, because I had never had that for myself, I knew that this marriage was not perfect. After the final straw of being shouted and sworn at, I asked him to leave and then had to endure a five-year process of court proceedings and a very messy divorce. He made things so difficult for me and every day of these times were filled with high anxiety and stress. I don't think I ever relaxed for one moment until it was all over.

WHEN I MET who would become my second husband, it was like a breath of fresh air. We had so much fun and began travelling the world together and doing the things I had never done in my previous relationships. It just felt natural and he was very good with my son.

AFTER A YEAR or so we started trying for a baby. He didn't have children and really wanted a child of his own, but it wasn't happening naturally. We started the process of IVF in Prague, but cycle after cycle failed and it really started to put a strain on our relationship. The excitement and hope of a new cycle only to be dashed by the disappointment of failure as the months and months flew by. It all felt so cruel. I already had already had a healthy pregnancy, so I really felt like my body was working against me. By the time we had been trying for nearly 3 years, I had started to come to terms that maybe it just wasn't going to happen, that my age was holding us back despite feeling young and keeping very fit and healthy. I couldn't change the age of those eggs inside me, despite reading the endless stories and posts of women getting pregnant over 40 on Dr Google. It remained elusive for me.

AROUND THIS TIME my younger sister was diagnosed with a high-grade bone cancer and had to have a year of aggressive chemotherapy and limb saving surgery, which meant her leg was amputated and a titanium leg was put in its place. She was working in Bermuda and had to move back the UK for treatment. It was a very stressful time and I spent most of the year travelling to and from Birmingham to support her.

IT WAS heart-breaking to watch your younger sister lose her hair and struggle to walk. But she made it through the treatment, made a full recovery and is now back working in Bermuda and is in remission. She maintained a positive attitude throughout and always believed she would be ok.

Meantime, my husband and I decided to give IVF one last try in Russia with a donor egg. Amazingly it worked, the egg began to grow, and we were filled with happiness. But as the weeks went by, I knew something was wrong, I didn't have the usual morning sickness and I was experiencing quite severe period pains. I just had a sense my body was trying to tell me something. I took myself of to hospital where I was given the devastating news that the baby embryo had stopped growing. The sadness between my husband and I was palpable. I felt that I had let him down and I knew in my heart that was our last chance and I couldn't put my body and heart through anymore. Cue more intense sadness and loss. I had to have a surgical procedure to remove the foetus the next week. It was harrowing as I was awake through the procedure, but little did I know then, that this had happened for a reason!

ABOUT A MONTH LATER, I was showering in the bathroom when I noticed a big hard lump on the outside of my breast. Now, I have had lumps and bumps throughout the last twenty years, so I wasn't overly concerned, but this lump was different. I made an appointment with my Doctor, who instantly referred me to the breast clinic, but this took several weeks. Eventually I was seen by the specialist who didn't appear at all worried and referred me for an ultrasound. A few weeks passed, and I was having my ultrasound scan, being told I just had lumpy breasts and having a cyst aspirated. Roll on a few more weeks, Christmas had just been and gone and I was back with the Consultant being told I'm ok and it is just lumpy breasts. But again, my gut told me otherwise and I said to the Consultant, "Look, this isn't right, the lump is growing, it's causing me a lot of pain and I have discharge coming from my nipple!"

AFTER A LOT OF STRONG WORDS, my consultant relented and sent me for an MRI. Weeks passed by, then I was back with the Dr being told the MRI showed the tissue was abnormal but that she still didn't believe it was cancerous but would do I biopsy. My intuition unfortunately was right. A week later I was sat in the waiting room and I saw the Macmillan nurse walk into the room before the Doctor and then they called my name. I just knew as the fear engulfed me, I walked in to the room. "The biopsy has confirmed you have cancer!" Those words changed my life forever. I was never to be the same person I was before that day. But I don't mean it in a negative way. I didn't realize in that moment, but cancer was the start of my rebirth. Treatment began quickly, and I would describe this time as an out of body experience. It didn't feel like I was me. I was on autopilot, on a fast train rolling through all the stations, caught on this journey of chemotherapy, drugs and appointments. I had switched off. My body was at war with itself!

BUT I COULDN'T UNDERSTAND why this had happened. I had a great diet and went to the gym every day, but I still got cancer. My gut feeling was telling me that I needed to heal myself both physically and emotionally. I can't pinpoint when the cancer may have started growing, or when my body first started changing but the specialists believe it had been several years.

WHEN I LOOK at the huge stress events in my life, the abandonment, the loss of my grandmother and fear of cancer, the loss of a close friend, the stressful relationships and the failed IVF, I can see how these all could have been a trigger. I had carried all that pain from those events around with me for years. It was always there inside of me. So, I knew I had work to do, but I still didn't know how!

I STARTED with a recommendation by a friend to see two ladies called Gloria and Hellie. I was so lucky to find them. All through my cancer treatment, Gloria taught me the power of positive thinking whilst Hellie gave me Reiki Healing. Week after week, Gloria, a trained hypnotherapist, would put me into a deep meditative state and repeat positive affirmations that told me my body was well, that my body was free of cancer and all power was within. My body started to believe it was well and I became stronger. I truly believe this got me through all the treatment and kept my mind from being overwhelmed with fear. I would repeat the affirmations every day and every evening before I slept and I'm still a great believer in affirmations.

AFTER MY TREATMENT FINISHED, I found myself in a strange place. I didn't have the safety net of hospital appointments and I was suddenly left to my own devices. What do I do now? I knew I had to do something more to continue my healing.

I HAVE KNOWN Tina for many years and have received fantastic readings from her at different times throughout my life. She has always been correct with her predictions for me and had actually sat in my lounge many years beforehand and told me my whole life would change at 43, which it did! I have watched her transition into the most amazing healer and teacher that she is today.

So, during this period of limbo after my treatment, I woke after dreaming about Tina. She came to me in the dream and we were walking on a beautiful beach together holding hands and I was feeling well. I had long flowing hair and a beaming smile, I felt so happy.

UPON WAKING, I knew it was a sign and I had to get in touch with her. Luckily, she fitted me in the following week. She gave me some Theta Healing and Reiki, I instantly felt the power of the healing. She explained to me about un-ease and disease and did some clearing on me. It was like a thunderbolt and I knew something had just happened. I decided to learn Reiki there and then. It is a decision that would change my whole life and it opened up so many doorways and introduced me to the most amazing souls who I now call my soul family.

BECOMING ATTUNED in Angelic Reiki was where my true healing began, and I was reborn. I felt like I had been enveloped in love and protection and now whatever happened, everything would be how it should, because the universe had my back. I could physically feel my body healing as the energies passed into me.

ON THAT VERY FIRST day of Angelic Reiki Attunements, I had travelled back from London after having a Pet Scan to investigate some pains I had been having. I was very frightened that the cancer had returned, and I was finding it extremely difficult to relax. But during my very first healing, I received a message and saw a group of angels surrounding me, telling me that everything would be ok. I instantly felt at ease. The fear subsided and a week later, I received the news that everything was clear.

As I CONTINUED with my Angelic Reiki Masters, I again received a beautiful and reassuring message from Mother Mary. She was holding a wicker basket and with her other hand was throwing out silver and gold butterflies indicating transformation and I knew this was a sign that my path had changed. My vibration had lifted and those feelings I'd experienced as a child were more powerful than ever. My psychic ability and intuition are so much stronger.

I HAVE DONE a lot of work on myself and continue to do so and I continue to heal. I have released the pain and beliefs that I was harbouring. I have met with my inner child and have given her a huge cuddle and told her what an amazing and strong woman I have grown up to be.

TINA and my family of soul sisters and brothers have provided me with the unconditional love that I needed. As my healing is a journey, I still have days where the fear can encroach and although I now have the ability to self-heal, I know that I can reach out to my soul family and ask for help, somebody is always there. It is a pure love that we all have for each other and there is no other love like it. I feel safe. I feel whole and it is a path that will only move forward and become better. I am always learning to be a better version of myself.

IF I CAN TAKE one thing from my journey it is that I truly believe that keeping a positive mind is the key. I always try and avoid panic and anxiety. Of course, that's not always possible, but if you can keep those periods to as smaller time as possible, you are helping your body to heal. If we suffer prolonged periods of anxiety, we are telling our bodies that we are not well. So, whether that's reading, yoga, fishing, Reiki, Theta or meditation, whatever you can do to keep your mind quiet, will only help. Take time to sit back and let the world keep turning, everything will be how it should be.

I BECAME AN ANGELIC REIKI MASTER & teacher and Theta Healer to firstly heal myself but in the process I naturally became a healer, and I am now able to help other people diagnosed with cancer and other life-threatening illnesses. I regularly give Reiki and Theta sessions as well as distance healing. Through this medium I can help people to keep their minds out of fear and to release the inner beliefs and experiences that have been preventing healing. I am in the process of organising healing weekends to inspire and to teach how I have changed my mindset and how I live healthily in body and mind with diet, exercise, complementary therapies and Reiki and Theta. I still remain in remission!

# ABOUT THE AUTHOR

## NINA WHITE

Nina White is an Angelic Master, Teacher and Theta-healer with a background in counselling. With a passion for travelling and meeting people from different cultures, Nina regularly hosts foreign students at her beautiful home by the sea. She also accommodates many students that are learning Reiki and Theta.

After leaving University with a degree in Natural Science, Nina deviated from the scientific path and began a career in supporting others. Alongside work, she volunteered for a well known charity and regularly supported young parents with a wide range of difficulties, which led to her training in counselling.

Always spiritual, Nina's healing journey really began after she survived a diagnosis of breast cancer. She realised that many of her life experiences and beliefs may have contributed to her ill health and began to work on her body and mind by utilising holistic therapies, exercising and changing her diet. This naturally led to her becoming a Reiki Master and Theta Healer.

She believes that the use of Reiki and Theta healing has been a fantastic medium for restoring her mind, body and spirit by allowing her to clear old beliefs that prevented her from healing and she now lives her life, thriving in a new positive way. This journey of self healing, led to her becoming a healer of others.

She has made it her mission to help and assist other cancer survivors to find a positive path after a diagnosis and she regularly offers Reiki and Theta to clients that have faced this life changing experience with amazing results. She plans to offer weekend retreats where you will be able to fully immerse in this healing and experience the amazing benefits of Reiki, Theta and other holistic therapies that have been part of her healing journey.

**Contact**
Email: Ninawhite2@hotmail.com
Facebook: Mavis Wanderlust
Facebook Group: www.facebook.com.groups/Orareiki
Instagram: Ora Reiki

# OLIVIA WONG

*H*ave you ever known there was more to this life than the here and now? have you felt the inner depths of despair and frustration and felt so close to walking through a death door? no longer wanting to be a part of this world? I have been there so many times, from as young an age as I can remember. I've never wanted to live this life, to learn these lessons, to be in this skin, to have those parents, those family members or those friends. So many times, I have wanted to give up, to walk away, never seeing the lesson, but being sucked up by the emotion and the desperation and the selfishness.

AS THE MEMORIES OF THE 'TRICKS' I used to do left me as I grew, one spiritual memory did stay with me and it was this memory that gave me hope and inspiration to there being another world, other dimensions and lessons to learn. I can remember my life as a baby a lot, but one thing stayed with me all of these years; the memory of me being no older than 15 weeks, laying in my carry cot on the sofa. I kicked my legs and my feet touched the bottom, so I started to push – this pushing enraged my parents and they began arguing about how they couldn't afford to buy me somewhere new to sleep – I vividly remember stopping crying and looking over my shoulder and seeing my wife and 2 children from the life I'd just left. I visualised myself as the husband and father that they had just lost, and I longed to be with them, I was so, so sad to be in this life with those terribly young and violent parents hardly able to deal with their own emotions let alone having a baby in the mix to care for.

I ALWAYS KNEW there was an energy, something greater than us, something which was 'in charge' but between the ages of 5 and 37 it was just like I'd forgotten, like my sense of this energy was just gone. I just wasn't feeling it or more than likely I'd forgotten it existed. As a child I was made to think I had an over active imagination, so I began to keep my conversations with 'God' as something I did in my private time, when I went to bed. I prayed he'd protect me, take all of this pain away but I truly felt like no one was listening and so I lost hope. That little girl with no one in the world but a Nanna and a God but the God just wasn't doing what I wanted him to.

As THE VIOLENCE GREW, I began to retract from this life, like I'd left a part of me there (later revisited and healed using Matrix) like I was truly alone. I was an only child up until the age of 12 and my parents were hard-core party goers, party hosts and recreational drug users and dealers. There'd often be drug shrapnel left after another long night and the house was always such a mess, with never any food in the cupboards. I guess my mum just didn't really 'do' mothering very well and there was definitely no intimacy between us, she'd kick me out of the house to play in the street as soon as I could dress myself. She would palm me off with my nan or friends or any baby sitter who would be willing to have me and I was grateful for that too; her violent rages would often leave me with chunks of hair missing, fat lips, bruises and more marked, a damaged soul which found it very hard to let anyone in.

GOING BACK to these memories using Matrix Re-imprinting have been the most cathartic. Seeing that 2-year-old who'd just had a temper tantrum in the buggy over dropping her ice lolly, remembering her mum promising her something nice when she got home, to then triggering the memories of the first time she was violently assaulted. Seeing things from her mum's perspective, and then remembering at that time her mum's own mum had recently died, has helped me with forgiving her.

BEING BORN an unwanted child of two teenage parents is a lot for a child to endure, the physical violence, the arguments and inconsistencies were reasons for any child to look for another world in which to lose themselves in. During this time, I made friends with spirits, I could read people and would know their names before I met them and knew whether someone was good or bad. I would feel energies and talk to spirits and move objects with my mind, I would tell people things about themselves and could easily see people's auras and could tell what was going to happen in the future. I role played with the boy/girl twins using my dolls, I practised being a mum, ready for when I grew up – I called them David and Dawn and held them awkwardly but affectionately in my arms. I kept these traits a secret especially as my mum would often tell me that she could see everything I did because she was a witch – I didn't want people thinking I was bad too!

NAN'S HOUSE and school were both safe havens from the world of neglect and abuse at home. My Nanna was as warm as apple pie, she loved me unconditionally, seriously let down by life and her husband

- a grandad who didn't believe I was his son's daughter and would jeer and torment me with his wooden walking stick regularly. At this time, I loved my dad but I didn't really know him - I felt a separation from him that would never be resolved – I knew he wanted me to be something I couldn't, although I never really knew what that was – possibly a son.

MOVING to the countryside from the city when I was 9 brought new triumphs and tribulations. On the plus side, we had a beautiful large new home with fields and streams all around. I'd spend the days playing with friends, borrowing and making, chopping and sawing, filling up the pond and fishing out fish from a neighbours to fill up ours. Dad still worked away but I had a new-found freedom from that of living in a city. It didn't take long for my parents to make their mark, my mum with her bright red hair and embarrassing dress sense quickly fell out with neighbours and friends leaving me feeling less popular and increasingly trying to keep what went on at home out of the public domain. Holidays to stay at my auntie's house in Kent were great and I'd come back being touched by the sun and with a renewed energy. At the end of the summer when I was 11 my mum met me from the train with the news that I would (finally) have a sibling early the following year, all being well.

AND SO, in April 1983 my baby sister was born followed by a move from my beautiful life in Lincolnshire to Kent. Three years later another sister was born – two biological younger sisters – I should have been so proud, but life really couldn't have been any worse in that awful terraced house away from the beautiful fields, beautiful friends and my beautiful Nanna, I just wanted to go home. I needed to get away from the arguments, the shouting, and my father, who I discovered had an affinity to alcohol and marijuana and a temper that went with it!

.  .  .

WHEN I WAS WORKING as a Saturday girl at Superdrug in 1988, I walked into the shop one evening after school to do a shift and I met the man who was to become my husband…twelve years after our first meeting… I knew as soon as our eyes met that he was the one. He swept me off my feet with gifts and lifts and money, and for a girl like me with nothing but an unsafe, abusive home to go to, no coat or scarf, he felt like my knight in shining armour.

A YEAR or so later when I was just 16, my mum asked me if I was still seeing 'him'. My dad told me to get on the pill and get out of the house. I couldn't believe the day had come that we could finally be together. I packed my bags and met my boyfriend at the end of the road, I told him the day had come, and that I was free to be with him – he was NOT impressed. I didn't have anywhere else to go, I spoke to my auntie who used to host students, I told her I could pay her the same amount as her students did if I worked every night after college – she said 'no' as she didn't want to fall out with my dad, so with great reluctance I moved into a place where I knew I wasn't really wanted. I left college as the logistics were a nightmare and began an A-level course the year after, whilst working full time in Mothercare.

LIFE WAS HARD, we could barely make ends meet, we went 2 years without a cooker, washing machine or a bed. But being the dutiful girlfriend, I found a way and tried so hard to make him happy. I hand washed all of the clothes, hoovered and cleaned and was quite house proud, I was really proud of this little life I'd created – or so I told myself…

THE ANGER WAS PRETTY quick to emerge, and everything was my fault, but I had nowhere else to go. I witnessed temper tantrums, verbal abuse and manipulation. I cried and cried myself to sleep, praying for someone to remove me from this torture but no one came, and I'd made my bed. I was a no one, living a nothing life and I needed someone to rescue me, I'd prayed as a child to be grown up, to get me away from my parents and this was all I felt I was worth – I made the best out of a bad situation and hung in because of the love I had in my heart for this man.

MY PARENTS WERE PLANNING on moving abroad to Canada when I was just 16, the day the taxi left the outside of my Auntie's house after the farewell party was the most momentous of my life. It was all over, all of it! I cried from the relief of them going, I really did, they were never going to affect me or my life again – I needed a mum, just not that one.

IN JANUARY 1993 our beautiful baby girl Grace Sui-Yan Wong was born. She was perfect in every way and I was the best mum to her I knew how to be because of the love from my Nanna. I adored being a mum and despite an out of body experience at the horrendous birth I knew she was a precious gift. Whilst her dad was away at work, we had the best times; I sang with her and played with her and cuddled her and she was everything I ever dreamed of. Despite her dad working away and not really engaging with our lives, I loved her unconditionally. I completed a degree and we married in August 2000 and in October 2000 our second beautiful, precious daughter Mei-Li Olivia Wong arrived by C-section. Jet black hair and the most beautiful nature, my care-free easy baby was born and I loved my girls more than life itself and cared for them the best I could.

WE'D SECURED a local business so that their dad could be more involved and we could live and work together but it wasn't long before the anger re-emerged and I was faced with a very angry man whom I couldn't speak my truth in front of. Things were crazy whilst we re-mortgaged the house and purchased our business and when our second daughter was just 7 months old, the day before we were due to fly to the Canaries, I had a scan confirming a twin pregnancy, I was in total shock at the fact I was going to have 3 babies under 15 months old. I laughed and then cried and then laughed and doubted that the pregnancy would result in two healthy babies.

MY NANNA WAS NOW LIVING in Kent. As a grown woman I didn't see her as much as I would have liked due to family difficulties. This is the woman who said she'd 'never have another man gift-wrapped' and pressed the unusual silver-cased coloured candle in my hand. Olivia Baynes, my Nanna, my beautiful angel, died in March 2003, aged just 83.

IZAAC YAT-FEI WONG and Alexandra Yin Wong were delivered by C-section on the 12<sup>th</sup> February 2002 at 38 weeks, my perfect boy/girl twins. I'd had a difficult pregnancy towards the end with pre-eclampsia and Pubic Symphysis Disorder. I have no idea how I carried them for so long, walking was difficult as was breathing and doing just menial tasks was hard, but I'd continued working for the family business towards the end of the pregnancy. I felt like a tired super-hero, not wanting to let my husband down. He had a lot on his plate but so did I, the early signs were there of him already being disengaged with the children and this was exacerbated once I'd brought the twins home.

LIFE WAS HARD, we moved into a beautiful Oast House on the outskirts of Canterbury and I was lonely, the house was awful to live in, I literally felt like I was being watched all of the time. Bringing up the children was hard work with no respite and having to rush to help out at the business with 4 children in tow. I thought he had grown up by then having four mouths to feed, but it was then that I saw the real essence of the father of my children, an emotionally inept man who would storm off in a rage and disappear for days leaving me holding the babies. I cried during endless nights from desperation, searching frantically for the Samaritan's number, for someone to hear me. I know I couldn't go anywhere because my children needed me, but I didn't know what I needed and who I was. I hadn't spoken with my parents since I was 20 after a horrendous trip to Canada.

I STARTED WORKING part-time as a teacher at a local independent school. It gave me a little sanity, pocket money and got me out of working for the family business. The children were in nursery two days a week and we were due to move again to a beautiful house right next door to the school, I felt we were finally heading somewhere with our lives. The following year I secured a full-time position at a local state school and the kids came along with me, I could keep them close by my side and take them to and from school, their dad slowly began to slip away. The contract was for a year so on completing my year I took a job at a very challenging school in Dover. I unfortunately put my kids on the back burner and thrust myself wholeheartedly into this intense role only to emerge some 4 years later with a few bad experiences under my belt. I was lost, lonely and utterly exhausted. I needed some time out to catch up with my precious children.

SLEEPING during this period was proving difficult, I was constantly worrying about how I was going to put food on the table and took to making bread and baking lots. I was in a financial rut and was managing just on my child benefit to feed and clothe the children. Their dad barely came home, and I just plodded along, needing something to help me settle, sleep and relax, I visited my local GP; when I walked away I had a prescription for a supply of citalopram; I stared at the box for 4 days. On day 5 I took one and stood there waiting for it to work – I thought to myself OMG, the doc thinks what I'm going through must be serious. I took another and waited. On day 6, I stood and looked at the box, what kind of example was I setting to my children and to myself? I put the packet in the cupboard and knew there must be another way, I knew I could make myself better, I knew that this difficult moment in my life didn't define who I was. I was strong, I was determined and I was my Nanna's granddaughter, I knew I must go on a mission to heal myself of these recent unfortunate events, of this unfortunate life.

I'D BEEN FORCED to sell my car so was pretty destitute, having barely enough money for the bus I took a ride to the local library. I filled my arms with self-help book, books on meditation, books on diet and sleep. I was armed to begin my healing journey, I was 37 years old and ready, ready for my life to begin.

IT WAS HERE the meditating began, I picked up a book by David Ji on different ways to meditate and when I reached the 'Candle Meditation' chapter, I took the unusual silver-cased coloured candle from the drawer and knew immediately that my Nanna was there with me, that she always knew this day would come for me. And so it began, I read and read and meditated and began to heal and sleep and get strong. A friend of mine had recently had a reading with someone she called The Angel Lady and I was intrigued. Instantly I found her on Facebook, it was around 2012, and I followed her in awe. Her messages stayed with me and I actually believed she was talking to me with what she was posting. I was fortunate enough to meet her at a Spiritual Fayre in Sandwich and just stood and looked at her, she was a being of 100% pure light, I could see her, feel her energy and I felt alive. I stupidly said 'Oh, hello, I'm friends with you on Facebook' and she just smiled a beautiful intriguing smile which warmed my soul.

I CONTINUED on my quest of self-healing, continued the meditating and using mantras and affirmations. I felt great but wanted more, I was desperate to see the Angel Lady again but I had limited funds, no child care and no transport, I watched from the side lines in awe wishing I could take the next step. I was better but I needed my thirst for this spiritual world quenching. My father passed away in the summer of 2016 – I still to this date don't know how or why but a Facebook message gave me the news; I knew right then that my marriage was over for good. I had nothing to prove and no one to please, I took my wedding ring off for the first time in 16 years, after 30 years of us being together.

WHEN MY DAUGHTER WAS 15, the constant inconsistencies with her father and me being in full time work took its toll and I received a call from her school recommending that she was taken to the GP and referred to CAHMS. I knew this was a slippery slope as I had been unwittingly given anti-depressants myself and had absolutely no faith in the system whatsoever. I knew my daughter needed help and knew that there was no way I would allow the system to get its hand on her. I finally plucked up the courage to message the Angel Lady – Tina Pavlou – and she agreed to help my daughter. I took her for some healing at The Alders Healing Sanctuary in Ramsgate and we both felt intimate divine love and healing and I knew I'd never look back. I knew that I would never have gone for myself but when one of your children is involved you'll literally do anything that's required. Tina took my daughter and held her and downloaded her with uncondi-tional love. The feeling was immense, my daughter left feeling like a new person and it wasn't long until we were both addicted – she completed her Angelic Reiki Levels 1 and 2 only a few months later.

. . .

IT WAS during these early meetings that I met Marcia. I didn't recognise her at first, she was bouncing around the room, talking of this business sale and that. She was really loud and spirited, donned in her Superdry hoody and her jogger bottoms, I liked her, she was energetic and cheeky.

I TOOK the kids to The Canaries for 4 weeks that summer, I needed my daughter picking up when I got back as I had a wedding to go to, so I messaged Marcia. We started to chat, I knew quite obviously that she was a lesbian – I liked her and thought about her lots whilst I was away. We began messaging and I began feeling like I actually missed her, like we had some sort of connection. When we got back she dropped my daughter off and my heart skipped a beat. As soon as she returned home she messaged and we agreed to meet the next day on some business that she had to do. In her car we sat and chatted, I was totally relaxed and according to her I was oozing sex appeal (ha ha).

WE MET AGAIN the next day and when we accidentally touched hands sparks actually formed. She knew I was the one and didn't want any secrets between us, right from the start she told me about her alcoholic drug ridden past and about her cheating; it was only the third time we'd been out but my God it was mind-blowing. We met the next day and we'd already agreed that we were falling in love, the feeling was so ridiculously intense, we haven't been out of each other's sight since.

I ALWAYS KNEW I'd be with a woman, I always knew I'd be with her, I desperately needed that tenderness and love that I'd only ever experienced from my Nanna. All of the times I'd driven past her house on the way to and from my teaching job in Dover, all of the times I'd sat alone peering down at Dover Town from beside Dover Castle when I would often sit and have some peaceful, reflective times, all those times she was down there waiting for me. She needed it too and I feel as though it's my role to show her that despite how cruel the world has been to her, it's such a beautiful place. I am totally and utterly in love with her, a love I have never ever felt before, a love so pure and so beautiful I feel like I have come home. My kids adore her but more importantly, I suppose, I have taught my children that being true to yourself and self-love is the most important thing in life.

AND SO OUR journey together began, as well as Angelic Reiki we have both completed our Theta Healing with Tina at our newly decorated Goddess Rooms in Ramsgate. We have completed Matrix Re-imprinting and EFT and Access Bars, we have completed many courses together on our healing journey and regularly work on each other as well others, we've got this! We regularly run Inner child meditations and workshops and we both help at a local charity using EFT and Matrix, for vulnerable and disadvantaged children. We have a real passion for working with the homeless and drug rehabilitators and have made some useful connections within the local community. We both have a passion to serve, to help others using our own experiences and ensure we can be the beacons of light that we needed in our deepest and darkest times.

THROUGH MEETING TINA, we have formed the most amazing sister-hood ever, we are the Chicklets and Roosters and we offer love and support and are there in times of need for one another. Tina has organised the most wonderful spiritual retreats in our spiritual home of Glastonbury offering workshops and healing that are so needed for us as a group. Spending this time together, without judgement or ego has enabled us to have an amazing network of friends, soul sisters and we help guide each other on our journeys.

IN JUNE we were on one such trip, staying in our little yurt at the bottom of the garden, we'd had sound therapy and were embarking on a Divine Feminine workshop; as we danced and worked on the light and shadow aspects of our personality we were led to line up ready for an Angel Walk. We were in two lines with a walkway between us. We took it in turns to touch and whisper to one another, the tears were flowing as we were told how amazing we all are and the love was certainly flowing. Met at the end by our beautiful Elizabeth all of us, including our teacher, Tina, were in a very emotional state. My turn came, with my eyes closed I could feel hands and hear voices telling me how beautiful and amazing I was. I got to roughly where Marcia was in the line and I heard the whisper of 'you are beautiful, I love you, will you marry me?' I had honestly never known until this day how loveable and important I was. My answer flowed before I even had time to think 'of course I will, my darling'. The love was astounding and people were so full of joy for us, the first Chicklet couple to come together out of pure love, it was truly an intimate, breath taking moment!

AND SO, finding Tina The 'Angel Lady', finding myself and healing from past trauma has enabled me to become someone with a story, someone with passion and ambition to help others on their healing journey. Some of the modalities we use are truly mind-blowing, we have both come such a long way and we love the fact that we now have the tools to empower others to do the same, to heal and get strong, and face the world head on without the fear of their past holding them back. We understand that the world as we see it is just an illusion, that we are all just spiritual beings living a human existence and that we are in fact just experiments; having everything we need in this word and getting greedier and greedier always wanting and feeling like we need more and more and more. We understand that the earth is becoming a split consciousness of the people who'll never wake and will have to live their live over and over until they learn their lessons, and the more evolved souls like us, who are here as beacons of light to help wake up the world through their alternative ways of thinking and healing.

FLUID MINDS IS A FULLY-FLEDGED BUSINESS. Our business which we are using to help those in need. To date we have helped vulnerable children and their families, cancer patients, those holding guilt and grief, those holding on to the energies of childhood trauma and those who are suffering various illnesses and diseases. We use Theta Healing, Emotional Freedom Technique and Matrix re-imprinting, Angelic and Usui Reiki, Access Bars and regularly hold Inner Child Meditations and EFT group sessions. We have some amazing reviews of the work we have done and are dedicated to continue in our quest to give people the tools they need to help themselves. We are happy to have both face to face sessions and also work over the internet with clients.

FLUID MINDS IS OUR BABY, our brain child, and we have great plans ahead! We will be working with further charities and schools teaching people how to help themselves by proving strategies and techniques to combat mental health issues and promote positive mental health. Mental well-being is our own responsibility, many of us have endured traumas such as deaths, divorce, abuse etc but just don't know what to do to keep the demons at bay; Fluid Mind aims to ensure that the children we work with, the adults of the future, and their families, are fully aware of the responsibility they have to keep themselves mentally fit and well, and we are passionate about providing the tools for them to do so.

. . .

THE CANCER INDUSTRY is a multimillion-pound industry as is the medical industry, it makes good business sense for people to be unwell, to be put onto pills and drugs that line the pockets of huge pharmaceutical companies. Whilst we are facing the worst mental health crisis of all time, people are being bunged up with antidepressants without anyone really asking why we are facing this crisis! Talking over problems with counsellors only serves to uproot problems without having them properly removed from the body, the energy of these problems stays with people throughout their lives if not removed or re-imprinted, thus being stuck in our energy fields which then assists us in attracting and re-attracting the same scenarios and dramas over again just with a different setting or a different person.

DURING A PAST LIFE Regression in March 2018 I was taken back to resolve the life before this one as it seemed I had brought so much resentment with me into this life. When I saw that beautiful wife of mine and those two kids over my shoulder I was asked if I knew them from this life 'look into the eyes' I was told and so I did. My twins were my children then and when I looked into her eyes my beautiful Marcia looked back and right then I knew my life was complete. In finding myself I had found everything I had been looking for my whole life.

WE ARE to Marry in September 2019 at the Goddess Temple in Glastonbury, I have never felt a love warmer, safe and real. You would be very proud of me Nanna x

AND NOW I can see the bigger picture in that all my life experiences today have served to make me who I have become, I am proud, very proud of myself and the battles I've had to face to get me to a place in my life where I feel happy to be me, in a place I feel strong enough to help others and share my experiences with the world.

I AM ME, I am Olivia, a 45-year-old Primary School Teacher, an awakened being, Owner of Fluid Minds, mother of 4 from Kent, who is alive and inspired to help heal the world.

# ABOUT THE AUTHOR

## OLIVIA WONG

Olivia is a 45-year-old Primary School Teacher from Kent who has four beautiful children aged 25,18,16 and 16 who she considers as her teachers, her friends and most importantly, her inspiration; she has been a single mum most of their lives despite being married to their father. Olivia's teaching career has meant she was able to be there for her children and although during very stressful at times, she has managed to successfully raise the four of them without too much difficulty; even though there was no extended family around to lend a hand.

Olivia has two, two-year-old sausage dogs called Martin and Zoe and loves to walk them in the countryside around her house. She loves cooking, baking and has been a vegetarian for over 7 years. Olivia is a happy go lucky character, who has learnt through experiences that we can always look within to find answers. Having once been prescribed antidepressants, she knew she didn't want to be another casualty of the system and began her spiritual journey.

The love of Olivia's life is her partner, Marcia, she is just the most loving, giving and loyal lady and Olivia feels like the luckiest girl in the world finally finding her soul mate. Together, Olivia and Marcia are lucky enough to be able to walk their spiritual pathway, they're both Theta Healers, Angelic Reiki Masters, Bars Facilitators and EFT and Matrix re-imprinters.

They both work together to deliver workshops and have recently become involved in working for a local charity, providing tools for local children and parents to support with mental health and well-being. They have a dream of eventually opening a beautiful retreat where both parents and children can have the most amazing healing and awakening experiences ever.

They can be found at their website fluidminds.com and they have numerous 'Fluid Minds' Facebook groups, where they promote EFT (Tapping), Theta Healing and Access Bars and run Inner-Child and Matrix workshops and meditations. Their dedication to working with the well-being aspects in local groups and schools continues, as well as working with groups and individual clients.

**Contact**
  https://www.fluidminds.co.uk/
  Email: molivia@fluidminds.co.uk
  Email: Fluidminds@mail.com

# ROCHELLE KARSLAKE

$\mathcal{M}$y earliest memory is one that has had a profound influence on my life. I was around 18 months old sitting on my bedroom floor in just a nappy, playing with wooden blocks. All of a sudden I became aware of a loving presence entering the room, it distracted me from what I was doing. I can't remember if I actually saw it, but it was more of just a knowing.

THE ONLY WAY I know how to describe it is that it merged with my energy, and it enveloped me. We became one for a moment. In that moment it felt like I lifted a couple of inches off the ground and I experienced an overwhelming feeling of love, so intense that tears of pure joy started rolling down my face. I realised that it was imparting wisdom to me. I instantly had a complete understanding of all things, it was almost like being on the outside looking in.

ALTHOUGH I WAS TOO young to speak, I understood everything the energy was sharing with me, and in that moment I knew that this was very special and that I would always remember it. That was the first time I became aware of the spirit world and the wisdom it gave me has stayed with me ever since.

I WAS BORN IN CALIFORNIA, USA and moved to the UK with my mother and sister when I was around a year old. My sister and I had different fathers but they both lived in the States, so we grew up without them in our lives. This had a bigger effect on me than I realised growing up as not only did I not see my father, but we had lost touch, so there wasn't any birthday or Christmas cards, or any phone calls. This definitely played a part in the beginning of my low self-esteem.

WE LIVED in a small village and went to the local primary school, I was quite a happy child really but slowly over time I let others' opinions of me become my own.

I ALWAYS FELT REALLY DIFFERENT. Everyone else had a mum and a dad and 'normal' names and ate 'normal' food. My mother is French and had lived in many different countries growing up so had a wealth of knowledge of different cultures and cuisines. Yet everyone at school was very 'English' as my mum would say. My sister and I were the only ones who came from another country and culture, and I realised early on that it was essential to fit in or bullying would of been inevitable. Somehow I managed to fit in as best I could. I still got bullied, not from my peers but my teachers. I didn't get diagnosed till years later but I have dyslexia, something that wasn't understood or even taken seriously then.

EVERYONE ELSE SEEMED to understand everything so easily but I just couldn't grasp what was going on or what was expected of me in lesson times. This resulted in being humiliated in front of the whole class regularly and sometimes in front of the whole school. The teachers would rip my work up, throw my work books on the floor, throw my glasses on the floor and call me stupid. It would be 'everybody stop what you're doing and look at Rochelle' then the teacher would proceed to ask me to spell something or for the answer to a times table, which of course I did not know and everyone would laugh. One teacher in particular was so mean to me that I would wet myself in her lessons. My mum ended up taking my sister and I out of that school and into a school that was alternative in its approach and education.

THE NEW SCHOOL was very different to what I was used to. Everyone was a lot more open minded. There were lots of people from different countries and backgrounds, I didn't feel quite so different there and my dyslexia didn't really hold me back as the style of teaching and learning was very different to a mainstream setting. Although I did fall victim to bullying again by my teachers. This time it was because my sister and I were the only ones from a single parent family. Times have changed so much now, it really doesn't matter how a family is made up, but back then there was still a lot of prejudice. This really hurt me as I so wanted to be just like everyone else. It really made me feel like I was not good enough, and as much as I wanted to be, it taught me that I wasn't as deserving or worthy as everyone else seemed to be. I did make some good friends at the school but it wasn't until the parents of a friend in my class split up that I had a friend that the teachers were happy for me to play with. We were always put together as we were both from a single parent family.

WHILE AT THE alternative school I had another profound spiritual experience. It was in the school holidays and my mother, sister and I went on a short holiday to Devon, where we stayed with one of my mum's old friends. On one day we went for a day out to this amazing place, some sort of national park or heritage sight. There were miles and miles of walks you could do and we set off on a long walk. Near to where we were walking was a river where you could do white water rafting, and the river was fiercely quick. We took a path uphill on a sort of edge with the river on the other side.

I WAS SO EXCITED to be there that I was running. My mum kept calling out to me to stop running, but I didn't listen and ran on way ahead. Enjoying myself immensely running along the top of the edge, I slipped and it was pretty much a straight fall down to the river and rocks, and I fell and fell. I managed to hold on to a long weed that was growing on the side of the drop which broke my fall.

THE NEXT THING I know I'm at the bottom, staring at a woman, she wasn't even five feet tall, and she was made completely out of white light. The light just radiated out of her. She was wearing white robes that were also made of light and had a white head scarf on. The only thing that wasn't white was a glowing red dot she had in the middle of her forehead. She looked to me to be an older woman, and it took me a couple of seconds to realise that she was standing on the water, which was moving so quickly, yet she stayed perfectly still. I couldn't quite believe my eyes and then she started talking to me. For the life of me I can't remember what she said, I was in so much shock, but I remember feeling like she was telling me off!

SUDDENLY I WAS BACK at the top of the hill which would have been impossible to climb. I don't know how I got back up there. I didn't get myself there, I was just instantly there. It all happened so quickly and seemed to be over in seconds. I waited there for my mum, her friend and my sister who turned up a few minutes later completely oblivious to what had just happened to me. I told them what happened as I was covered in mud and scratches but they didn't believe me. Needless to say I walked the rest of the way.

WE SPENT three years at the alternative school and then we went back to mainstream. My sister was now secondary school age and went on to a grammar school, I went back to the local primary school I had previously attended. It wasn't as bad second time around as I still had my friends and different teachers that were nicer. It was ok.

AT THAT TIME in our lives something amazing happened. My mother, who had also grown up without her father, and didn't have any contact with him her entire life, had suddenly received contact from him. This was amazing for all of us as the grandparents we knew had passed away a couple of years before, which really hit me hard. We had very little family, our auntie lived in London so we would go and stay with her in the holidays and she would come to visit us. It was always so much fun but that was all we had when it came to family. I remember when he came into our lives, it was really special.

THE GRANDFATHER I HAD KNOWN, that had been there all my life, was my grandma's husband and not a biological grandparent. Still, I loved him just as much and was wary about my new grandfather trying to take his place. I decided I wouldn't call him grandpa but I would call him by his name, and we would be good friends, and we were. He was a sailor and lived on a boat in Paris, but he would sail his boat all over the world. He would come and stay with us for short visits and then go off for a few months and then come back for another visit etc. He would take us out for dinner and buy us treats and trips away, it was so nice.

· · ·

THEN ONE TIME when he came and visited it all changed. I remember sitting with him in the living room and he put his hand up my top as I had started developing. I didn't quite know what to make of this, it felt weird, he would do this whenever he got the chance. Then things progressed and he started kissing me with his tongue whenever I kissed him goodnight or goodbye. Of course this only happened when we were alone. He told me not to tell my mum, and that it made me really special and a good girl. I was very confused as I knew that this didn't feel right, my other grandpa never did anything like that. Still, I thought about my mum. I thought how I would feel if I had just found my dad and then something like this happened, I'd be devastated. So, I decided to do what he said and not tell her.

HIS NEXT VISIT, my mum and sister needed to go away for a few days, and they left him to look after me. It was awful. I slept in my mum's bed as I felt safer in there but he would get into the bed with me. I remember one time asking him 'why are you doing this to me? I don't like it' but he would just tell me it was because I was special. I felt sick and after those few days I decided I wasn't going to let him anywhere near me again.

MY NEW FROSTY attitude towards him was noticed by my mum and sister and they were really upset by it, they couldn't understand why I had gone from being so happy and loving toward him to being completely cold and guarded. I remember one day my sister saying to me that we hardly had any family and she didn't understand why was I treating the family that we did have so coldly. I didn't respond, and I really started to withdraw at that time. He would still come and go but I never let him near me again. The next time my mother and sister needed to go away and leave him to watch me I insisted on staying with friends.

A FEW YEARS later after many more visits had come and gone from my grandfather I did open up and tell my mum what had happened. I remember feeling awful, that it was my fault that she wouldn't have her dad in her life anymore after only knowing him a short time. She was really upset and said that she would deal with it. He was off somewhere on his boat at the time so I left it up to my mum, I felt so guilty and full of shame.

AROUND THE SAME time my mother had some friends, a couple, who we had known for years. I had always really liked them both, and we would often have them round for dinner or we would go to them. One evening, the husband of this couple came around by himself for dinner which happened every now and then, as the wife worked away a lot. We were sat in the living room watching TV after dinner and he started putting his hand up my top. My mum was in the room but she couldn't see. I froze as I didn't know what to do, then he got my hand and put it on his privates. I felt completely betrayed again as I had really cared for him before, almost extended family, we'd spent Christmases together and everything. Unlike my grandfather we never spoke about it. From then on, I tried to keep my distance whenever he was around but somehow, he always managed to sit next to me and fondle me. This time I did tell my mum, but I don't think she believed me as they would still visit often.

AS A RESULT of this I started experiencing a lot of self-loathing, feeling so guilty and full of shame and anxiety. The only men that had been in my life had done this to me and no one really seemed to care that much. The lesson I learned from this was that men only wanted one thing, and that I was completely worthless.

ONCE I STARTED secondary school I was really trying to learn the ropes quickly to fit it again. It was a big school and there was no way I was going to get bullied. A lot of the pupils were quite rough and ready with a lot of attitude, I hadn't met people like this before. I made mental notes of what type of behavior and attitudes were acceptable to my peers and I made it my own. I was always in trouble, always getting detention. I hated school, but I was so desperate to feel accepted that I would do pretty much anything. At this time I was suffering with really bad depression, I had no self-worth and no self-esteem, I didn't care about my future. I absolutely hated the way I looked. I had discovered makeup which I fell in love with as I could completely change the way I looked. I couldn't bare looking in the mirror without makeup, so this became my coping mechanism. I could face the world with a made up face and I could be someone else. Plus I started to get a lot of attention from boys, which I liked, but didn't know how to behave around them as I was so messed up from the molestation.

WHEN I WAS 14 years old I met a young man who was 21, he became my boyfriend. I lied about my age of course, but he soon found out and didn't seem to mind. I knew my mum wouldn't approve but I was also way too embarrassed to bring any potential boyfriend back to my house. At that time, I felt my mother was so different in an eccentric, bohemian kind of way that people would think we were weird. I wasn't allowed to do what most of my friends were doing, like go to the local night club for teens. If any boy rang the house they wouldn't ring again because she would have scared them off.

. . .

THIS PARTICULAR YOUNG man and I became really close really quickly. I was in such a bad head space, feeling caged by my mother's control and desperate to be free, as well as longing to be accepted and loved. We saw each other whenever we could. He drove and bought me cigarettes and I thought that was cool. Then things started moving in another direction. We started smoking weed, which I liked, and then he introduced me to cocaine. It gave me that buzz I had been longing for and not even known. I liked it. I felt invincible when I was on it. One night when I was sneaking out to see him, I decided to jump from my bedroom window and I ended up fracturing my foot. Within a couple of weeks my mum had made plans for me to go to rehab.

I DIDN'T KNOW I was going to rehab, my mum told me I was going for a counselling session, but when I turned up there were people there with slippers on. It was all a bit strange. They sat me down in a room with two counsellor's who told me that I had to stay for the next six weeks, and that if I left the premises I would be put straight into care until I was 17. I was still 14 at this point and so angry that I had been led there under false pretenses. They forced me to sign a document and showed me to my room. My mum left, and I was so angry with her that I never wanted to see her again. I cried so much that first night. You weren't allowed any phone calls for the first week, so I couldn't speak to anyone I knew.

LUCKILY THE OTHER people in there were really nice. I was the youngest by far, the others came from so many walks of life and had so many amazing stories. The staff, on the other hand, were all a bit pretentious. It soon became clear from the inside looking out that actually it was all about money. They would keep patients there until their money ran out. I don't actually know how helpful it was for me or anyone else but I decided I might as well try and enjoy myself while I was there. It turned out it was better than being at school. I was there for three months in total and I had my 15th birthday in there too. I ended the relationship with my boyfriend whilst I was there. Looking back now as an adult, I still don't think being placed into rehab was necessary. It was a very extreme measure and perhaps all I needed was some long overdue help and support from the people closest to me. Within a week of leaving rehab, I flew to the States all by myself to meet my dad for the first time.

JUST BEFORE I had gone into rehab my mother had managed to track down my grandma (my dad's mum). She was living in Southern California. We spoke on the phone, and she passed on my dad's information. So, I contacted my father and he used to call me while I was in treatment and we slowly started to form a relationship.

I FLEW out in the summertime, my dad met me at the airport, I didn't know what he looked like, so I was really nervous. My mum had told him what I was wearing so that made it easier for him to spot me as he had no idea what I looked like either. I saw a man put his hand up, he was smartly dressed and wearing a San Francisco Giants baseball cap. I instantly recognised my facial features in him. It was MY dad. The emotions that ran through me were overwhelming. I ran up to him and hugged him and cried and cried. We embraced for what seemed like forever and then I wanted to get another look at his face. He had my eyes, my nose, my chin! I stayed with him for two weeks before coming home. In that time my grandma and my aunt flew in to meet me, and we spent the 4th of July together. Growing up with my mother and sister, they didn't wear much makeup and they didn't wear acrylic nails. I on the other hand loved all of this and would spend hours getting my hair and makeup just right, as well as perfecting my nails and tan. Now, there was my grandma and aunt exactly the same as me! Lots of makeup, big hair, nails. I finally understood where I came from and it felt so good after being criticised on a daily basis for choosing to express myself this way.

DURING THE WEEK that followed I got to know my dad quite well. He was a deeply spiritual man, and belonged to the Pentecostal church. He would tell me about all the spiritual experiences he'd had. He had seen angels and demons, had visitations and witnessed some amazing things. It turns out the whole of my dad's side of the family were like this. He turned and said to me one day 'you know this is in you too'. I instantly knew he was right as I had always felt a spiritual pull and was aware of so much, I just didn't have anyone to guide me.

IT WAS A TRULY amazing time visiting my dad. He showed me love in a way that only a father could and, at this point in my life, I felt he was the only person who truly loved me, and now it was time to go.

AFTER RETURNING home I went straight back to my old ways. Still deeply confused and messed up, I started college and became very promiscuous. I would get with anyone I found remotely attractive. I had no self-worth, no self-esteem, and although I didn't realise just how bad, I was suffering with severe depression. I didn't even feel worthy of having a guy take me for dinner or a drink. I would sometimes even say to them 'save your money for someone who's worth it, I'll give it to you anyway'. My thinking was, if I give it to you then you can't take it from me. Somehow in my messed up outlook, it was me taking control. Needless to say I got pregnant, and the whole experience was absolutely awful. I didn't have any support from anyone, and was forced into a termination. I was 16, and the whole thing left me physically and emotionally scarred.

. . .

IT WASN'T until a year later that I realised that it was the right thing to do but wished I had been given the time and freedom to make that decision for myself. However, after the termination something inside had shifted, I felt even more self-loathing and the depression got worse. I dealt with this as best I could, but I couldn't seem to break the cycle of sleeping with more guys to validate myself, because for that moment in time, somebody wanted me.

NOT LONG AFTER I turned 17, I moved in with a family friend Who had known me nearly all my life. She was like another mother to me and it was really nice. I had the freedom and respect that I had been yearning for. I was still at college and had gotten myself a job and for a while I felt really good. It was whilst I was living there that I felt the freedom and space to start looking into my spirituality. I knew there was a God (or whatever you feel comfortable calling source), and I started trying to form a relationship with this energy.

ABOUT A YEAR after living there I met my now husband John. He was very different from all the other guys I was used to. He treated me with respect and despite my advances insisted on taking me out for dinner! He's since told me that he realised how emotionally fragile I was but saw something in me that I didn't know was there myself. He's also said many times that he believes he was guided through the first couple of years of our relationship as I had no idea how to behave or what was appropriate while in a relationship, but I was committed.

AFTER A WHILE I did become very dependent on him. I knew that I was getting my validation from him now and I needed it constantly reaffirmed. I now know that this is not anyone else's job but my own!

·  ·  ·

WE DECIDED to move away from family and start our very own adventure. We moved up to the midlands and for a while had a really fun time. We had lived there for around a year when I started having awful headaches. I didn't think too much of it at the time as they kind of came and went, but after a month it just seemed to be there all the time. It felt like my head was in a vice and my vision was distorted, also facial pain and pressure. Plus I had really bad lethargy. I went to doctors and specialists and no one could find anything wrong with me. So I ventured out to homeopaths, healers you name it I tried it, and nothing seemed to help. This put my life on hold as I didn't feel well enough to work and I withdrew so much that I stopped looking after myself.

THE ONCE FUN, bubbly person that I had become was now deeply depressed again. I couldn't get out of bed, I stopped wearing makeup and brushing my hair and gained weight. I also started having panic attacks, first monthly, then every couple of weeks till they became so regular I was having them every day. I felt on some level that 'of course' this happened to me, just as life was starting to go well something had to come along and mess it up. I wasn't worthy of being happy and having a happy life. My husband (partner at the time) didn't know what to do, the woman he'd fallen in love with had gone and all that was left was this emotional wreck that had something wrong with her that no one could figure out. This ended up lasting for four years. Four years of constant pain and discomfort, and apart from close friends and family, no one seemed to care. Again, I felt this was just validating my unworthiness.

DURING THIS TIME I found out I was pregnant. It was not planned and our relationship was not good because of the strain my headaches were having on John and I. Having children was not something we had planned on just yet and I didn't feel ready, but something inside me said that this baby was meant to be here. Looking back I now know my son saved my life. If I had chosen not to have him, eventually John would have left because I was so hard to be with and I would have probably ended up in an institution.

WE MOVED BACK DOWN to Kent to be nearer family after he was born. Not long after John and I spilt up for a few months. My son and I moved in with friends for a couple of months, who I will always be eternally grateful to. It was a really hard time for me. It was not my decision but I respected why John felt the way he did, and I believed I was now completely damaged goods. Who would want me now? After experiencing real love I couldn't settle for anything less. After a couple of months we decided to try and get back together. I was initially so happy but realised that John didn't quite feel the same way. It was heartbreaking and my headaches were still really bad, I had learnt how to cope with them, and I still managed to get up and do everything a new mum needs to do.

IT WAS at this time that I went to see a healer who truly was incredible. She gave my whole body an MOT and she diagnosed me with trigeminal neuralgia. Unfortunately nothing she did or gave me actually helped with the discomfort or pain, but to have a diagnosis made me very happy, I wasn't insane!

WE DECIDED to move back up to the midlands and try again with our young son. We thought that a fresh start was exactly what we needed. Although this time it was very different as we felt completely isolated and realised how important it was to have family around. I fell even deeper into depression to the point that I decided I was going to end my life. I couldn't live like this anymore, feeling that I was a burden on my family and struggled to see an end. Some days when my headaches were particularly bad I took comfort in the fact that one day I'd be dead, and at least then the pain would stop.

I DECIDED that after my sons 2nd birthday was when I would do it. I'd made my mind up and actually felt at peace because this pain was going to end. One night I spoke to one of my best friends on the phone and said I was going to do it and to keep it to herself, she said things that were so lovely about me and got another one of my best friends to call who also said amazing things about me that I had completely forgotten. I had been in such a dark place it hadn't dawned on me that anyone would actually miss me and that I was loved and admired by others. It's amazing how the universe works, because a few months after that my headaches started clearing up and soon they were completely gone, just as quickly as they came. It was amazing. I had dreamt and prayed that this would happen for so long but once it finally came, I soon learnt that I really struggled with the transition of feeling normal!

NOT LONG AFTER that I found out I was pregnant again. Again it was not planned but we were really happy. It wasn't working for us being so far away from friends and family so we decided to move back to Kent again. We moved to the coast and settled very quickly. John got a job almost straight away and we loved our new house, always having friends and family over it was exactly what we wanted. Our second son was born and it was a really happy time. When he was 9 months old I found out I was pregnant again! This was a complete shock, and again not planned, but we were happy and excited. My third son was born just before Christmas and it was a very busy time. After he was born I had quite bad postnatal depression, not that I realised at the time.

·  ·  ·

MY DEPRESSION HAD NEVER REALLY LEFT SO I didn't think anything of it. I went back on antidepressants and carried on as best I could. John was a restaurant manager and seemed like he worked all hours as he was hardly ever home, and I began to struggle with the boys all by myself. I didn't feel I could take all three of them out by myself and didn't drive at the time, so I felt trapped at home. When John was home we'd have days out and I had amazing friends who would come and visit me at weekends, and I would look forward to that all week.

WITHIN A COUPLE of months John and I decided that three boys was enough and that he should get a vasectomy, which he did. However, his vasectomy failed and I discovered I was pregnant again.

THREE MONTHS prior to this discovery I had decided to do something myself about my depression and anxiety. My auntie had introduced me to the law of attraction about 10 years previously, and I understood the basic concept of it and I decided to look back into it. I stumbled across Abraham Hicks (the most prominent teacher on 'law of attraction') this was the beginning of my spiritual awakening. I was in complete awe and soaked up every word they said.

WHEN I FOUND out I was pregnant I knew I wanted this baby. It was by pure fate I thought, what were the chances of a vasectomy failing? John was really worried how we were going to manage but I decided that whatever happened, I was going to have this miracle baby. Due to staff cuts I didn't get a chance for a scan until I was 16 weeks and the news was not good. It turned out that he had something called 'non immune hydrops', and basically everything that could be wrong with him was wrong, and he wouldn't live much longer. I remember being absolutely heartbroken, and John and I cried the rest of the night. At nearly 19 weeks I had to give birth to him. The night before, John and

I talked to him in my tummy. I hardly ever felt him move because he had no energy. John put his hand on my stomach and told him, in his mind, how much he loved him and I instantly felt him move. So much so it felt like he might come straight through my stomach. I had never felt him move like that before. I told John who could feel him moving and he told me that, this moment was the purest moment of love he had ever felt in his life.

THE NEXT DAY was grey and I had to give birth to him on the maternity ward, where I had had two of my other children. I could hear babies crying. It was truly heartbreaking. He was born that afternoon and I had the Chaplin come in and say a blessing. I was allowed to stay the night with him. John went home that evening. I remember holding his tiny body and taking him up to the window to look at the stars so that whenever I looked up at them again, I would think of him. The next day saying goodbye was the hardest thing I've ever done. I couldn't leave him, so John had to ask one of the midwives to come and take him away. I don't remember much more about that day, but I remember feeling even then that this had happened for a reason, and I was determined to learn what ever there was to learn from this and that it wasn't just going to be a bad experience.

A FEW MONTHS LATER, my middle son got diagnosed with autism. Without going into all the ins and outs, it hadn't completely come out of the blue, but the process of getting him assessed and then obtaining the relevant documents he needed to go to a special school were way more than I anticipated. It was an emotional rollercoaster, that I felt even more so, as I was still in the grieving process of the baby I'd just lost. That's when my spiritual path really opened up for me.

So I STARTED at the only place I knew, my local church. I started going every week and did Bible study, and soaked up as much as I could. One thing I knew was that I was breaking the pattern of depression and stepping out of victimhood. I was going to develop a relationship with my creator so that when the hard knocks came I could lean on my faith. I got a lot from church and eventually became baptised and confirmed. I completely surrendered myself to God and knew it was time to yield to the spiritual calling that had always been in my life.

IT WASN'T until my youngest son got diagnosed with autism that I nearly lost it. I had thought he was copying his older brother and was so consumed with getting everything in place that his brother needed that I just wasn't seeing what was right in front of me. However all I seemed to get at church was pity, there wasn't really any faith filled people there telling me 'you'll be fine, you've got this' people just didn't know what to say to me.

THIS WAS A VERY important time for me. I had a decision to make. I was aware I was at a crossroads, where I could either start going down the same road I always had emotionally, believing it must be my fault and that I don't deserve what everyone else has. Of course it had to be me with two autistic children. Or I could instead realise that my children were a blessing and going to be my biggest teachers. I once heard a phrase that said 'God doesn't give you more than you can handle'. My husband and I often laugh and say God must have a lot of faith in us!

IT WAS ALSO at this time that I started to notice how far we still have to come as a society. I'd never really questioned society before because it hadn't had an impact on my life. That was until society said that my children weren't 'normal' (I hate that word!). This definitely contributed to me becoming a bit of a recluse but, at the same time, pushed me even further into the alternative and thinking 'outside the box'. Around this time, I had realised that although I had gotten a lot from church, it wasn't quite filling me up any more and I sensed that there was a lid on it.

I REMEMBER years ago one of my mum's friends went to a spiritual church and I thought perhaps they might be more open minded. By this point I was listening to YouTube all day, just to get myself through the day, people such as Abraham Hicks, Wayne Dyer, Mike Dooley, Lorna Byrne etc. looking for inspiration. I was aware that most people around me were still 'asleep' and that without intentionally feeding my mind with nourishing optimism and faith on a daily basis I would get sucked back into the woes of the world and the low vibrational things. I was very mindful of where I wanted to be emotionally and that became a daily practice.

LIFE'S EVENTS had made me really question who was in my life, and I pretty much stopped seeing everyone except family for about a year and a half, while emotionally I was trying to process everything that felt like it had come at once.

IT WAS at this time that I looked back and remembered discovering Abraham Hicks, and thinking it was like opening Pandora's box. I should have left it alone. Yes I was depressed before but life was just ticking along, all run of the mill. It wasn't until this year on a Theta Healing course with Tina that I realised it was a grace period, allowing me to open my mind a little more and have a greater understanding before the life changing events came so that I would be better able to deal with them from a broader perspective.

· · ·

I FOUND my local spiritualist church and attended a service. It was nice, I found out that they did a development circle for psychic mediumship. It wasn't exactly what I was looking for but it was closer than what my local church offered. I started going every week. I enjoyed the meditation and learnt about the chakras and met some interesting people. Over time I got better at trusting my intuition and was able to give good readings. I remember one particular evening we were in meditation and I was still slightly in two minds with how what I was doing conflicted with the teachings I had learnt at church. I asked in my mind 'is this God's love I'm feeling or is it....?' and before I could finish my sentence in my head it felt like I was physically punched in the upper abdomen. There was a sucking sensation that felt like my solar plexus was absorbing in the energy that surrounded me and then my whole body started buzzing. It felt like I was in a cocoon. I knew that was source energy and I've never doubted it again.

AFTER ABOUT A YEAR and a half of attending this circle it stopped fulfilling me and there was quite a bit of ego there. I was still searching for my spiritual home. I knew there was a healing sanctuary in my local town but it hardly ever seemed open and didn't have a website. One day I was trawling through 'spirit what's on' and saw there was a law of attraction workshop there with Tina Pavlou. I couldn't believe my luck! I thought surely I'd have to go to London to find anything like this, to think there were like-minded people like me right on my doorstep! I immediately booked a place.

I COULDN'T WAIT. Finally the day arrived and I went with my mother-in-law. I remember meeting Tina for the first time. I loved her the second I met her, she was so warm and radiated love. I loved being around her energy. I remember saying to her that day how happy I was to be there, and she replied saying that she put out to the universe for the right people to come, and they did!

. . .

AFTER THAT EVENING I realised that I had been lost and after meeting Tina and the Chicklets I knew I was home. The energy was fresh and vibrant and exactly what I had been looking for. I couldn't wait for the next workshop. Tina put on a few more workshops in the coming months and after each one I left feeling completely inspired and exhilarated. She understood me and I wanted to learn all that I could from this amazing woman, she really inspired me to be the best version of myself. I clocked on quite quickly that one of the things I loved about her, was that she really does walk her talk, and her genuine mission in life is to help people, teaching them to work on themselves through healing and raise the vibration of the planet. How does it get any better than that?! I honestly did, and still do, feel so blessed to have Tina in my life as a teacher and a sister. Her classes are a truly incredible and magical experience.

THROUGH ANGELIC REIKI and the gift that is Theta Healing, Tina has taught me how to start healing my life, through love and the powerful act of forgiveness. She taught me that I would never find validation for myself in anyone else, that I was enough, that I had always been enough without having to do or change anything about myself. That unconditional love had always been there just waiting to be tapped into, and that I no longer needed to live my life driven by fear. On top of this, Tina has brought so many amazing women into my life. It is a true sisterhood and I am beyond thankful for every single one of them. Tina has helped me to become my authentic self, knowing it is safe, and for that I will be eternally grateful.

I HAVE GROWN SO MUCH in the last two years, and have dedicated myself to my spiritual path. One of the biggest revelations for me was hearing that our circumstances don't have to dictate how we feel, that we still have a choice! This has been life changing information, as no matter what happens I can still choose to feel good and focus on the many blessings that are in my life. As the late Dr Wayne Dyer said, 'when you change the way you look at things the things you look at change'.

I AM STILL on my healing journey and am so thankful for the undying love and support from my husband, who has stuck by me through it all. He has always believed in me and seen the best in me even when I couldn't see it myself and who has made this part of my life a possibility through being such an incredible father and husband, I love you.

# ABOUT THE AUTHOR

## ROCHELLE KARSLAKE

Rochelle Karslake is a wife and mother of three boys two of which have severe autism. Rochelle has always been able to see auras and she is now an Angelic Reiki Master and a Theta Healing Practitioner, she is also a developing psychic medium.

Rochelle has had a colourful life and her experiences lead her to rock bottom. She decided she couldn't live like that anymore and after nearly fifteen years of depression she decided to change the way she looked at things and slowly learned, just like Dorothy (from the Wizard Of Oz), that she had always had everything she needed inside of her. Not long after that she met her soul family, Tina and the chicklets, and has never looked back.

Rochelle now wants to educate and empower people, to teach them not to be defined by their circumstances, and that your past does not determine your future. We can be whatever we believe we can become. Rochelle is a passionate vegan and animal lover who lives on the coast in the south east of England.

**Contact**
rochellemari18@gmail.com

 facebook.com/rochellemari

# SALLY JONES

## DIVINE TIMING

*W*ell this is different! The fact that I have always had my head stuck in a book (mostly fiction) and dreamt of being a proof-reader as a career, and even joking to my children that we should write a book or screen-play about our lives as the Jones Family, I did not realise that one day, I would be asked to contribute to Tina Pavlou's collaboration book.

FOR ME AT the time of writing, it has been difficult to get focused and stick to deadlines, something I used to pride myself upon in the work-place, working with data all day. I had a vision, years ago that all data, would be kept in a central place, which each relevant department would access for information, but any updates would be checked and verified as correct before data was updated. This eventually became my job.

I HAD WORKED within the local hospital for 29 years. I had thought, wow, so lucky, I have a job I love, lovely colleagues and excellent work environment, something not usually seen in an old hospital building. Also, we had a laugh! I admit, I have acquired my late dad's loud, fun laugh. I also thought I had a job there for life, or until pension age which these days would be for me another 13 years. I had just received a promotion and salary increase according to my job role. I had a husband who worked too hard, always working and something I worried about, as both our fathers were equal workaholics, and who equally passed at the age of 57 (one with heart problems, the other with lung cancer), you can imagine, as we reached our 50s, the more I prayed that something would change the tide, of men dying young in both our families. I hoped I would see more of my husband and spend more quality time together.

So, brief back-ground history ticked. My Bio and photo for this chapter ticked. Now to start my story:- It only starts in June 2017. Not long you may think, but so much has already happened and continues to do so.

June 2017, Kelvin my husband, was hoovering up, yes I am blessed that my husband shares the household chores, however, on this particular day, I neglected to spot the hoover lead and tripped up well and truly, crashed into the wall opposite badly knocking my head. I was dazed and felt my neck already beginning to tense. I gave myself healing, and did not travel to Wales that weekend to help Kelvin collect our youngest daughter from Cardiff Uni for the summer. Next thing I am aware of was at work, the spot which I thought was on my pc monitor was in fact in my left eye. An emergency eye test, next day, revealed nothing, not even a change of prescription, which I might add surprised me, as since my hours using the PC monitor increased and doing more detailed work, I was increasingly convinced that my eyesight was deteriorating. So, the floater disappeared after some self-healing.

· · ·

WITHIN THE NEXT WEEK, more and more floaters had appeared. I googled it and read that it is very common in my age group. (Word to the wise don't google your symptoms). I was in the process of bringing a brand new data system online with my manager and couldn't leave her in the lurch. So I kept on working. I was conscious even more that my eyesight was changing, my eyes were getting tired more quickly, dry and sore. No matter what I did, it didn't alleviate the symptoms. I remember lunching with a friend after a long dog walk, as I looked up what I thought was a flock of birds, was in fact, floaters in my left eye. So, are you getting the picture? I ignored the warning signs!

DURING THIS TIME, Tina was working at the Alder Healing Sanctuary, and had been since September 2016. During this time, I watched her working so much on her self-healing, and self-development. I was drawn to Angelic Reiki as the next step in my healing journey, and my future career (my dream). The morning after my first attunement Kelvin, very casually asked, "can anyone be attuned to Angelic Reiki?" He had previously started on his spiritual healing journey at a low point in his work, life balance and before he re-trained as a plumber and started to work for himself in building up his company. I asked why, feeling hopeful, his reply was, "You look so different today, you're glowing"!

THAT WAS a Saturday in August 2017. During that day we did a past-life healing practice with a fellow student, I felt this bubble of emotion pushing to the surface from very deep within me. I started to sob. Boy, did I cry, no I wailed... I couldn't stop for ages. All I felt was a massive wave of human suffering, the likes of which I could not imagine. It certainly did not come from this current life-time.

. . .

BY THE END OF AUGUST, I became aware this time of a bright white light most times I closed my eyes. WOW, I thought, this is amazing, I'm finally seeing stuff. Hahahaha, although I've been on my hands-on spiritual healing journey for years, I was still exasperated over that fact, that I couldn't get colours or visions while meditating. I just learnt to accept that everyone is different and what works for some, doesn't work for others.

DURING A LUNCHTIME TREAT OUT, I just happened to mention the white lights to Kelvin. He groaned. He knew what was coming... giving me strict orders to get myself to the doctor's first thing in the morning. So off I went, the next thing I knew, I was being referred up to Moorfield's Eye Hospital in London, with a massive tear in my left retina. Armed with my crystals, meditation music on my phone and headphones, we headed up to London the very next day.

EVEN THEN, I wasn't scared or frightened, I had asked for healing over the airwaves, and I could feel the love and support of all my family, friends, colleagues, Angels and Creator all around me. There was another lady there, who was in shock, as she had only popped into A&E a couple of hours earlier, she had no-one with her. I sat with her and spoke to her and gave her one of my crystals. I find it always helps me to help someone else more in need. Everything about this experience was totally new to me. I had only given birth twice, both times with gas and air and help of a tens-machine (mothers will know what I mean) though I had sat through many other operations on my loved ones, and remember the anxiousness I felt, it did feel surreal that I was the patient this time!

. . .

NOW THOSE OF you who are aware, some eye operations are usually carried out by local anaesthetic, mine was no exception. I was awake the entire time and heard everything. It took a lot longer than normal and to the best of my knowledge had to be re-done. I know the sedative had almost worn off by the time I was brought out. Kelvin was getting very worried, as others in the waiting room, came and went and still no sign of me! After grabbing a sandwich and cuppa it was a taxi to the railway station and home. We were met at the station by our eldest daughter Abi (a successful young woman and of whom we are so proud, as any parent would be). Abi presented me with a bunch of Sunflowers and a big hug. Something I have always noted when Abi hugs, since I was pregnant with Izzie, I suffered even worse sickness bouts, but always Abi as a toddler would come over and hug me. It always made me feel better. I even remarked on it to the Health Visitor once!

TWO WEEKS later I went back up to London with a friend for a checkup, as you can imagine I was still not seeing very well at all. Eye pressure was 45, when it should be maximum of 21. No wonder it hurt and I had a constant headache. The next follow-up appointment I planned to go on my own. I was a big girl, I had this, I was only to be discharged! I had an eye-sight test, as I was still struggling to see with the right eye. I couldn't see anything out of the left eye. I did not realise until that first operation, how much better I saw in my left eye, compared to my right. The optician noted that I had in fact a small cataract forming in the right eye. My mum who is twenty years older than me, had just been told the same. No previous history of cataracts so early in our family. So armed with new glasses I could see to get myself to Moorfields. I had a scan, and this revealed another tear.

THE HEALING PROCESS of the retina had puckered it up and it had torn somewhere else. I had to have another operation and quickly before it became detached completely. Once that happened I could be permanently blind in that eye. WHAT? – Another operation NOW? Errrr NO! I was not prepared to have it there and then, so came home in shock. My youngest daughter Izzie (who again we are so very proud of, as through one thing or another she had taught herself pretty much through her GCSEs and A' Levels, getting into her first University of choice, Cardiff reading Biochemistry), juggled her commitments and came home to wait with me for the phone to ring.

WE WAITED for a week and on 31st October I had a call to get up to Moorfield's for the afternoon. So off we go up to London again. At this time, Kelvin was in Wales taking his mother for a scan as she had not been well for some-time. We received a call while on the train, she had just been diagnosed with bowel cancer. Kelvin and I knew about this likelihood but had been sworn to secrecy by his mum, as she didn't want to worry the girls unnecessarily.

AFTER THAT OPERATION, my eye was so sore, and when I closed my eyes, I could still see some white light. There was still something wrong. I lasted a couple of days, my eye was so painful and nothing at all like the first time. After another emergency appointment at my local NHS trust, the consultant said my retina had now become detached and I needed yet another operation the next day.

THAT NIGHT, I found myself in my spiritual, healing home. (The Alders), Tina was there, and she gave me some Theta Healing, followed by beautiful Angelic Reiki. As she was working, she suddenly saw me in a past-life. Tina saw me in Atlantis and Creator had shown her I was a seer. (Seer – is an old fashioned word for a wise person, usually a woman who could see the future and one of the many reasons, lots of us were hunted down and murdered for being

345

witches' in a time of darkness, ignorance and fear). During the healing, I realised then what the immense human suffering was which I had felt whilst having my past-life healing in August's Angelic class. It all made perfect sense.

I HAD SEEN the fall of Atlantis in my visions, and I was there at the end. As a result I vowed never to see clairvoyantly again. Through a recent Theta Healing course Tina had just attended, she had learnt that we see the future with our left-eye and the past with our right-eye. As we had been working so much in getting me to see clairvoyantly through my third-eye, my left eye was reacting to stop me seeing the future. We both got tingles which confirmed we were correct.

THE NEXT DAY, I had my third operation. The Consultant would have rather done the operation with general anaesthetic, I was still wary of GA, as I'd never had it before. I still opted for the LA option. I felt most of that procedure and I apologised to the poor man whose hand I crushed, joking I hoped he had been at a childbirth prior to this, so he could understand. After the operation I was informed that I would need another one in 8 weeks to remove the cataract which grows very rapidly after eye surgery, and to have the oil which was inserted to keep the retina flat, so giving it time to heal and seal without tearing.

ONE THING I remember after that time was the fact I did not need any pain relief whatsoever. I was on a total high. I could still feel the healing energies all around me and to have finally discovered more about myself, my true self, my soul. Everything suddenly became clearer. I knew that something else was going on. Something bigger was afoot!

·   ·   ·

ALTHOUGH OFF WORK, due to poor eyesight and constant operations or so it seemed, I still managed to hold onto my sanity with my healing work, my meditation group and my fellow sisters & brothers AKA 'The Chicklets'! Two weeks after my first operation in September, I manifested through the Angels that I would be able to join the first Angelic 3&4 course Tina was teaching. Kelvin had gone to Wales, (ohhh, did I mention the fact he is Welsh? Suppose my surname Jones gives it away). He was taking Izzie back to Cardiff Uni and called in to see his mum in Porthcawl).

BY NOW MY vibration was rising and rising. I loved this healing modality and wanted so much to offer this to people to help them in their spiritual/self-healing journeys, I was and still am hooked. It is an awesome energy feeling and to be honest, you really don't want to leave it and go back into the 'Matrix' – the Real World, or is it?

ONTO DECEMBER 2017, had my fourth operation and first with general anaesthetic. Yes finally, I could see just in time for Christmas. Still early days with the lens I had received. The day after Boxing Day, the doctor and hospital both called me in for a post-op appointment the following morning. Off we went again to William Harvey Hospital in Ashford. My third operation was done there and it was easier to travel to and cheaper than a train into London each time. I had my scan. The senior registrar looked and looked, then left the room. I was called into another Consultants office to be told, that yet again the retina had began to lift and tear. I needed another emergency op the next day. She explained that this rarely ever happens and that due to the amount of previous operations and damage, I was unlikely to get much central vision back. But she could try and save my peripheral vision and so enable me to keep driving.

. . .

THIS IS when I finally flipped! I was devastated! I had previously exceeded my families and friends' expectations on how calm and positive my attitude had remained all those past months. To be honest, I had been rather impressed myself on just how well I had been coping. But this was the straw that broke the camel's back, so to speak.

I'VE HAD a lot of these moments in my life, I have found life very stressful and hard to cope with at times. When I was a young mother, the return to full-time work just didn't work out for me. I hated the fact that I had to leave my beautiful baby daughter at home, (all be it, with my mum), and go to work all day. It really got me down. I wanted to spend quality time with Abi, and enjoy the experience, not be totally stressed out in a now demanding job. Certainly, anything which kept me away from my daughter I would have felt the same. One day, I got as far as the staff car-park and could not make myself walk into the office. I had frozen. I ended up at the GP instead and onto Prozac. It calmed me down and helped me focus and have some clarity.

THINKING BACK, I must always have had some chemical imbalance of the brain, as I have tried so hard on many occasions to slowly wean myself off these drugs. Even in the course of writing this chapter, I really thought I had finally cracked it, I had done some self-healing, I should be ok now, right? Wrong! It has taken both Kelvin and Izzie to point out that I was again suffering from a major dip in serotonin. The fact that my mum has been on anti-depressants for years is also an indicator that there might be something lacking in our DNA/Genetic Gene pool.

SINCE MY AWAKENING, my spiritual & self-healing journey has been tough at times. But at each time, I had a network of beautiful souls to support & love me. They recognise in me, who I truly am, something which I have had a struggle to actually see myself. I am always in awe and wonderment, with what people write and comment about me in cards, feedback and in general. I used to think 'WHAT ME?' It's taken this past year and working with Tina and my Soul Family to finally start believing in 'MYSELF'.

So, back to the fifth operation on 29ᵗʰ December 2017. The lady consultant who I had seen before and during the operation had lasered away all previous scar tissue and put in silicone oil. This stayed in my eye until December 2018. I was luckily enough to go to Spain in the October, but due to the flight and the length of time the oil had been in my eye holding down the retina, the pressure was increasing and became very painful, at times I honestly felt like my eyeball was going to explode. Boy, did I pray hard and ask for healing. This was my last chance of sight. I needed this to work. I kept making pacts with the Creator, "So you want me to serve you? Then please give me my eye sight back 20/20 vision".

I HAD ALREADY DISCUSSED and decided with my manager that I would not be able to return to work, doing the same job as before. In fact, as the year progressed it became more and more obvious to me, how little I could do on the PC. I was always mistyping. When you work with figures, you don't have the option to spell-check. I find it hard to read a book as after half an hour my right eye gets watery and I struggle to focus. To cut a long story even shorter, I was given the option of retiring early on ill-health grounds. "Yes, I can do this, I am being called to work, to heal, teach and help others. I cannot turn back now". If I did ignore my calling, my destiny, call it what you will, well I don't want to even contemplate it now.

. . .

HAVING MADE A MASSIVE DECISION, I thought things might actually settle down for me, I would work from the Alders Healing Sanctuary, in Ramsgate. But no, the Universe had not finished with me just yet. It was on my first Theta-Healing course, Basic DNA which Tina was teaching at the Alders in late January, that someone appeared at the door and handed me a letter. I was the only member of the Alders there at the time. It was a letter saying we had three-months to vacate the building. What a huge shock! The Alders had been going for over 60 years, and in a building, which was purpose built for us by the Alder family. However, due to reasons I won't go into, the building was bequeathed to a charity in London and they had decided to sell the place.

THERE WAS no way we could afford to buy it. We all worked there out of love and donations only. To be totally honest, the last 20 or so regulars left had all retired, some were in their 80's and had worked there for years and years. I was gutted, but you can imagine how the others must have felt. They all thought they would see their life-time out there. In March 2018, we vacated the premises. Some of us had already thought that this was the Universe yet again, working in its mysterious way, and getting us working out in the community more. I moved my meditation group into my home, and started doing healing sessions from there too, another one of us started up his Shamanic Drumming Circle in a seaside café after closing time etc. It was very much trial and error, but I thank my loyal group for sticking with me.

ON A VISIT to South Wales that spring as I took in the coastline and realised yet again, how beautiful nature is, I suddenly knew I had to work there. My vision to open and run my own healing centre & retreat had started to take seed. But my feet were well and truly buried deep down in East Kent, plus my mum was there too. I didn't really want to move away did I? I had a beautiful home, lovely friends and many soul family members which had kept me going through the bad times.

In June a group of Soul Sisters went on a Goddess Retreat in Glastonbury, this was my first ever retreat with other women and as I was getting into the car, Kelvin, who was driving me and two other sisters on his way to Wales pointed out the milometer on his car. 111111 – New Beginnings. How excited we were, a jolly bunch of chatterboxes all looking forward to our first retreat and a break from everyday life for a few days, enjoying totally us time. It was an excellent weekend and cannot wait to do another Tina retreat.

From January 2018 to February 2019, , I kept up my Theta Healing training. Having undertaken Advanced DNA, and those of us in the first wave of Tina's teaching were looking forward to Dig Deeper that April. When you start on this journey with a group of others you become so close, as you share your innermost self with each other. A strong bond is formed, I have never really felt this before. When recently asked why I felt the pull so strongly to be with my Soul Family, I replied instantly "they just get me, no judgement, just pure love".

During our Dig Deeper course Tina looked at me and she could sense that I was beginning to resist something deep within me. We call this a 'Trigger'. When a deep emotion is struggling to come up to the surface of your sub-conscious self, and your conscious-self tries to fight it. It comes up to be healed. Tina then asked me to sit down and allow her and Creator to work with me. I suddenly saw myself as the Seer in Atlantean times, (the one Tina had seen the previous November the night before my operation) this time I was standing amongst a pile of rubble.

I TRIED and tried but couldn't see/sense anything else. Tina guided me to the end of that lifetime and saw me take my own life. As soon as she said this, I knew again, that this had happened, I felt the guilt and the shame. Something I had been carrying around with me in this current life-time, but no idea why! We cleared it and I felt relieved. Still though, at the back of my mind, I needed to know what I was doing in the rubble!

MOVING onto another Theta course in October, Family Ties, (have you guessed yet, that I am in fact hooked on these amazing out of this world energy?) Those of us who attended this course all experienced huge shifts. Once again, I saw myself standing amongst the rubble in a white robe with my arms outstretched. The anger and frustration I felt was immense. I had caused the temple to collapse, I saw myself pleading with the High Council of Atlantis and trying to get them to understand what I had seen in my vision, that all of Atlantis was going to fall. They refused to believe me, so in my anger and frustration I took it out on the temple. When I saw this, I started to cry (again), I had finally seen clairvoyantly one of my past lives. I could feel it, see it. It was totally awesome!

THEN THE VISION SWITCHED, and the temple was standing again, people in brightly coloured robes where walking up and down the steps outside, and others were coming up to me with arms outstretched, welcoming me home, and so happy that I could see them after eons of lifetimes later. I cried with the sheer joy and happiness. I didn't want to come back to be honest with you! (Might have had something to do with trying to wean myself off the AntiD's again).

. . .

I HAVE ALWAYS BEEN conscious of acts of injustice. I remember vividly as does my oldest friend, of playing in my garden as 7-year olds, a policeman arriving and saying that my elderly neighbour had called him and accused me of poking sticks at her dog through holes in the fence. I was so mad at being wrongly accused I remember literally jumping up and down on the spot screaming at the policeman that I had not done it. This has always lingered in the back of my mind, and only in November last year, did the relevance of this make sense. As a result of not being taken seriously in Atlantis, I have brought over from that life-time to this life-time and more than likely other past life-times in between, the all consuming passion I feel when an injustice has occurred.

MOVING backwards in time to the first weekend of August 2018, Kelvin had been trying to call his mother. However, there was no answer on the Friday or Saturday. She had been a fit 87 year-old who was always out and about most days doing one thing or another. Her neighbour had taken a weekend trip away, so we couldn't contact her either.

AFTER CALLING AGAIN Sunday morning at 7am and still getting no answer, Kelvin was in the car speeding to South Wales, he met up with Abi somewhere along the M4. I couldn't go with Kelvin then as we had some English students staying and one more arriving later in the day. I then spent the rest of the day trying to get friends to take over and it included looking after our dog and cat. As I was racing around, getting everything and everyone organised, I suddenly became aware of the number 222 which kept popping up. 222 – Divine Timing – Interesting!

THE POLICE GOT THERE first and found his mum on the floor in the kitchen. We all thought she had just fallen. She had a life-line, but like so many others, it was sitting on her bedside table. It turned out she had had a massive stroke. I went over on the train the next day, with some clothes etc and Kelvins medications, as he had panicked and not taken anything with him the day before. The following Saturday, Betty (Kelvin's Mum) suffered another stroke before our very eyes. But she had been left with little or no vocal communication, so none of us quite knew what was happening, Kelvin and I just asked the Angels to send healing to her.

DUE TO THE touch and go scenario Kelvin stayed in Wales. He put his business on hold and lived up there the whole time she remained in hospital. If it had not been for him, checking in everyday and sitting with her she would never have left the place alive.

AS IT NOW IS, she has defied all medical knowledge and is back living in her home, with very little help. I managed to stay up with Kelvin for the first three to four weeks. During those first weeks, I saw Kelvin struggle with the shock and he could not have tried harder to help his mum. We both explored various ways in trying to communicate, I thought about how good she has always been with numbers, so bought in a pack of cards, that and singing seemed to help us all. One can only imagine how hard it must be for her and others like her to be trapped and unable to get across what you want or need.

BY THE END of the third week, I started to struggle with it all. Prior to this event, Betty had made it clear that she was not to be placed in a home. Kelvin felt he had to become her full-time carer. That was how it was looking then. I could not understand how I had gone through all the past year, thinking, working on myself, dreaming of my vision, and with various messages from psychic friends that everything in my life up till then was as it should be, and all will be well. I would be a success, would be a great healer, help teach and assist others in their journeys too, to suddenly seeing my future change and mapped out caring alongside my husband for his mum full-time in Wales.

AT THIS TIME ALSO, my own mother (Marion) was going through a bad bout of depression and our relationship became strained to the point we couldn't speak to one another without hurting each other. I also, missed my dog and cat. Medena is a cross-terrier dog we rescued from Croatia in 2013, and I knew she was not coping too well being passed around various friends. She has always been able to pick-up on my moods, it seems even from a distance.

AN INTERESTING FACT COMING UP, did you know that dogs take on their owners' illness? Unfortunately, dogs do not know how to release said illness and they themselves can become ill. However, a cat can do the same, but it instinctively knows how to release it. I will give you two examples which have occurred with me and my pets over the past year. On one occasion in 2017, after I had the 2nd eye operation, I came home from hospital to find Medena had an ulcerated left eye. That week we were both like the partial blind leading the partial blind on walks. Following on from my most recent eye op, I found it quite hard with the pain this time. Is it I'm getting older and taking longer to heal?

WHATEVER, I was in bed clutching my crystals and the cat jumped onto the bed. Dragon is a rescue too. Usually when he is on the bed is when he's most affectionate. He is all over me and yes, dribbling like a baby. Yuk! But this time I noticed he did not come near my face, perhaps the eye guard put him off, but he just snuggled up to me and I could feel the pain energy pulsating out of my body and into him. I lay there in total awe. It was an amazing feeling and one I shall not forget. I even drifted off to a healing and much needed sleep. I always give my pets healing, they love it.

So, after three or so weeks I ran back home to my roots, to my beloved animals and yes to my mum too. September flew by, I ran my second Angelic Reiki course, I attended another Theta course, 'Manifesting and Abundance.' All of us had been waiting a year to sit this one course! I had to do this course if nothing else this year.

I HAVE CHANGED SO MUCH in the past 17 years, but none so much as this past year. I am thankful to Tina for coming into my life and for guiding me along the way. We have helped each other, we all help each other. That's the sheer beauty of connecting with like-minded people who are willing to do the work, and put in the hours and yes, expense when required, to become a higher, more positive, healthier person.

So, now I'm in late November, Kelvin has been in Wales since August. I have my 6<sup>th</sup> eye operation coming up, I been trying hard to get my healing business up and running but kept meeting various obstacles. I needed to earn money to pay the bills. More and more, the idea of a retreat/healing centre was taking a grip, but still I ignored it. Then finally, I was drawn to have a reading.

DURING THAT READING, I was told:-

- a) What was I doing having a reading? I already knew what I needed to do.
- b) My Dad came through and said he couldn't tell me what to do. I had to decide myself.

- c) I said I needed confirmation that I was doing the right thing in moving away and leaving my mum and all my friends and soul family.
- d) The medium then started to pull cards out randomly. A move away, green, green grass of home started playing in her head, a centre was being opened that was mine. I was being sent to do this to help others, that it was a new beginning. That there would be no regrets, only joy, happiness, abundance and family around me.

I LEFT the room feeling relieved, and re-motivated, as still my future was being reassured. The Creator and Universe helps those who help themselves. So, by the end of the following week, I had the house valued and started to tell my friends of my decision. Of course, I told Kelvin, he had already started saying a few years ago that he would love to move back to Wales, so things were beginning to look brighter. We would finally be clear of mortgage and debt, we could start over again.

IT'S NOW the 31st December, Kelvin is now home, and the house has been on the market just 10 days. In those 10 days over the Christmas period, we received 3 offers.

DIVINE TIMING IS STILL PLAYING a big part, but we have both been struggling with stepping into the unknown, leaving a place we love, friends, soul family. We are working on it, isn't there a book out there somewhere, entitled, 'Feel the Fear, and Do It Anyway?' We have now passed the New Year, and both Kelvin and myself are in another period of self-healing.

. . .

WE ARE DETERMINED NOW MORE than ever, to deal with the shit, that has held us back in both of our lives and in which we have affected our daughters' lives too. Only last week I treated myself to some therapy, which I had previously 'had a problem with', this changed how I have been feeling for over 52 years, and I will come off the antidepressants. It is also a genetic thing but it is not untreatable, as I once thought, even a few weeks ago. So, we are embracing the New Year as a New Beginning, A Fresh Start and we will move to South Wales in the late spring of 2019. Just waiting for the right house, in the right area to present itself to us when the time is right!

I WANT to say a HUGE Thank You to my husband, Abi and Izzie, Mum, our many friends and Soul Family who have helped us over the many years. Without you all we would not be here today.

I LOVE YOU ALL xx

# ABOUT THE AUTHOR

## SALLY JONES

Sally is a 54-year-old, mother of two beautiful grown-up daughters and has been married to Kelvin for 27 years.

She has always been intrigued and fascinated with all things spiritual since a teenager, when, on the passing of a young Aunt, her mum gave her a Doris Stokes book to read, if you haven't heard of Doris Stokes please look her up. She was an amazing medium many years ago.

Although Sally worked within the NHS for 29 years until 2018, she still felt something was missing from her life. She had a secure job which she loved, she had a loving husband and family, pets, home, everything, but she still didn't feel totally satisfied. She knew there was more, but was unsure how to find it.

In 2001, she lost her beloved father to lung cancer at the age of just 57. She had spoken to him about trying other methods of healing, and he promised to visit a local healing sanctuary. Unfortunately, he never made it. However, following on from that promise Sally paid the place a visit. It was just down the road from her home and she passed it every day en-route to the girls' primary school in Ramsgate.

Upon walking inside, the peace and amazing energies wrapped themselves around her and she never looked back. She started attending the Spirit communication services each Sunday, each time the same message was given to her from Spirit, 'One day you are going to be an amazing healer.'

She attended every Monday evening for a meditation circle and regular healing. Sally found this a very healing time and the lovely people there became her second family.

Sally met Tina Pavlou for the first time at an Angel Workshop, in 2013, when Tina caught her eye and told her that she was going to be very successful one-day!

Sally is always keen to learn and explore all things weird & wacky, and from 2009 she started training as a Spiritual healer, learnt crystal healing in 2013, then explored Usui Reiki. After that, things had started to change at the Healing Sanctuary, as Sally became more and more active.

Being the youngest there she took on more and more responsibility. In September 2016, Tina came back into her life, this time on a more permanent note and they became friends. Within just two months Tina had started running courses at the Alders and Sally attended most of them.

Sally has her own unique blend of healing which incorporates her many healing gifts to which she has had much success and feedback over the years, to not only humans but animals and plants too.

She also runs regular attunement courses in the beautiful Angelic Reiki, Spiritual Awakening/Awareness Classes.

Sally is also a Theta Healing Therapist and teaches/runs various meditation groups and classes across the local area, including teaching Mindfulness to hospital staff where she worked for so long.

Sally has adopted a saying "Before you can help others, you must first start to heal yourself!"

**Contact**

    Email – <u>sally178@talktalk.net</u>

    Website - www.sunflowerenergyhealing.co.uk

    LinkedIn – www.linkedin.com/in/sally-jones-sunflower

    Facebook Group:

    https://www.facebook.com/groups/228035934393661/

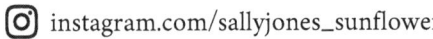 instagram.com/sallyjones_sunflower

# SARAH JANE FITZGERALD

*H*ave you ever just sat and contemplated what life is all about? How do we get here? Why are we placed within these specific bodies, and why do some have a stereotypically great life, yet others have it a lot harder? I always used to ask myself, why is this happening to me? Why do I have to face one thing after another? Why can't I just have a nice family, a nice quiet life? Of course, after having come so far, I finally understand that I wouldn't be the person I am today without all of the life lessons.

Now, here I am, fortunate enough to be able to share just some of the pieces of my story with you (though diluted down somewhat); some of you may resonate with the experiences of my past, just as some of you may have gone through harder circumstances, and some easier. After all, each of us face different trials in our lives, and I just hope that someone, somewhere, will be able to take something away from me sharing my personal journey with you.

. . .

I HAD what you might call a challenging childhood: I grew up in a poor family living in North West London; I struggled with bullying in school; had a mother who left when I was four years old, leaving us with a violent, angry father. Needless to say, my life was filled with challenges from an early age, and I constantly used to daydream about my 'real parents' coming to rescue me one day.

MY ONE SAVING grace while I was growing up was my beautiful grandmother. Whenever I was with her I felt safe, (even when she was telling me off!). The bond we had was unlike anything else I had ever felt, she truly was my guardian angel, my protector. To this day, I still remember the amazing ability she had to wipe away my troubles just by stroking my hair. I used to sit on the floor by her feet and lay with my head on her lap, and I could just feel the positive energy and love flowing through her hands. I knew no matter how bad life was, or how many bruises were inflicted upon me, that just a single minute in my nan's arms would make it all better.

ALTHOUGH MY CHILDHOOD wouldn't be winning any world records for 'best upbringing', I had become accustomed to my routine, no matter how turbulent it was; so, my world was thrown off-kilter at the age of 11 when my dad married a woman who didn't want us in the picture and sent us to live with our mother in Kent. My world fell apart. You might think that it was a lucky escape from my father, but my only thought was that I was being taken miles away from my nan, the one person who I knew loved me and made me feel safe. I know my Nan was devastated too: we sobbed our hearts out saying goodbye the first time, and every time after that when I visited, even when we spoke on the phone. Saying goodbye was always the hardest thing to do.

LIFE with my mother was inconceivably different to what I was used to. I went from living in a poor London home with a controlling father, who only fed us the cheapest, most basic foods and dressed us in second hand clothes, to living with an estranged mother who was always out at work and thought that love consisted only of feeding us nice foods and providing us with material things. It was so bizarre to experience two different ends of the spectrum, and to know that neither of them were right. My sisters were happier, but I didn't want to be there; I was angry with my mum for walking away when we were little, and I was so heartbroken about being so many miles away from my nan, that I rebelled. I stopped going to school, hung out with the wrong people, got into drinking and other dangerous substances and put myself in very vulnerable situations… anything to block out the pain. My life was a mess. I learnt to be tough, to switch off my emotions but the truth was, I had never felt so alone.

At the age of fourteen, I ended up in voluntary care and was placed in a children's home. I was happier there; looking back I think it was because I finally felt that I fitted in somewhere. I was with other unwanted, misfit kids and, oddly, I felt safe. I had structured routines, proper boundaries, and people who genuinely seemed to care; for the first time, I had hope! Hope that things would get better, that I could make decisions about my life and choose where I wanted to live (unfortunately my nans wasn't an option, but I did get to speak to her more often). I knew it wouldn't work if I returned to my family so I chose to go into foster care, and it was the best thing I could have done. In the two years that I was with them, I learnt what it was like to be part of a 'normal' family. They taught me useful life skills, showed me the importance of going back into education and I was encouraged to work towards a career.

It was this turn around that helped me realise that I wanted to be a social worker; I wanted to help kids like me. I went back to school half way through the last year, sitting exams in Maths, English and Science, and although my grades weren't amazing, they were good enough for me to get into college. So, I enrolled in a two-year Social Care course. I had my doubts I would be able to cope with the academic study as I'd missed so much school but somehow, in my heart, I knew it was the right path for me to take. At the age of seventeen I moved into a bedsit to be nearer to college, which allowed me the opportunity to discover who I really was. I was excited about living on my own, being able make my own decisions and taking charge of my own life.

SURPRISINGLY, two years of college passed quickly, and before I had even graduated, the residential home which was my last college placement, had already offered me a full-time job and I was ecstatic, despite knowing it wasn't what I wanted to do in the long term (I was drawn to working with children but at eighteen I was too young to enter the field). By the age of twenty-one, I was in a steady relationship, had gotten my driver's licence (which allowed me to see my Grandparents more regularly) and I had finally gotten my dream job working with children at a Barnardo's residential school. It was the happiest I had been in a long time; I finally felt I had come into my own.

So, I was heartbroken when, in August 1995, the worst happened. To everyone's shock, my beloved Nan was diagnosed with late stage ovarian cancer and went into hospital. I sat there helplessly day after day, holding her beautiful hand - the hand that radiated love, that had stroked my hair countless times - and I watched with dread as she slowly slipped away. She fought to the end, waiting until all the family were there before she finally let go.

· · ·

I HELD her hand as she took her last breath. It destroyed me; my heart was completely broken. At the funeral the attendees were spilling out into the Churchyard, so many people paying their respects to the beautiful spirit that was Edie. I was so numb that I don't recall the service, but I remember to this day the pain I felt in my heart.

THEY SAY that great heartache changes your perspective, and I think that was true for me, because it was from that day that I started to see her. The first time, she was stood in front of the coffin in the church, as if she'd risen out of the coffin and wanted to see everyone. She was looking around the church, looked at me and smiled... I cried and cried. Was it grief or did I really see her? From then on I felt her presence beside me, and at night as I lay in bed, I'd see her stood beside me, I'd talk to her and recall the feeling of her stroking my hair whilst I cried myself to sleep.

LIFE BECAME NUMB ONCE AGAIN, and I went around in autopilot. Eventually my marriage came to an end and I moved away. Fortunately, I was offered a secondment to another Barnardo's School in Berkshire, which came with a promotion to Deputy Unit Manager of a nine-bed unit. I needed the distraction and the challenge of something new to rise again. I threw myself into work: long shifts, sleep-ins, staff meetings, reviews... time flew by...

THEN SEVEN MONTHS later I was pregnant! (Okay, yes; obviously it didn't happen quite as miraculously as a bump just appearing after seven months, but I thought I'd spare you the details). My bump was not planned but the most amazing news. I was terrified as I'd always said that I would never be a single parent (a prime example of accidently manifesting your fears), but the best life lessons are born from the embracing the unexpected.

I felt sure I could rise to the challenge I had been given, and was motivated to prove that although raising a child alone is a tough job, it could be achieved properly and not in the manner that I had been brought up.

IN DECEMBER 1997, after two whole days of labour and a broken coccyx, Jade Elouise was born! She was the most beautiful baby I'd ever seen (yes, I know all mothers are supposed to think that). She was perfect, and after already being days late, she seemed determined to assert that she would work to no man's schedule but her own, as she slept for a twenty-four hours straight (a skill which she still likes to utilise now).

THOUGH I KNEW it would be a struggle, I had come to terms with being a single mother (Jade's father wasn't up to the task of being a devoted dad), but it did sadden me that my nan had never gotten to see Jade. I used to take her to see my grandad, hoping she would pick up on her energy and feel close to her. Those early years of mother-hood flew by, and it wasn't long before I realised that Jade was gifted; she was walking before the age of one and talking non-stop at the age of two. It was around this time that I realised just how special she was.

ALWAYS THE INDEPENDENT, she loved playing alone in her room with all her toys, and one day I went to check on her and overheard her talking to someone through the closed door. Stood outside listening, I heard her laughing, chatting and being her beautiful bossy self. When I opened the door and asked who she was talking to, her reply was music to my ears: she calmly said, "Nanny silly!" as if it was obvious. I no longer needed to feel sad that they hadn't gotten to meet, and it comforted me to know my nan was with us.

. . .

BEING a single mum changed my life in a lot of ways, from changing my job role so that I could spend more time with Jade in the evenings and weekends, to struggling to make ends meet financially. Between parenting and working full time, it also meant that I rarely got the opportunity to meet people. Which meant that I met my next partner in what might be considered a rather unorthodox fashion: in an online MSN chat room of all things (yes, that was a thing once). One evening as I was signing off to go to bed a message popped up from 'anyonewilldo' who's opening line was "I like your name" (MsGenuine69). As I recall, my reply had been a little flippant "Wish I could say the same about yours!".

WE CHATTED BRIEFLY THEN I signed off, not anticipating that we would start chatting as regularly as we did. We really connected but I didn't think anything would come of it as he was in the army, living in Germany. Little did I know then that Mr Anyonewill do (aka Pete) was going to be my rock in time to come!

AFTER EVERYTHING that I had been through, I hadn't anticipated that I would fall ill. One of the downsides to working in a school environment was the constant spread of viruses, it was common place for staff to come down with something during the term, and 2002 was no exception for me. In October I came down with a cold, which turned into Bronchitis, and I couldn't seem to fight it off. Everything ached, especially my legs; lights hurt my eyes, the slightest noise went piercing through me and anything requiring any level of physical or mental exertion completely exhausted me. This wasn't me, I was a 'get up and go girl' - always busy, always doing things, but now I couldn't even get out of bed without it hurting: just lifting my head up was exhausting.

.   .   .

FINALLY, after eight months of pleading with the doctors for help, I had a diagnosis: Myalgic Encephalomyelitis, more commonly known as M.E. I'd never heard of it, so I started looking into it, and I wasn't consoled by what I found; there was no cure, no quick fix and the medical profession were baffled by it.

Left to manage my symptoms alone, I did a lot of research about M.E. I soon learnt that my body could no longer deal with any processed, unnatural foods or products. I had to change my lifestyle completely, a real challenge at times as preparing food and being organised was a physical struggle. I knew that positivity and determination was key; however, remaining in that mind-set was a challenge in itself when most days I'd struggle to get myself out of bed due to widespread pain and severe fatigue.

THE HARDEST PART was not being able to look after Jade in the way that I believed a mother should. It took all my energy just to get her ready in the morning and take her to nursery, and I would have to come home and rest before going to collect her again in the afternoon. It was an existence not a life. I know kids are naturally resilient and Jade adapted well, but this wasn't the life I wanted my beautiful child to experience, and at three and a half she had become increasingly independent, almost acting as my nurse at times; it shouldn't have been that way and I felt extremely guilty.

EVENTUALLY WITH PERSEVERANCE, I started improving but I had to accept that things weren't going to be the same. I lost my job when occupational health decided I couldn't fulfil my role, which meant I also lost my house as it was owned by Barnardo's. My debt piled up as I couldn't pay my car loan and I lived on credit cards to pay bills. I felt like everything was spiralling out of control, and I was initially distraught when I found out Jade and I were going to be placed in a council caravan in a country park. I had worked so hard to provide a better life for us, and suddenly it felt like I had hit rock bottom.

Throughout it all, my one saving grace was Pete. He would listen to me complain and cry but never lost interest; he even surprised me with regular visits every six to eight weeks. I was over the moon when he told me he'd asked to be posted back to the UK. I honestly believed that my nan had sent him to help me, and when he was posted at a Barracks only 20 minutes away, we were able to see each other all the time, and soon became an item. Not only did he play a significant part in my recovery, but he also stole my heart.

Jade initially struggled with someone else being in the family, but she soon came to love Pete and eventually decided she wanted to call him Dad. In October 2004 we got married, and Jade decided she wanted to change her surname so that it was the same as mine, we truly felt like a proper family.

Finally, the wheel of fate seemed to be turning in our favour again, as we were eventually given a maisonette near a really lovely village school. I was still working hard on my recovery, having regular Reflexology, Massage and Osteopathy to help improve my health, and three years after first becoming ill I was finally feeling ready to go back into work. I joined an agency that really supported me in my integration back into the working world, whilst working with them I undertook a job suitability questionnaire and ironically my ideal job came up as a Reflexologist!

Having had first-hand experience of the benefits of Reflexology, I actually felt that this was something I could do, as it would allow me to help people without putting too much stress on my body. The training was expensive but with the help of Pete's parents I was able to fund the course.

In 2007, after training at the Oxford School of Reflexology, facilitated by a wonderful couple (Geraldine and Keir) I became a qualified Reflexologist. Geraldine is a truly inspiring lady who was very supportive of my journey, and I know I was meant to train with her; I couldn't have asked for a better teacher (we still keep in touch to this day)!

I felt a great sense of achievement and couldn't wait to start my own business, and as Pete was due to be posted to Maidstone in Kent, we decided to make the move and have a fresh start. We were given a lovely house near a good primary school, and Jade settled in well. Unfortunately, the recession had hit at the same time and my dream was struggling to take off, so I sought alternative employment. I went through a few different job roles as I was struggling to find a job I would both enjoy and physically manage, but I eventually ended up working for a 'Meals on Wheels' company, starting off as a delivery driver and working my way up to Contract supervisor. I still practiced Reflexology on family and friends as I knew one day I would start my business back up. After three years I was prompted to make a career change once again, as the stress of the job started to cause a number of M.E. relapses.

I missed working face-to-face with people, so I decided to go back to working with adults with learning disabilities, at the same time that Pete was retiring from the Army after 22 years. This was another significant period of upheaval for us all (though by this point I think we had all acclimatised to the prospect of constant change). Pete and I bought our first home together, moving to a more affordable area just outside of Maidstone. I started work in a Day Service, and Pete was given employment with Waitrose as an HGV driver. It seemed as though our period of transition had worked out for the best: money was tight at times, but we were content as a family.

HOWEVER, over time the dynamics of our home began to shift once again. Though Pete did enjoy his job, he worked long shifts with really early starts, which started to take its toll on him (and my sleep); and over a period of a year or so, Pete's behaviour started to change. His mood was constantly shifting from clingy to distant, moody to overly hyperactive - something so different from the dependable, happy man that I knew and loved.

BY 2013, we had started having progressively intensifying arguments, something which we'd never really done in the nine years we'd been together. In the July we had an argument so monumental that I started questioning if we would get through it. I decided to go away to my sister's house in the Isle of Wight to give us a break from one another, and though we agreed to give each other space, Pete continued to call and text me.

HE SUDDENLY BECAME like a different person on the phone, saying I would regret my decisions. At the time I was confused by what he meant - I thought he was just angry for me not coming back when he asked. I tried to call him the next day but he didn't answer. I rang Jade, and she told me he went out the night before to his friend's house and didn't come home. Initially, I assumed he got drunk and was sleeping it off, but a bad feeling began to form in the pit of my stomach; he wouldn't normally leave Jade overnight. For whatever reason, I knew I had to get home, so I took the next ferry back to Southampton.

. . .

I WAS on the outside deck when I received the worst phone call of my life. I answered to the question 'Is that Sarah Fitzgerald?' and my heart began to sink. He identified himself as the police and from that moment I knew. Out of my mouth rolled the words "Please don't tell me he's dead."

BUT MY WORST fears were confirmed.

I'M NOT REALLY sure how the rest of the conversation went. I was an emotional wreck and only made it home with the assistance of the kind ferry staff and a police escort. At the time, all I could think about was how I was going to tell Jade, and after that hurdle was crossed, I was unable to focus on anything for days, overwhelmed by the feeling that it was all my fault. My husband had killed himself, and I was consumed by regret. I cried for days, but by the time the funeral came around I had run out of tears: self-preservation had kicked in, and I knew I had to be strong and resilient so I wouldn't crumble.

AT THE WAKE many of Pete's army colleagues approached me to share the experiences they (and Pete) had endured on operational tours and it was their belief that Pete must have been suffering from PTSD. Some of his retired colleagues had been employed as drivers upon leaving service but they had found this too difficult and isolating, stating that spending twelve hours a day alone in a truck gave them too much time to reflect, and that past experiences would come flooding back to haunt them. For me the pieces of the jigsaw started to slot into place, such as his change of behaviour after a day at work. I also found out that when Pete was just eighteen his Staff Sergeant was found in a hanger having taken his own life the same way Pete had. As horrible as it was to hear all this, in a strange way it helped answer some questions.

REBUILDING our lives was a challenge like no other. I was no stranger to grief, I'd lost my nan (1996), followed by my grandad (2001), and then my dad (2008) but this was a new kind of pain. No one can prepare you for everything you go through when someone commits suicide, from the emotional turmoil and unanswered questions, to the stigma associated with taking your own life. I only got through by taking life a day at a time and compartmentalising my feelings. To some, to most in fact, I must have looked cold (I felt it) but it was the only way I could cope.

LIFE DESTROYING moments like this change you in lots of ways. They break you down, and when you are finally able to start rebuilding again, the person you become is different to who you once were. Though I had never been religious, there had always been a spiritual side to me - call it great empathy, or latent psychic ability, whatever you like – which had allowed me to feel the presence of my loved ones after they'd passed away. However, unlike with previous experiences, I hadn't felt Pete's presence around me after he died, so I tried to reach him through a Medium on a couple of occasions. Other loved ones would come through like my nan, my nephew and dad but not Pete - I was told it was too soon.

THEN MY LOVELY FRIEND, Nicola, told me about Tina Pavlou. She said she was a truly gifted psychic medium and that I would benefit from seeing her, so trusting her judgement I tried to get in touch with Tina. She was very busy, but I found out she was at a Psychic Fair in London so Jade and I decided to go and see if we could get a reading with her. Unfortunately, she wasn't doing readings that day, but was instead holding Angelic meditation group sessions, so we signed up for next session. While we were waiting, I happened to see Tina heading to get a drink. Feeling increasingly like a stalker, I followed her and introduced myself in the hope that I might be able to get something from her. I introduced myself, explaining that my friend had recommended her, and her first words provided all of the confirmation of her abilities I needed.

"HELLO DARLING," she beamed in that way of hers. "Who's that stood behind you, wearing a hat? He's got big ears and a smiley face!" I knew she meant Pete, it was a perfect description! As my eyes filled with tears, she touched my hand and said, 'Darling you are going to be absolutely fine, honestly!".

THE ANGELIC HEALING Meditation Tina gave was beautiful, and Guided Angel Meditations soon became my saving grace. I would meditate morning and evening, and any other time I felt I needed angelic support. I have to admit I struggled at times with believing in Angels as I was not at all religious, in fact I'd always said I didn't believe in God; it was difficult to wrap my head around the idea that a higher power would allow so many bad things to happen in the word, to allow people to suffer. People often asked how I could believe in Angels but not God, but I eventually gave up trying to find an answer; I believed what I believed, and I didn't want to over analyse it.

OVER THE NEXT few years I worked to build my life back up again, deciding that I wanted to start my own complementary therapy business. I dropped my hours at work and started training in Massage to compliment the Reflexology. I undertook many CPD courses to bring my knowledge and skills up to date. I decided that I wanted to be able to open my own therapy room, so started looking for a home with a space which would be suitable for a business, which is how Jade and I ended up in our current home. It had basement space with its own entrance and two rooms, ideal for a new business, and although it needed a lot of renovation, I had faith it would work out somehow. A move in date was set for January 2015, and both Jade and I were excited for the change.

On New Year's Eve 2014, Jade had a party at the house, and I had a couple of friends over, during which time they both encouraged me to set up a Tinder account. I wasn't overly enthused by the idea, but I let them talk me into it. I continued to swipe left face after face, uninterested in anyone who came up... except one man whose face caught my eye. He had a genuine look about him and a kindness in his eyes which convinced me to swipe right before closing the app and not giving the matter any further thought.

When I woke on New Year's Day there was a message on Tinder from the guy with the kind eyes (more commonly known as Paul). We started exchanging messages and I was enjoying our conversation, so we decided to speak on the phone. He had a great sense of humour and made me laugh...and I loved the sound of his voice (bonus!). He asked me out on a date, and we met up two days later (after a thorough grilling from my then sixteen-year-old daughter on the dangers of online dating!) I was really nervous and had my guard up, which he mistook for me not being interested but once we'd had a few drinks we both relaxed a little more. There was something about Paul that intrigued me: I'd look into his eyes and it was like I could feel the true nature of his soul.

I just knew he had a heart of gold and was certain we'd been brought together by fate! Though he was a D.I. in the Met, Paul also had a passion for building and renovations, and despite only knowing each other for a few weeks he helped us move into the new house, and went around the house telling me what work needed to be done, volunteering to help.

PAUL SPENT the next two years of his spare time renovating my run-down house, and building my treatment room, as well as working on his own home. He really is truly gifted and extremely generous and supportive. He has three amazing kids of his own, each with very different personalities: the boys are petrol heads like Paul, one creative and one sporty, where as his daughter is a nurse by day and girl's girl by night.

I HONESTLY DO BELIEVE we were bought together to complement (and challenge) one another. We're at two different ends of the spectrum at times, and Paul still struggles to understand my beliefs around Angels (which you can't blame him for) he jokes that my herbal medicines are 'potions' and refers to Angelic Reiki and Reflexology as 'witchy stuff!'. Nonetheless, he is incredibly supportive and always encourages me to do what I think is right (even when he doesn't agree with it) and having his support means a lot to me whilst I continued my spiritual journey.

AND WHAT A JOURNEY it has been so far. Tina and I had stayed in touch since our encounter at the psychic fair. She told me about Angelic Reiki, and she added me to the Chicklets and Roosters page so I could find out more about the healing work they did as a community. I have to say I was fascinated by what others were saying about Angelic Reiki and how it changes your life. Soon enough, everything fell into place, and I found myself on a course to become a level 1 and 2 Angelic Reiki Healer.

THE EXPERIENCES I went through during this process were profound. One such particular moment took place during my second attunement, I remember feeling a deep aching in my upper back throughout the process, before being overcome by the rushing growth of angel wings, like a warmth spreading across my back. They enveloped me, held me close, and I felt the love of a thousand angels surrounding me. It brought me to joyous tears (well actually I was sobbing!) and I felt something within me change for the better.

I LEARNT a lot about self-development on the course and found pieces of myself which I had been missing for so long. The experiences had left me wanting more, and I knew that I wanted to eventually go on to teach Angelic Reiki in the future, as I wanted to share the healing beauty of it with others. Becoming a Reiki healer had allowed me to connect with Angels and experience the true meaning of unconditional love. Having never received it from my parents, I had always lacked that wholesome feeling of knowing real love, having only ever felt a love like that before in the arms of my nan; I had missed it so much. It also allowed me to truly connect with myself, something I hadn't really achieved before.

EVEN THOUGH I was getting to know others within the healing community Tina has created, I still felt a little bit of an outsider. I think it was because I had always struggled with building relationships with others, especially with women, I really struggled to trust them (mother issues!). It wasn't until I went on a Tina's Glastonbury retreat with a group of Chicklets and allowed myself to be vulnerable and face these barriers, that I finally felt I had found a place where I belonged. I will never forget the trust and connection that I developed with these wonderful women during our time together in Glastonbury, as it was a huge breakthrough for me in terms of building relationships with others.

I FEEL I should share that each time I move onto the next step of my spiritual journey, I find myself entering a space of real reflection and introspection, during which time I feel like detaching myself from others, it's a strange feeling but it I know it allows me to process and move further on in my journey. Yes, there have been moments of doubt along the way, because the idea of believing in a higher power, in Angels, is something which is difficult to come to terms with. But I couldn't deny the experiences I'd had, or the shifts in emotional state within myself.

I WENT on to do Angelic Reiki 3 and 4 (Masters) which was an equally beautiful and profound experience. I found that the more I went into that healing space, the greater my intuition became, something which really assisted me in my work as a complementary therapist. Part of my development includes assisting Tina with other groups, and on a few occasions I have witnessed Tina clearing negative energies and entities using Theta Healing. It was that which prompted me to go on to do Theta, in order to learn how to clear any negative influences which may present themselves during my healing work, and possibly teaching, in the future. So in late 2018 I started the process of becoming a Theta Healer and have completed the basic DNA course, another life changing experience!

I FEEL TRULY BLESSED to have met Tina and the Chicklets, and I am so grateful for the support they have given me. It's comforting to know that you can reach out for guidance, clearing, or just for a chat whenever you need to. I've always been a caring and loving person but I feel like I've finally learnt to receive love in a way I could never have imagined.

LOOKING BACK, I realise that all I have been through has taught me valuable life lessons which I had to experience to get to the stage I am at now, and although it has been challenging, heart-breaking and unbearable at times, I understand that it was also necessary. I look forward now to continuing on this path of positivity, and to helping others through my work as a healer and complementary therapist over the years to come.

# ABOUT THE AUTHOR

## SARAH FITZGERALD

Sarah Jane Fitzgerald is a mother first, and entrepreneur second, and has devoted her life to raising her daughter Jade over the past two decades.

Sarah is an empath and intuitive Complementary Therapist. She is also the owner of Relax Rejuvenate Repair, a growing Complementary Therapy business based in Maidstone, Kent. She is an experienced support worker, with over thirty years' worth of experience within the health and social care sector, having undertaken various roles with both vulnerable adults and children with special needs. She has also gained diplomas in a number of sectors, from Massage and Reflexology, to Social Care and Care Management.

Sarah uses her talents in reflexology and massage to help people through physical and emotional difficulties in their lives. This entails working with a variety of clients: from peri-menopausal women who wish to reduce their levels of stress and anxiety; to clients in need of lymphatic drainage; and oncology patients who are looking for an complementary method to help relieve symptoms of cancer treatments and reduce levels of pain.

After a challenging and inconsistent upbringing, Sarah eventually ended up in the social care system herself. Her difficult start in life, and the many obstacles she has faced since, from physical and emotional abuse to great emotional loss, has guided her into a life dedicated to helping others in need; not only in a professional capacity, but also in her personal life.

Sarah currently splits her time between growing her business as a Complementary Therapist, and working part time as a support worker for adults with learning disabilities. She has recently gained funding to set up a Complementary Therapy provision within the Day Service where she works. The prospect of being able to bring together the two roles she loves into one space is something she has always hoped to achieve, and now with the power to manifest at her side, it seems her wishes are finally coming true.

Sarah has undergone great change in her life over the past few years, after becoming an Angelic Reiki Master and starting on her journey to become a Theta Healer, she has experienced massive shifts within herself and how she sees the world. She is now firmly on the path of positivity and unconditional love, and aims to spread that message of self love and healing to all whom she crosses paths with.

**Contact**
Email: sarahr-r-r@outlook.com
Website: www.relaxrejuvenaterepair.co.uk

facebook.com/RelaxRejuvenateRepair
instagram.com/relaxrejuvenaterepair

# TRACEY STEMBRIDGE

*I* am telling you some facts about my life, that I hope will help you, or someone you know, get through a bad point in life, to believe there truly is a light at the end of a tunnel, no matter how dark things get. Maybe it will just be enough to help you see that nothing is that bad, that no matter what happens, there is always a way forward, a way to live your life after anything.

FROM A YOUNG AGE I remember always feeling not quite right, not fitting in with my family, almost as if I was not really a part of it. My brother and sister were very close and would always seem to be together, whilst I was the baby sister that just seemed to get in the way. I never really understood why I felt like that, somewhere inside of me just felt different. I would say I was a difficult child, I didn't really follow rules that well whilst growing up and would get into trouble a fair bit, especially during my secondary school years. I loved animals though, well animals, creatures, almost anything that wasn't human. When there were school holidays coming up, I'd always volunteer to bring something home, newts, frogs spawn, mice, well it was a mouse, but over the holidays it turned into several mice. Once, I even let a little kitten in the house and made out I knew nothing about it.

MY MUM THOUGHT it was lost, so put an advert in the local shop. Turned out it wasn't a kitten, but a very old little cat with hardly any teeth and it belonged to an old man, they were reunited. I thought I was being helpful giving the kitten a new home. I think my parents knew I'd always end up bringing something different home from school, or just from outside. I loved horse riding too, the smell of horses was just pure bliss to me. I ran away from home once and was found in the stables with the horses, where I felt very safe. So, yes, I think I was trouble for my parents and that also made me feel I didn't fit in, belong, as I just didn't act in the normal, expected way.

IN JULY 1979 my parents moved us to Ramsgate in Kent, I didn't want to move as I had just turned 16 years of age and had just left school. I didn't take to this move well, I didn't know anyone, which probably made the move even harder than it should have been for me. After around 11 months, my parents sold their house in Ramsgate and purchased a hotel in Cliftonville, Margate. I met a few people there that weren't really that good for me. They got me out and about, instead of being on my own, it wasn't that good though, as I ended up getting into the habit of drinking alcohol to pass the time. I became bored with these people and the drinking and moved on to find some new friends. This is when, one night while out, I met my first husband.

IN SEPTEMBER 1981 I gave birth to a beautiful baby girl, she was perfect, everything I'd ever dreamed of since I was a little girl myself. I finally had something, or rather someone, I could love and spend my time looking after, whilst at the same time feeling I had a purpose in life. I wasn't just Tracey the oddball, the black sheep of the family. I was a mummy, I was needed, someone truly relied on me, and it felt good. I wasn't overly happy with my relationship, but I believed that as I had a child with my then partner, I had to stay with him, I felt it was expected of me.

I DIDN'T WANT JUST one child, so I had planned to have another baby, just one more daughter, to make my life complete. I used to think that 2 daughters were the perfect family, so that's what I wanted. I didn't quite know how to tell my mum I was having another baby out of wedlock. I sort of put it off, but when I went for my first scan, I was told I was having twins, I was in shock and thought I really have got to tell my mum now. When I telephoned her that day, I remember the conversation like it was yesterday, 'Mum,' I said, 'you're going to be a grandma again.'

'YES, I KNOW,' my mum said, 'I've just been to see Julia (Julia is not her real name, but this is the name I will refer to her as, she was a medium my parents used to visit) and she saw a baby girl and a baby boy coming.' I remember thinking, no way is that right, I was adamant I was having girls, I said to my mum 'She's wrong, I'm having twin girls and they will be identical.'

IN APRIL 1983, I gave birth to two beautiful baby girls. The first born, was a little smaller than the second. There was a slight complication with giving birth to the second baby, I had to be given a general anaesthetic, so she could be delivered by hand. She'd managed to get caught up and needed to be freed. The twins were taken to the baby special care unit, due to them being a multiple birth, they were cold and small, I didn't see them until I had fully recovered from the anaesthetic. I was taken down to see them on my bed and held them for the first time, for what seemed like a few seconds, but was a lot longer than that. I was then taken back to the ward, away from my girls.

AFTER 3 DAYS, I was moved into a mummy's bedroom in the unit to be with them and after 8 days we were allowed home. I had an 18-month-old daughter and new born identical twin daughters, I was happy, my eldest daughter Zena (Zena is not her real name, but this is the name I will refer to her as) adored her new sisters. I remember saying to mum 'See, Julia was wrong, I have twin girls, not a girl and boy'.

NOT LONG AFTER they were born, I started having feelings that there was something wrong with one of them, I didn't know which twin, or what was wrong. I used to telephone my GP's surgery for appointments or the out of hours Doctors, I even used to take them to A & E to see the Doctors there. I kept telling them there was something wrong with one of my babies, I didn't know which one, or what was wrong. In the end, I was diagnosed with post-natal depression. I was only just 20 years old, the month after the twins were born, and there was nothing visibly wrong with either of the twins. I was given some sort of medication to try to help me cope. The medication left me in a zombie like state, I couldn't function whilst taking them, so I stopped taking them. The situation became unbearable. I couldn't get anyone to listen to me. I just kept being told it was me, not the twins.

I HAD a thing about odd numbered children, so in December 1983, I decided to have a chat with my then husband about it, we decided we would try for another baby when my contraceptive pills ran out in February 1984, allowing for a fourth baby to be conceived around the end of February beginning of March 1984.

. . .

ON SUNDAY 26TH FEBRUARY 1984, I was cooking Sunday dinner which I'd invited my mum & dad to come over to. I had a very strong feeling something was wrong with one of the twins but didn't know what or which one and so I called for a Doctor to come out and check my girls over. The Doctor arrived, she told me 'I was an over protective, interfering mother and I didn't know what I was talking about.' She went on to add, 'She would not come out again.'

ON THURSDAY 1ST MARCH 1984, Zena woke up and said she needed to go to the toilet, I checked the time it was 7.20am. I remember sitting her on the toilet and while waiting for her to go, I noticed how quiet the twin's room was. Normally, they would be laughing, and you could hear the cot moving as they kicked each other's feet, they wouldn't sleep in separate cots, so one was always empty. I left Zena on the toilet while I went into the twins' room opposite. I first went to Diane (Diane is not her real name, but this is the name I will refer to her as), she was laying on her stomach at the foot of the cot, I turned her over onto her back, she was wide awake but just looking at me not making a sound. I then went to the top end of the cot, where the youngest twin was also laying on her stomach. I reached into the cot and as I turned her over, I knew without a shadow of a doubt my baby girl was dead, Kimberley was no longer breathing. There was blood all over the sheet and all down her front and covering her face, there was also some sort of lumps which I assumed was food. I ran downstairs, screaming, no words, just screaming, out the front door to my neighbours house and woke her up to call for an ambulance.

MY LANDLINE HAD BEEN DISCONNECTED and I can honestly say, I have never been able to be without a phone since, the sheer panic of losing the use of a telephone has left me feeling something awful would happen. I still remember to this day, the ambulance crew going straight upstairs, and the police not allowing me to go up there, they wouldn't let me see my Kimberley, I was made to stay in the front room, along with my husband. I then remember my dad arriving, asking what had happened.

AT SOME POINT a Doctor was called. The ambulance crew wanted me to be given something to take away the shock, initially given by injection, to speed up the result they were aiming for. The Doctor arrived, it was the same Doctor who came out on the previous Sunday, this Doctor did not administer an injection but left a prescription on the hall table. I was taken into my kitchen by a couple of policemen, to be questioned away from my husband. My dad followed me into the kitchen.

THE POLICEMEN ASKED all sorts of questions, when did I last feed the twins? Which one did I feed last? What did I give them from their bottles? Who was the last one out of myself and my husband to see them alive? There were lots of questions and some questions were repeated. My dad became quite protective of me and became loud towards the policemen, who informed my dad they had to ask these questions, due to the nature of the death. I wanted to see Kimberley so much. I was refused. One of the last images I have of my baby girl, was when she was carried out of the house, in a black bag, that looked like a record bag and placed in the ambulance, not a normal one, but a black one, all dark and lonely inside.

I CANNOT REMEMBER how long everyone was in my home, but when they'd all left, I went upstairs. Firstly, I went into the twins bedroom. Everything was gone, all their toys, the bedding, the mattress's, even their bottles. I then went into my bedroom, I thought I was going to die. The pain in my chest was unbearable as I looked at my bed, I saw several tubes and swabs with blood on them, just left on my bed. It was obvious they'd been used to try and resuscitate Kimberley, but it was no good, she was gone, gone from my life forever. My sister arrived at some point and I remember that she stayed with me, my husband, Zena and Diane. We went down the town to the shops, I could not tell you anything else about that day other than smoking so many cigarettes my throat was sore. We had in fact smoked over 200 cigarettes that day between us.

THE NEXT DAY came and just seemed to happen around me, as if I wasn't really there, I wasn't really living it, my mind was somewhere else. It was like nothing was real, people are there, but they just don't look real. It was almost the end of office hours, it was around 5pm, when we were informed the coroner had completed the autopsy on Kimberley and what the findings were. Kimberley had a diaphragmatic hernia which ruptured, that was why there was so much blood and stomach contents in the cot and on her little body. Kimberley was born with it, and because Diane was Kimberley's identical twin, we would need to take her to the hospital first thing Monday, to get her checked over and have an x ray to make sure she didn't have one as well.

SATURDAY 3RD MARCH was a long day, a day I don't really remember other than my brother got married and I felt so guilty because I thought I'd ruined his day. He told me I hadn't, which at the time I found hard to believe, but I know it wasn't my fault that Kimberley died just two days before he was married.

MONDAY 5TH MARCH, my mum took me to the hospital with Diane, to see the consultant that the twins had been under for around 6 months of their lives. He was not happy that we were there asking for an x-ray. He said they had had them when they were born. He added, it was common practice for multiple births, and babies that go to special care for other reasons to have x-rays at birth. He was quite rude to be fair and sent for the twins' hospital notes. When they arrived, the consultant checked both sets of notes. There were no results of any x-rays being done, they had not had the x-rays at birth or at any other time. My mum asked, if it had been known that Kimberley had this hernia could anything of been done? The consultant said 'Yes, they could have operated.'

I SPENT the next few weeks wanting to die, wishing I was brave enough to kill myself, I didn't want to live anymore with so much pain. I didn't want to live without Kimberley, but at the same time, I couldn't leave my two baby girls behind, motherless. I couldn't bring myself to end my life, so I had no choice, but to live with the guilt I felt over my Kimberley's death, I should have made the Doctors listen to me. I should have pushed harder. I should not have allowed the Doctors to fob me off, make me feel as if I was the one that was ill, ill in the head.

MY FEELINGS towards my husband were cold. I didn't feel worthy of being with anyone, I shouldn't be happy, I didn't deserve a life. Yes, these were my thoughts they weren't rational thoughts, they were thoughts coming from a broken mummy who didn't want to live but didn't want to leave her living babies alone either. My life was a living torture on a daily basis, the pain inside was covered up by fake smiles and fake laughs. The hardest part was putting on a brave face for Diane's 1st birthday. The guilt became bigger and weighed me down more. I felt I wasn't doing the best for her, all I felt was pain. I spent so many days running away to cry in my bedroom, or the bathroom, where no one could see me.

.  .  .

In April 1984, I found out I was expecting my 4<sup>th</sup> baby, I would still end up with an odd number now that Kimberley had died. On 19<sup>th</sup> May I was taken to hospital with a threatened miscarriage, I felt so useless, why me? What have I done to deserve this? I was kept in hospital on complete bedrest. I had a scan to see if they could see if I was still pregnant with a live baby. I was, I was approximately 7 weeks pregnant. The next day was my 21<sup>st</sup> birthday, I spent it in bed, in hospital, not knowing if my unborn baby would make it or not. A few days later I was allowed home but had to take things easy throughout the pregnancy. December 1984, I went into labour, I was petrified. I was convinced if I gave birth to my baby, the baby would die. I didn't receive much help from my husband, he just didn't seem to understand how I could feel like that and was vocal about it. I gave birth to the most gorgeous baby boy. My first-born son, he was perfect, he made me want to carry on living for my children, two girls and a boy. Julia, the medium, my mum had been to see when I was pregnant with the twins was correct, I did have another girl and a boy after my first child.

Around a year had past and I realised I had no love for my husband. I felt nothing, I wanted him out of my life, but I wasn't sure if it was the right thing to do or not. My parents took me to see Julia, this was the first of many visits and I started believing in the unknown. She described my Diane perfectly, she was holding onto my skirt, but this was my Kimberley and she'd grown since her death. Julia told me I would have 6 or 7 children, but she wasn't sure, and a second marriage to a man with either blonde hair or who was bald and that his name began with an S, I was thinking of Christian names, so Steven, Simon and the like. At the time I went to see Julia, I was in my first marriage and had had 4 children. She thought I must have lived with someone as well, but I hadn't. Then she asked how old I was and realised she was reading into the future instead of the now.

I FINALLY PACKED MY FIRST HUSBANDS' stuff and gave it to him one day in October 1986. The reasons our marriage fell apart are not for public knowledge, but I do believe losing Kimberley helped me decide it was a mistake to carry on in a marriage which was too broken to glue back together, and to be honest I didn't want to.

I MET my present husband in November 1986, and we had our first daughter in November 1988. We married in July 1989. I recall my mum saying to me 'See Julia was right,' as she looked over to my second husband and added 'His hair is really light and fine it can hardly be seen, and his surname starts with the letter S.' Our second daughter was born in September 1990, which was on the same day as her dads' birthday, he always says laughing 'I wanted a router but got a daughter.' My husband really wanted a biological son, but he ended up with two gorgeous daughters.

MY FATHER-IN-LAW LOST his life in an RTA (road traffic accident), this was a seriously hard time, he had been a fantastic man, great father and brilliant grandfather. I recall saying to my husband, a while after his father's death, that I believed if we tried for another baby, it would be a boy as his dad was up there and able to give him what he wanted this time. So, Christmas Day 1993, I hadn't had a pregnancy test, but I knew I was pregnant, I just knew. On that day, I was telling friends that I was pregnant, and I would have a boy, born on 23rd August and he'd be named after his granddad. My second son was indeed born 23rd August and he was named after his granddad.

.   .   .

THERE HAVE BEEN several times throughout my life where I would dream about things and then these dreams would be day visions, that then, in turn, became reality. I didn't like it, as it was nearly always it was me seeing someone's death, or something not nice.

MY YOUNGEST DAUGHTER developed a lump on her neck at the age of 16, on Christmas Eve 2006 she was told by the A & E Doctor she had tonsillitis. I wasn't happy with the diagnosis, so I pushed and took her to the Doctors and the hospital until I someone would listen. Finally, in February 2007 she was diagnosed with Hodgkin's Lymphoma. I had learnt my lesson with Kimberley, and I was not going to lose another daughter from being ignored. My baby daughter is a survivor and beat the odds to eventually live her dream of becoming a mummy to her very own baby 12 years after her diagnosis.

WHEN I WAS ROUGHLY 45 years old, I found myself in a medical crisis, I kept collapsing, then one day I couldn't get out of bed. I was diagnosed with several back conditions relating to the spine and discs. Around my 50th birthday, I had a thought, a vision, appear in my head, that I was diagnosed with these problems to make me sit down and listen to what I was meant to be doing with my life, that I was to start developing my psychic abilities.

I FINALLY TOOK the next step and joined a circle to develop whatever gifts I had. I had a lovely teacher and friend who taught me a lot. I had tasters of different things to see what I could do and what I liked doing. I was interested in quite a lot of things, I became a professional tarot reader, using clairvoyance and I also tried healing, which I found really lovely and once I'd started doing a little healing my hands stayed warm to hot all the time, whereas before I'd tried healing, they were always so cold.

I HAD COME to the end of what this teacher could teach me, so I then started to think about what I could do next, I knew I liked the feeling of healing but wasn't sure where I could go with it. Then I thought about doing Reiki. I spoke to a few people teaching Reiki, but they all said the same, that you need to be able to stand up to do it. That was my downfall, I couldn't stand up for any length of time. I was disappointed but decided I would have to forget this and just do the things I'd been shown. I was happy with the things I was able to do, but I just didn't feel complete, there was something missing. I just wanted to help people, so, I kept going with readings, mainly for friends, as I was unable to get out much.

AROUND A YEAR LATER, in February 2018, my #2 daughter was on social media asking if anyone was able to teach Reiki. I saw this, and also noticed someone had posted that a lady, by the name of Tina Pavlou taught Angelic Reiki, I'd never heard of this before. I had an instant thought pop in my head, I had to message Tina to find out more, what was Angelic Reiki? and could I do it sitting down? Well, to my surprise, Tina told me I could do this sitting down and even told me there was a course for Angelic Reiki 1 & 2 starting on Friday 13th April. Friday 13th, I was like wow, I have to do this. Friday 13th April came, I went to the first day of the course, I met Tina, wow, she was so lovely, she made me feel at ease and at home in no time. By the end of that first day, when it was time to go home, I realised I had been sitting for hours and I wasn't in pain, this was a first for a long time, for years in fact.

WHEN I WENT HOME, I slept so well, no pain, none, I was so amazed at how fast I was benefitting from this new-found healing. I went in for the second day of Angelic Reiki and told Tina and the others on the course how I'd been without pain all night and slept so well. It was truly a fantastic form of healing, we were channeled by the angels and the healing was given to our clients, but we also receive the healing and it was just fabulous. I wish I'd have known about this before, the benefits from it were wonderful, the amount of people who have commented on how better I looked and how much easier I seemed to move around now. I loved this course so much I signed up for Angelic Reiki 3 & 4 with Tina and have since become an Angelic Reiki Master, I hope one day to become a teacher. I am totally hooked with healing now and love the fact I can be a channel for the angels to heal others.

TINA LATER PUT on courses for Theta Healing, I felt the need to sign up to these too. Theta is an awesome way of healing, not only can we heal ourselves using Theta, but we can heal 7 generations back and 7 generations forward just by working on ourselves. I have done 6 different courses in Theta to date, and can't wait for more to follow, this is the best addiction ever. I have, in less than a year, found a brilliant teacher, friend and soul sister in Tina and found and connected to a new family, my soul family. We help each other, we heal each other, we love each other in a way that is the purest of pure. There is so much to learn and so many people to help. I have reduced my medication to next to nothing since I first met Tina and started working on myself, I sleep so much better than I have for many years. I have also done a course on crystal healing, which works very well with Angelic Reiki and Theta Healing. Tina Pavlou is an earth angel, she teaches, heals, gives readings and also puts on retreats. She is such a hard worker who gives her all and I'm grateful to have her in my life.

THERE IS someone else I feel has played a massive roll in healing me and that is Marcia Staples, I have had several sessions with her in EFT (Emotional Freedom Techniques) and Matrix re imprinting. One of these sessions took me back to the day my daughter Kimberley died, I literally relived the day, but by using EFT I could do it without the pain and trauma. I have managed to finally lay to rest the pain from that day, I removed images that have haunted me for over 34 years. Marcia, had me talk to Kimberley and ask her questions, also I got to cuddle her, this was weird at the time, but not anymore. I gave Kimberley a cuddle, but it was after she had died, yet she was still alive. A picture was then taken and downloaded into my memory. I can now see this picture whenever I like. I am able to talk about that day now without pain, without getting a lump in my throat and having to stop talking as it would choke me up too much. I can say Kimberley's name without feeling upset, without a heart wrenching pain. I will keep having sessions with Marcia as they are so worth it, changing things that have happened to something better is awesome and I am truly grateful to have her in my life.

I AM TRULY BLESSED to have been shown life can be beautiful, life is for the living, it is to be lived and loved. Sometimes, life throws us problems we don't know how to deal with, but if we work on ourselves, we can overcome almost anything. We are able to manifest a life of pure love and happiness, a life we all deserve, not just a life that we get by in, but one we truly enjoy. I love talking to people, especially my family about Angelic Reiki, Theta Healing and Crystal Healing. I am open about my feelings and my beliefs. What I love the most is how everyone I know comments on how much I've changed, how well I now look, how my mobility is improving. I don't see my mum that often, but we talk on the telephone a lot and I felt proud of myself when she said, 'She can tell by the way I speak and my manner that I've changed so much for the better'. My journey since meeting Tina has been amazing, I wouldn't change it for the world.

WHEN I LOOK BACK over the years, I see a child that was troubled, different, but could see things others couldn't. A teenager, who felt out of place with visions and thoughts swirling around her head and feelings that couldn't be explained. A young mum who was ignored by professionals that should have listened to her instincts, her gut feelings. Then I see this mature person, who has changed so much, but, at the same time is in fact the person she always was but has awakened to the reality of what is really going on in life. I have a life I am happy with, a family I am proud of and a peace in my heart that can only come from being free to live your life the way you want.

# ABOUT THE AUTHOR

## TRACEY STEMBRIDGE

Tracey Stembridge is a twice married 55 years old mother to 7 children, grandmother to 24 grandchildren and soon to have her first great grandchild. She is an Angelic Reiki Master, Theta Healing Practitioner, Crystal Healer and Professional Tarot Reader using Clairvoyance.

The youngest of three children she was born in Billericay in Essex, moving to Bexleyheath at preschool age and then at 16 years of age moving to Ramsgate on The Isle of Thanet with her parents & siblings for around 11 months, then moving to Margate also in Thanet which has been her home town ever since.

The first few months of life were spent being looked after by her maternal grandmother due to health issues with her mother after her birth which left a stronger bond with her grandmother than anyone else, it also left long lasting issues surrounding self-worth and feelings of being unwanted & unloved.

From a very young age her mother thought there was something wrong with her mentally as she would drift off into a day dream state where she would not respond to anyone trying to talk to her, she was thought to be a problem child with a lack of real friends so became isolated from the real world.

Her lack of self-love & self-worth left her drawn to people of a similar low vibration which left her being treated badly which in turn left her feeling she was worth even less. The vicious circle of sending out poor thoughts about herself would then bring even more abuse & ill treatment.

There came a massive change in her life in her mid-40s where she was diagnosed with a spinal condition that had a huge impact on her life. Just after her 50th birthday she joined a spiritual development group and spent a couple of years gaining knowledge in using tools like pendulums for clearing & cleansing, using clairvoyance to read tarot cards, and also had a taster session in healing to name just a few things that were tried. After these sessions the need to heal had become quite strong however, unable to learn Usui Reiki due to poor mobility & not being able to stand for any length of time seemed to put an end to this.

Then in early 2018 was when things really took off after seeing a post on social media that Tina Pavlou was teaching Angelic Reiki, unlike Usui Reiki you don't have to stand to learn or be a practitioner. Finally, Friday 13th April 2018 arrived, a new way of life was just about to start all thanks to a post on social media. Since starting the Angelic Reiki course with all the healing received, there has been a big improvement in her health & mobility. The biggest changes are taking place from the Theta Healing and sessions of EFT (Emotional Freedom Techniques) & Matrix Re-imprinting with one of the soul family sisters Marcia Staples.

Naturally Gifted is the name of her business that has been launched in 2019. You can contact her at tstemb@aol.com or

f facebook.com/NaturallyGifted.co.uk

Printed in Poland
by Amazon Fulfillment
Poland Sp. z o.o., Wrocław